Praise for *Miracle Country*

"*Miracle Country* is a soaring homage to California and to the sparsely populated and drought-prone Eastern Sierra. Blending family memoir and environmental history, Kendra Atleework conveys a fundamental truth: the places in which we live, live on—sometimes painfully—in us. This is a powerful, beautiful, and urgently important book."

—Julie Schumacher, author of *The Shakespeare Requirement*

"Truly something special and refreshing. Kendra Atleework's powerful debut, *Miracle Country*, is the rare trifecta that seamlessly blends personal narrative with historical nonfiction and highly charged, activist-style rhetoric with rarely a misstep or heavy hand . . . Whether you're in it for the emotional roller coaster or want an armchair view of an area of California not on your radar, *Miracle Country* works on multiple levels. It reminds us to hold our loved ones close, conserve our resources, treat the land as sacred and stop putting our collective heads in the sand when it comes to climate change."

—*San Francisco Chronicle*

"Atleework captures how the history of the landscape affects how people feel in the present in prose charged with emotion . . . [and] scenes imbued with importance and urgency . . . *Miracle Country* is a beautiful read, Atleework's prose steeped in her passion for the region and her striking observations. Even more, though, the memoir is important because it reveals Atleework's deep understanding of the region, of a life defined by an absence, and she points us to the power in this understanding—it can be a tool to stay safe in a desert or on a cliff, a way to connect with other people, a call to counteract climate change, or, as in Atleework's case, a reason to return home."

—*Ploughshares*

"Essayist Atleework recalls her family roots and explores the history of California's arid Eastern Sierras in her ambitious, beautiful debut . . . [Her] remarkable prose renders the ordinary wondrous and firmly puts this overlooked region of California onto the map."

—*Publishers Weekly* (starred review)

"Kendra Atleework has written the most beautiful book about California I ever have read. The author locates the mystery and beauty of her life in the small town of Bishop, on the eastern slope of the Sierra, decades after Los Angeles has stolen the water. Her poet's prose, on every page, honors the dry land and breathes Nature to life."

—Richard Rodriguez, author of *Darling: A Spiritual Autobiography*

"[A] shimmering memoir . . . A bittersweet tribute to home and family in breathtaking prose that will appeal to lovers of memoirs and history, as well as anyone who enjoys beautifully crafted writing."

—*Library Journal* (starred review)

"Few writers manage to capture the essence of the California that exists beyond the images typically offered up by film and television . . . Echoing the works of Carey McWilliams and Mike Davis, Atleework's assertive love letter to this geography paints a vivid picture of a place, and a family, that has weathered countless storms, fires, and cataclysms both large and small . . . Its elegant prose, deftly balanced narrative, and careful research are sure to make readers fall in love with *Miracle Country*."

—*Los Angeles Review of Books*

"Atleework pays tribute to the drought-ridden California desert of her childhood in this gimlet-eyed memoir . . . Nature lovers will immerse themselves in Atleework's vibrant prose and meditative musings."

—*Booklist*

MIRACLE COUNTRY

A Memoir of a Family and a Landscape

Kendra Atleework

ALGONQUIN BOOKS OF CHAPEL HILL   2021

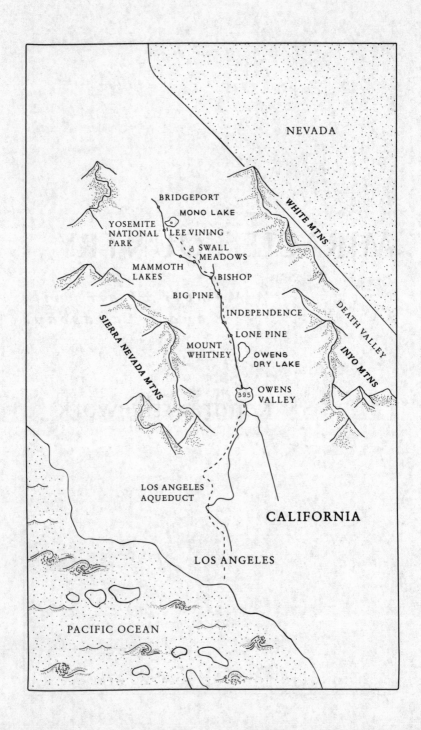

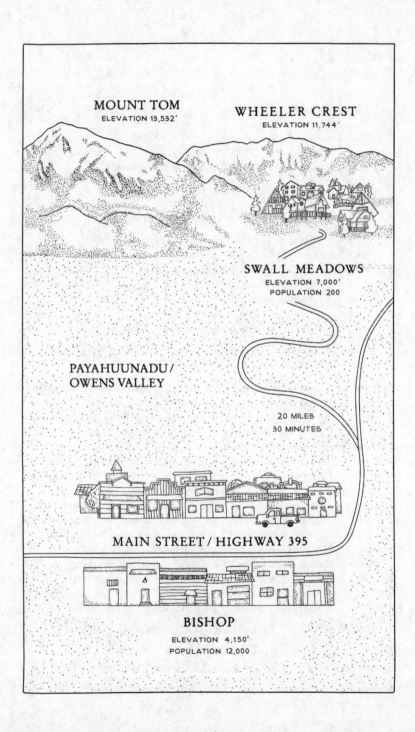

Published by Algonquin Books of Chapel Hill
Post Office Box 2225
Chapel Hill, North Carolina 27515-2225

a division of Workman Publishing
225 Varick Street
New York, New York 10014

First paperback edition, Algonquin Books of Chapel Hill, June 2021.
Originally published in hardcover by Algonquin Books of Chapel Hill in June 2020.
Printed in the United States of America.
Published simultaneously in Canada by Thomas Allen & Son Limited.
Design by Steve Godwin.
Maps illustrated by Em Gallagher of Taurean Trade.

Portions of this work first appeared in *Territory*, *Hayden's Ferry Review*,
The Pinch Journal, and *Best American Essays 2015*.

The Library of Congress has cataloged the hardcover edition of this book as follows:
Library of Congress Cataloging-in-Publication Data
Names: Atleework, Kendra, [date]– author.
Title: Miracle country : a memoir / Kendra Atleework.
Description: Chapel Hill : Algonquin Books of Chapel Hill, [2020] |
Summary: "*Miracle Country* captures one family's spirit and losses in a harsh
landscape that has been shaped and exploited over hundreds of years, and chronicles
the author's journey as she realizes that there's nowhere else in the country,
no matter how green and welcoming, that feels like home"—Provided by publisher.
Identifiers: LCCN 2019053878 | ISBN 9781616209988 (hardcover) |
ISBN 9781643750552 (e-book)
Subjects: LCSH: Sierra Nevada (Calif. and Nev.)—Biography. |
Women—California, Southern—Biography. | Bishop (Calif.)—Biography. |
Coming of age. | California, Southern—Description and travel.
Classification: LCC F868.S5 A75 2020 | DDC 979.4/4—dc23
LC record available at https://lccn.loc.gov/2019053878

ISBN 978-1-64375-141-2 (PB)

10 9 8 7 6 5 4 3 2 1
First Paperback Edition

Contents

Preface   xi

Part 1. Wind
    1. Kindling   3
    2. Search and Rescue   25
    3. Whiskey's for Drinking   40
    4. Flight Plan   74

Part 2. Wildflowers
    5. Lupine Land   103
    6. Miracle Country   121
    7. Last Days of the Good Girls   135

Part 3. Rivers
    8. The Indestructibles   157
    9. Locals Only   166
    10. A Child's History of California   189
    11. Dust   205

Part 4. Moonrise
    12. Rim of the World   217
    13. Walk Home   236
    14. Dawn of Tomorrow   246
    15. Sunset   254

Part 5. Summit
    16. Three Points of Contact   261
    17. Wings   280
    18. The Hardest Part of Flying   295

Research and Inspiration   304
Acknowledgments   305
Questions for Discussion   306

For Pop

PREFACE

I HAVE A PHOTOGRAPH of my mother on a rock ledge over water somewhere in the mountains. Basalt rings the lake. My mother stands naked at the edge of the precipice looking across desert, arms around her pregnant belly, as water scatters sun.

A century before, the writer Mary Austin caught a split second of sublimity, before loss, before trouble, when she walked one morning on a windblown hill and stood at the foot of a walnut tree. Suddenly earth and grass and tree and sky and her child self "came alive together with a pulsing light of consciousness."

She remembers the foxglove at her feet, a lingering bee, the "swift, inclusive awareness of each for the whole—I in them and they in me, and all of us enclosed in a warm lucent bubble of livingness."

And I remember the night I wandered with my mother in full moon up Mountain View Drive, when we threw off our clothes and walked in only our hiking shoes, me a child and her cutting the waters before me, as if she could ferry me to safety, and for a while she could, and she did.

PART 1

WIND

1. Kindling

THE VALLEY LAY DRY that winter, and wind roared over the mountains.

February 2015 marked the fourth year of bad drought in California, the worst in more than a millennium, and the jet stream raced over the Sierra Nevada range and hit the floor of Owens Valley as it usually does a few times a month in winter. But on the afternoon of Friday, February 6, the wind moved with enough force to strain the wires draped between the old power poles that stretch along the base of the mountains. Maybe these wires swung like heavy jump ropes. Maybe the wind knocked a branch across a weak point. Regardless, just before 2 p.m., a wire broke and sparks trailed through the dry brush, there on the floor of the valley, fourteen miles from the little hospital where I was born.

Owens Valley is part of the region we call the Eastern Sierra, or the East Side. This valley is high desert, a long brown sliver of sagebrush and bitterbrush cupped between ranges—to the west, the stark granite escarpment of the Sierra Nevada, casting its rain shadow across our towns; to the east, the Whites and Inyos, those ancient desert mountains, rippled and purple—rising two vertical miles, over fourteen thousand feet at the highest peak. Fire, drought, flood, and blizzard visit the Eastern Sierra often. Perhaps this is why the nearest place with a population over thirty thousand is two hundred miles away.

Just northwest of Owens Valley, here on the East Side, Mammoth Mountain spits steam and rumbles with a belly full of magma. The wind knocks big-rig trucks over regularly. In our living room a scorpion once stung Mom's toe, and black widow spiders lived in the wooden frame of our old hot tub. Our neighbors' dogs died from the bites of rattlesnakes, and their cats died in the mouths of coyotes and mountain lions. Our neighbors themselves fell from cliff faces and froze in immense, immovable snow. Some crashed airplanes into mountains during storms. Others lost themselves in the desert without water.

Annual rainfall in the Owens Valley town of Bishop averages five inches and in drought years measures closer to zero. And so the brush that covers the valley is always dry, but that February it was drier still. Usually snow lies over the mountains, but lately the days had been eerily warm, and snowpack was at a record low. My gardener grandfather on the central coast of California fretted about his yellow pasture. In Bishop, my father—jack-of-all-trades with hands like leather, split fingertips wrapped in duct tape, wrinkles on his cheeks like scars—told me that even in February he was working outdoors in a T-shirt beneath the sky-pricking point of Mount Tom and the long gray line of Wheeler Crest.

My father saw the fire when it was still small. He drove north from Bishop toward the stone wall of the mountains, toward our old neighborhood, Swall Meadows. He did not drive to investigate the fire but to do some work on the place, to split some kindling he'd harvested on the side of Wheeler Crest. As he drove, he saw smoke rising and had to detour around a cottonwood the wind had knocked across the road—the wind blew a steady fifty miles per hour with stronger gusts, shifting directions, throwing dust, whipping brush. At that time, the fire had just been called in, and a crew of volunteer firefighters swarmed around it. A small brush burn, my father thought, and continued up the mountain.

On that February afternoon I didn't yet know how the ground becomes naked where fire passes over, how tree trunks cake in their own blackened bark and clumps of boulders lie bare and singed in the sand. Though I was halfway across the country, a graduate student in snow-crusted Minnesota, from my father's telling I could imagine what he saw. After all, I am always thinking of home.

BEFORE THAT FRIDAY Swall Meadows consisted of about 120 houses and two hundred people tossed across the steep east-facing wall of Wheeler Crest, surrounded for miles by sagebrush and ragweed and desert peach. In Swall Meadows there are no streetlights and no sidewalks—no need for streetlights with so many stars and no need for sidewalks with so few cars—and every road slopes and sloughs down the mountain, eroding before our eyes. Here, the house where I grew up rests on Mountain View Drive, well up the incline of the Sierra Nevada, seven thousand feet above sea level and three thousand feet—a thirty-minute drive—above the nearest town of Bishop. To get to Bishop, follow an old wagon route, paved over now, that swoops and wriggles through pinyons and crumbled piles of pale volcanic rock, a road so unruly in its curls and curves that as you drive you see the green patch of town twenty miles down, then the wall of Wheeler, then you spin again to the rising bulk of Mount Tom, shifting shape and shade and expression.

These days my father lives in a house on the outskirts of Bishop. Swall Meadows is just too isolated, he says, for a person alone. But the house in Swall where we grew up was not a place you left behind all at once, and his tools still cluttered the garage. Sometimes he rented out the rooms to vacationers, and sometimes the rooms sat empty. The house rested on the mountain, neighbors on all sides within shouting distance but farther than I could toss a stone, its long driveway narrow and unpaved, and around it grew blue spruce, aspen, cottonwood, Jeffrey pine, apple trees. Below the house the mountainside swooped into an acre of brush, a woodpile, and a shed where my father and brother once kept dirt bikes. From the living room big windows gazed over the valley and at night revealed Bishop far below, a patch of streetlights in a great darkness.

The house was sided in redwood. It had a wooden porch, where I used to get splinters and carve my name, and a corrugated sheet metal roof I climbed in summer. In the cement steps that led down the mountain to the little apple orchard were imprints pressed by my sister, my brother, and me when our hands were small. In the bedroom downstairs, where my mother died when I was sixteen, a window overlooked the ridge of Wheeler and, beyond that, the perfect pinnacle of Tom.

FIRE HAPPENS OFTEN in California during summer, the driest months. Strange, my father thought, to see smoke over the valley in February. But this was a drought winter, absent of the snow that usually covers Swall Meadows and stops just above the Owens Valley floor. My father parked the pickup outside our house beside the rounds of wood he had chainsawed and rolled into a trailer when a pine fell, and he split logs for an hour until the sheriff, Joe, came by and said everyone in Swall had to evacuate, that there was a fire seven miles down the mountain and no one knew which direction it would go.

Pop told Joe, "One more minute, I've just gotta grab some kindling," and Joe chuckled and said hurry up. My father went into our house and gathered the photo albums and some jackets from the closet in the mudroom, passing by the painting of two trees leaning into each other over a stream, the wooden salad bowls that were a wedding present, the stacked cassettes of flute and fiddle music—Joni Mitchell, Cat Stevens—that my mother had loved. He threw the jackets and the photo albums on the backseat of the truck and he drove down the mountain.

He didn't really believe Swall Meadows would burn.

He'd planned to move the photo albums to his house in Bishop anyway; otherwise, he might not have grabbed even those. Had he believed the house would burn, he would have

called me before he was already back in Bishop, watching the
mountainside from the valley floor. Had he called me sooner,
I would have told him to get my mother's T-shirt printed with
wildflowers, take the pictures off the walls, save the soft toy
frog she gave me when I was small.

The wind became more and more a wild thing as the sun
moved west toward the ridge of Wheeler Crest. In Owens
Valley the wind gusted to seventy miles per hour, to ninety,
to one hundred, shoving cars across the highway and pitting
windshields with blown sand.

Anyone who lives in the Eastern Sierra knows this wind
and its moods. On the beaches of the Pacific, gusts arrive
laden with salt spray, whooshing with enough force to make
your eyes water, a persistence perfect for launching kites. By
the time that breeze reaches Owens Valley, it has raced over
the coastal range, up the western, windward flank of the
Sierra Nevada, and it has turned powerful. Dust devils tear
up the dry surface of what was once Owens Lake, tossing
toxic particles miles into the sky, into the lungs of the people
who live near the old shoreline. The wind blows from the
west over the mountains, and the willows along the river lean
east. It scatters pollen in a golden film over backyard ponds.
It stretches curtains across bedrooms.

When a cold front moves off the Pacific, wind hurtles
over the crest of the Sierra Nevada faster than a hurricane.
In Bishop it splinters pine boughs, shatters windows, breaks
the little airport's wind speed indicator. Wind this wild is
called the Sierra Wave, and it tumbles over the valley like a
wave breaking. I have hiked on a day when the Sierra Wave

pummeled the sky, have leaned into a gale so strong it negates the work of gravity and I can almost lie down on air, can fall forward without really falling. I have found myself caught in a canyon when the Jeffrey pines above me thrashed their branches like furious giants and the Wave hurled stones and pine cones and I ran for my car.

While my father drove south toward Bishop, this wind fanned what was no longer a small brushfire up the mountain.

AT 7 P.M., fifteen members of the Wheeler Crest Volunteer Fire Department drove to the little station in Swall Meadows and changed into structure protection gear, which is heavy and built to withstand heat and smoke. The youngest of the fire crew was in his forties, the rest past retirement. The volunteers drank some water and left the station. Fire reached over the blacktop and around their tires. They drove through a river of flame.

My father stood in the desert on the outskirts of Bishop. Even from twenty miles away, to look directly at the burning flank of Wheeler Crest hurt his eyes. The gale knocked him to his knees. He watched to make sure the wind didn't turn, because a fire line like this could whip through Bishop and torch everything—his house; the mobile home where my brother lived with his girlfriend and dogs; Great Basin Bakery; the mountaineering stores; the whitewashed Methodist church where a man named Caddy presided every Sunday; and the two-bedroom house on which I had made a down payment a month before, on Keough Street, its roof shaded by the long white boughs of a liquidambar.

But the wind did not turn toward Bishop. It blew up the mountain, tipping bare willows in the direction of Swall Meadows like pointing arms, and as soon as it became clear what would burn tonight, my father got in his truck and drove.

He parked at the sheriff's roadblock near the base of the mountains and tried to calculate how high the flames had climbed. The wind blew his hair and pressed his flannel shirt against his shoulders. In the early dark he could not make out the house of his friends Dan and Linda, who were traveling and had asked him to send news, and he could not make out our redwood house where it sat higher up Wheeler Crest, just below a row of towering Jeffrey pines. What he could see was every tree, everything that could burn, burning.

The big spots were houses, glowing longer than trees, black pillars rising from the roofs. The frames lit up as if by X-ray, and the windows blazed. Dan and Linda had a natural wood house, like ours. Amid darkness and whipping flames, it was impossible to tell one from another, impossible to know what the firefighters might save.

What my father heard: the wind shrieking in the bare cottonwoods along the creek that ran up the mountain and into the fire. Then voices from the scanners of the officers manning the roadblock, chewed with static: firefighters withdrawing, the community of Swall Meadows fully engulfed.

DECADES BEFORE I was born, a retired engineer from the Los Angeles Department of Water and Power built the redwood house on Mountain View Drive. I know little about this engineer, except that he dredged an entire wrought-iron stair-case from a hydroelectric plant on the bottom of Owens River Gorge, which now spirals into our basement. He designed a lofted second story from which I could look down on the living room, the entire house open and barn-like, a house where sound drifts. He built the exterior walls, porch, and ceilings from old-growth redwood, the cores of trees, rot-resistant heartwood salvaged from enormous tanks that once held water for Los Angeles 250 miles south. He built a greenhouse and a sloping metal roof to shed snow and framed six exterior doors, none of which have ever, as far as I know, been fitted with a key, and he affixed those rambling walls to a steep part of the mountain at the end of that long dirt driveway. This was a house so strange it could never be rebuilt.

Pop watched the mountain burn. And he remembered buying the house with my mother after the engineer left Swall Meadows, after the place had begun to crumble in the slow way of a dry country. My parents pulled desiccated birds from the radiators. Their friend fell through the half-finished floor of the second story and landed in a heap in the living room. Outside on the bare mountain, my father planted saplings.

Now he breathed smoke and pictured the piano, the beds, the curtains, as I did, burning. The dried roses from a high school boyfriend resting in a vase, heads tipped toward the ground. The bedroom window, glass melting my view of Wheeler and Mount Tom. The little model airplane Pop and I built together, still sitting on my desk. Mismatched couches, one green, one purple, one upholstered in fabric printed with maps, chosen by my father because it is his job to map these mountains. The cherrywood cabinet he'd gotten from a carpenter in exchange for a ride in his hot air balloon. Those wide windows overlooking the valley.

When houses burn, embers lodge in doormats, in pine needles on the ground, in leaves in roof gutters, in vents without screens. Heat breaks windows and flames enter. Second floors collapse and rafters fall. Softwood—redwood, cedar, pine—burns faster than hardwood. A house reduced to ash has burned for hours.

I took a red-eye flight home to California and met my father at his house in Bishop. All night he woke with thoughts of objects left behind, the smallest things, a lifetime's accumulation of tools. "I really couldn't sleep last night," he told me. "I kept thinking, Shoot, I should have grabbed my drill. I need my drill to put up a fence."

Saturday morning, near sunrise, a neighbor on the volunteer fire department got into Swall Meadows before the evacuation order was lifted and drove the streets. There are not many streets in Swall Meadows to drive. The neighbor tried to match faces with the houses that were gone.

His daughter called me. She had been my classmate; how many afternoons had she walked Mountain View Drive to sit on my bedroom floor and listen to the bands we loved? Still there, she said tearfully, of her own house with its wooden porch, though the cabin across the street was a lone stone chimney. And what about the redwood house, standing on the brush-covered hillside below the line of guardian pines?

Her father had snapped a photo: a neighbor's new cabin, gleaming pine, which had perched just above ours, was ash and buckled sheet metal. In the distance, hazy with smoke, our roof rose unharmed.

WHEN LINDA SAW me for the first time, the day we were allowed back into Swall and one by one cars rolled up the mountain, she hugged me for minutes, her standing knee deep in what was once her foundation, me bending over to grip her under the arms. Two firefighters looked away.

Our neighbor Linda is sixty years old, small and blonde and pretty. Her kids went through school with my brother and sister and me. On winter breaks her daughter Jessie ice skates with us on frozen ponds; we talk about how much we miss home when we are far away. Through sifting ash I learned the contents of this family's life, more through memories than what could be reclaimed.

Linda stepped back from my arms and looked behind her. She wore a stranger's clothes, her hair mussed under a baseball cap, her face dusted with ash. She pointed to the charred metal of what I realized were a washer and dryer, to the skeleton of her little red car, melted glass sloshed over its doors. A stone wall that had been the garage squared off against the mountain.

"Look at it," she said, tears cutting tracks down the gray of her cheeks. The firefighters stirred the ash with the toes of their boots and looked at the ground. They were young men, sent by Cal Fire from the city of Bakersfield, four hours away. Now they paused to crouch in the ash in their yellow suits and pick out tiny warped beads. This was the first day and it hadn't yet occurred to the rest of us that a burned house is toxic, and so we wore no gloves or goggles or respirators, and the white ash made a low smoke over the shattered foundation, which was really just a blueprint now, a house-shaped border marking where floor and walls had been. As we reached for handfuls of Linda's house, we brushed soil and rocks that had lain buried beneath the foundation for twenty-five years. Three days after the fire, the earth was still warm.

Leaning on her elbows in the rubble, Linda said, "It's our place in the world, our mark." The house was evidence of her family's life among mountains—planks of cedar, windows overlooking a sweep of brush to the ravine from which the flames rose, walls once surrounded by gardens, a fish pond, and trees. Now the needles of the pines were blackened, and the branches reached stiffly in the direction the wind had blown. Living fish flashed orange in sooty water as Pop splashed with a shovel to drive oxygen below.

THE LAST TIME I came home, before the fire, I helped my father run his usual errands around Bishop. We rode bicycles around town and he restocked the map rack at the visitor center. Besides selling maps, he has tried just about everything you can try in the Eastern Sierra, not an easy place to make a living: mucked out the bottoms of streams, pumped gas at the little county airport, babysat, taught kids how to ski, rented out storage units, run a Greyhound office, delivered pamphlets by bicycle, run a gym, run a used car lot, built an airplane, flown a hot air balloon. On that afternoon in January, a few weeks before the fire, we picked up windshield wipers for my brother Anthony's truck and a parakeet in a cardboard box for a neighbor. The parakeet went in the saddlebag on Pop's bicycle along with everything else, and we rode back to his house over root-cracked asphalt.

My father is six foot eight inches tall and gangly—a beanpole, he calls himself, who takes ballroom dance lessons and accidentally wore ladies' sunglasses for years, who gives extra money to the school district because he thinks property taxes are too low. He wears bike shorts and a flapping long-sleeved shirt and rides in an old canvas hat instead of a helmet, because up here the sun burns you in minutes. He runs into so many acquaintances it takes a half hour to pick up some hummus at Manor Market.

On one of Pop's maps, downtown Bishop is a tiny grid among the swooping lines of river, highway, wilderness boundaries, and a long steel pipeline running south. When I was a kid in Swall, the lights of Bishop on the valley floor met me when I woke from nightmares. You could look out the living room windows and see those lights sparkling, just a sprinkling on the black blanket of desert below. Pop grumbled about light pollution, but in the midst of darkness, Bishop was there.

Weeks before the fire, we stopped for bagels at Great Basin Bakery and ate them at a picnic table in the Bishop park as ducks swam in the creek. And then we biked to the Inyo-Mono Title Company, where I sat at a small wooden table with my father and an escrow officer named Stephanie, and sun fell across the papers in front of us, and I signed for the house on Keough Street.

• • •

HERE BESIDE THE vanished southern wall, Linda's jewelry box had once rested on a dresser. We found traces of its contents scattered, as if propelled by an explosion. The house was not so much rubble as powder. The powder that was once the childhood bedrooms of Jessie and Ryan and Chris combined with the powder that was once their parents' room, and so we found fishing lures from the boys' tackle box mingled with Linda's shattered beads, a tiny white scallop from the shell collection that had lined Jessie's desk among bits of broken tile.

I cupped as much ash as I could hold in my hands and sprinkled it across a wire screen. As I shook the screen, powder lifted and swirled. The air smelled of sulfur, a smell that got into our clothes and would not wash away. I coughed. Linda coughed. We sprawled out and propped on our elbows to better study the debris, the chunks of things that snagged on the sifting screens. We were looking for a diamond from the anniversary ring Dan gave to Linda. We were looking for anything that retained its shape.

Every shard of porcelain was precious now. "I want all of it," Linda said. "Maybe I can make something out of it." And I imagined a shrine of relics raised in a quiet corner beneath a window, a view of Mount Tom, years from now when a new house stands inside the memory of the old.

Pop and I left Dan and Linda and turned up Mountain View Drive. In our own driveway I saw dry leaves piled by the wooden walls. The pines were green, the spruce blue. We replaced a melted portion of drip line. This is what we lost: that thin black strip of plastic, a few patches of brush, part of the woodpile. We threw bread and carrots onto the brown lawn for the mule deer, who picked through charcoal meadows and looked up in confusion, too stunned to recoil from cars.

I swept ash out of the doors, ash driven through cracks by the wind. A bad seal, my father said, and made a note for repair, but it seemed to me the wind could spread ash without limit. In the dirt of the driveway and snagged in the brush below the apple trees, I found bits that had drifted as houses burned: a piece of window screen, a flake from a solar panel. Upstairs I vacuumed the faded blue carpet, and this act was now a great privilege. I remembered dragging a futon across the carpet to the side of my parents' bed, where Mom let me sleep after bad dreams. One nightmare repeated: the blackened face of a dime, oversized, burned or dirty, horrible for reasons I didn't understand.

Dan and Linda will live in our house for years while they rebuild. Jessie and Ryan and Chris will stay in our bedrooms upstairs when they visit home. That day, Pop and I changed the sheets so they wouldn't smell of smoke. We printed pictures of our neighbors and put them in our frames. We put a vase of flowers on the table.

To UNDERSTAND THE place we call the Eastern Sierra, you must be able to see what is no longer here. See what hides, change your definition of big and empty and small, of good and bad. Bend and search the desert floor for the near-invisible petals of a crowned muilla and then look up to mountains that seem to rise forever. This dusty margin of California draws and then replicates the kind of people who have never completely adjusted to a human scale. They don't quite fit other places, be it the orbit of their ideas, good and bad, or the size of the sky they require in order to carry out their lives. The author Mary Austin wandered west from Illinois in 1888, fell into the California desert, and remained for a long time. She wrote of the place, "You will find it forsaken of most things but beauty and madness and death and God."

Mary Austin came to the Eastern Sierra in 1892. She lived in a brown house in Independence, one of the little towns strung along the highway in Owens Valley, where she wrote novels and essays and stories and plays about the strange presence of the land. As she told it, there was something about this country—"something that rustled and ran, that hung half-remotely, insistent on being noticed, fled from pursuit, and when you turned from it, leaped suddenly and fastened on your vitals."

I walked around Swall Meadows, and it was not the same. I looked from my bedroom over the old view, the ridge of Wheeler blackened and in places still smoldering. I could not arrange myself anywhere in Swall so that my field of vision did not include evidence of fire.

But once the smoke cleared from the valley, the days after the burn were perfect blue and warm. We were first evacuated from Swall when I was too young to remember much besides snow lying over the mountain and burying our driveway, my father pushing the snowblower, a plume drifting over his shoulder like the tail of a white bird. That February, twenty years ago, we drove to Bishop in case of avalanche, which had swept houses off foundations in decades past. An avalanche had flipped a landmark on Wheeler Crest, a hundred-ton granite boulder Pop nicknamed House Rock, so that it pointed toward the sky.

I had evacuated for wildfire before, too, but that was in July. "Beautiful country burn again," wrote the poet Robinson Jeffers in 1926, words that have become famous in California.

If the mountains are burning in February, my neighbors ask, what will summer bring? The streams that encircle Swall Meadows haven't rushed the way I remember in a while. How starkly different each season once felt. In high school I remember wet feet because I refused to wear boots. The roof over our lockers collapsed every year under snow. Lately, when I visit home in December, it seems I have traveled to a land of constant warmth, the myth of Southern California stretching north. Back in Minnesota, I tell people, "When I was home this summer . . . ," then recall it was winter.

Swall marks the border between desert and sky. Mostly the mountain is dry, the valley brown, but meadows spread to the west where my brother and sister and I used to roam. There, rose hips grow thick enough to tear denim, and a grove of water birch and willow hugs a snowmelt creek. Years ago my father discovered a clearing beneath a roof of leaves, water running over crumbled granite. Grasses on the banks were flattened by the sleeping weight of mule deer or mountain lions. We called the place the Fairy Glen, and on summer afternoons we walked there with Mom to make mud balls and grass crowns and to pan for fool's gold in the cold water. Pop bent green water birch branches into our hands, let go, and we launched twelve feet into the air. With my friend Daniel I pulled the tailgate off an old truck burned in a fire in the 1980s and abandoned to the brush. We dragged the tailgate to the Fairy Glen and laid it as a footbridge across the stream.

After the fire Daniel wrote to see if my house was okay. He grew up thirty minutes northwest in another Eastern Sierra town deeper in the mountains, called Mammoth Lakes. Now he lives in a wet, green place and works with trees. Sometimes he wants to move home. Then he thinks better of it.

"California is gonna get really scary, I think," he said. "Crazy how things change in a decade . . . fires in February."

Beautiful country burn again. I told Daniel what the Fairy Glen looks like now: mostly gone. My hand ghostly against the blackened trunk of a water birch.

Walking the neighborhood, I saw women and men standing on driveways in front of warped water heaters, half-melted sewing machines, skeleton motorcycles, a spiral staircase leading nowhere.

"It's not *if* it's gonna happen again," a volunteer firefighter told me. His house, once resting beside poplar trees across from ours, had vaporized. He watched it burn as he fought the fire, saw flames spilling into the street as his fire truck rumbled toward his driveway—thought *no*—then turned his back and went on to other houses. "It's not if, it's *when*," he said. "It might be thirty years. We could lose twice as many next time." A pause. Smoke drifting from a hot spot on the mountain.

The firefighter reminded me that in the past four years Big Pine, a tiny town just south of Bishop, had burned once and been threatened by fire three times. The fire that burned Swall Meadows swallowed seven thousand acres in all. That's the size of Bishop, including its unincorporated areas and the Paiute reservation. Everyone understands what the future promises. "But people are here," the firefighter said. "People want to stay. I'm gonna get my house back. I'm gonna get my business back. Those meadows you're looking at—they're gonna be much greener than they were before."

That first day, a Red Cross truck roamed the streets, distributing sandwiches in Styrofoam boxes that sat unopened while Dan and Linda searched the ash. Linda did not pause to eat or drink or wrap herself in something warm. The sun set behind Wheeler and the air chilled. My father brought a jacket from our house, worn and practical—Mom's. He said, "This is Jan's jacket. She would want it to keep you warm."

Linda wrapped the jacket around herself. "My sweet Jan," she said, and I looked up for that glow above the ridgeline, the one I saw when I was sixteen, when I turned to the mountain to save me from grief and from fear.

Linda said, A house burned is like a death. And I wondered what it meant to go to smoke. This land demands that you consider—makes you think you'll find an answer, but you never can. And where do we turn after everything burns? What light do we find, or not find, just over the summit?

As we pulled twisted half shapes from piles of white powder, Linda held each object in her palm like a marble. This, a friend gave to her in high school. This, Dan gave to her on a trip to the sea. Remember, remember. We blew ash off a tea-cup and saucer, a ceramic boy painting at an easel, Dan's class ring. We never found the diamond, although once a piece of cut glass fooled us.

North of Linda's house, at the place where Swall Meadows and Sky Meadow Roads meet, the community bulletin board stands on two legs, a wooden slab everyone passes as they come and go, pinned with announcements like *A bear in my home last night!* (We don't bother to note when our cats go missing.) In the days after the fire, the bulletin board remains. Packs of dust masks and trays for sifting are stacked around its legs, and someone posts a notice for a community meeting to be held at the Wheeler Crest Fire Station.

The afternoon of the meeting is warm, even hot. Most of Swall gathers, a blackened meadow at our backs and, beyond that, the mountains. My sister, Kaela, has driven home from Santa Cruz, beads in her dreadlocks, less rattled than I some-how, a strange pattern etched into her arm with frog venom, a ritual of some significance I don't understand.

We sit under red vinyl tents and eat a Red Cross lunch. A woman in a white uniform sees me struggling to hold a ketchup bottle and takes my wobbling plate. She says, "Let me help you," her voice tender and helpless, and I think of the ash I can't wash off my hands.

The fire chief speaks. The sheriff speaks. The county super-visor speaks. My father puts a hand on my shoulder and ges-tures at ravens riding thermals, circling against Wheeler Crest.

A small wind rises, billowing the tents, and people reach to trap paper plates. The volunteer fire department wear navy blue hats and collared shirts embroidered in gold, and they are called to stand while everyone cheers. And then a woman takes the microphone and asks that we rise and hold the hand of the person next to us as she reads the names of the people whose houses burned and the names of the streets where those houses once stood.

Valley View. Rimrock. Pine. The wind moves softly like something alive, and I think of the stories of people driving past the roadblock, evading the sheriff, throwing goats, dogs, cats into cars. I think of the man with a coop of chickens who stayed as long as he could, cutting brush away from his door, who heard a whistling and turned to see a tornado of flame, watched it touch down and rise, touch down and rise. I think of the man who could not get his horse in a trailer and so walked her back and forth around patches of burning grass until finally he had to let her go and drive away.

Late on the night of the fire, my brother told Pop he was going to save our house. He could get into Swall the back way on an unpaved road where the two of them once rode dirt bikes together for countless hours, even during the bad years, when Pop was a newly single parent and Anthony was pure cooked-down rage. They both knew that road, how it led from the highway through pinyons and Jeffrey pines, pitching and falling over the base of Wheeler, and let out near Mountain View Drive.

"Anthony, no," my father said. "Do not. This isn't like other fires. The wind is too strong."

"I'm going," said my brother, and later his girlfriend told me she begged him to stay. He drove the dirt road in the dark in his Chevy pickup, two-wheel drive. And then he saw the fire, saw it moving through the pines, hopping between stands of brush, this fire that had raced up the mountain at what might have been fifteen miles per hour. He tried to turn around. His wheels sank in sand and spun. The fire advanced. My brother got out and ran.

Later, in the bright living room of his mobile home in Bishop, dogs running in and out of open doors, he sat on his couch and told me he'd never been so terrified in all his twenty years of life. His brindle pit bull, Bear, rolled on the carpet. On a bookcase a picture of Mom stood; in it she wears her green jacket, and a tiny Anthony leans into her, as if out of the wind. "I could feel the heat," my brother said. "I was choking on the smoke. The wind kept knocking me down."

I don't know what he thought of as he drove up the highway and turned onto that dirt road or what he planned to do once he got to Swall. Sometimes there is just the impulse to return.

The firefighters gathered before the red tents, and behind us the mountains glowed. For now, there is the horse that found its way to a safe patch of meadow, the cat coaxed from a rock pile, paws lightly burned. The toy frog sits on my bed and regards the ridge of Wheeler with sad glass eyes. And the wind blows from the west, from the ocean and over the coastal range until it whistles in the peaks above our heads, troubling a clear sky.

2. Search and Rescue

OUR PARENTS LEARNED OF Mom's diagnosis with a rare autoimmune disease when I was six years old and Kaela five and Anthony not yet ours. They did not know if, or when, the disease would turn to cancer and kill her, but they knew it could. They chose not to tell us this possibility until, when I was sixteen, and Kaela fourteen, and Anthony eleven, the cancer diagnosis was handed down by the specialists in San Francisco. Perhaps they decided we would live enough years with fear. And so they separated fear from caution, making caution an ingredient for joy.

Every family cultivates a culture and lives by its own strangeness until the strangeness turns normal and the rest of the world looks a little off. The Atleework children are alone in the world with this name because our parents made it up. Who needs a hyphen? Robert Atlee met Jan Work and there you have it. Our parents kept their respective last names, making us the only three. We're difficult to pronounce—AT-lee-work, somehow endlessly bungled—and embarrassingly easy to look up online. We got to know life without television, our only radio the valley's beloved country-western, thirty minutes from any town, a day's drive from what might be considered a city—under, or at least in the shadow of, a series of large rocks.

Once, the five of us posed for a Christmas card photo, perched in the branches of our apple tree. The next year our parents put us in matching plaid shirts, we three Atleeworks looking like miniature lumberjacks, and the year after that we all sat on the sofa in plastic pig noses. At my middle school graduation, girls walked between rows of folding chairs in the gymnasium wearing leis of purple orchids while I carried a single orange blossom Pop had heisted from the flower bed in front of the school.

In our living room Pop hung a trapeze. We dangled from our knees. We bounced off the couches. We flew.

Our family matched the strangeness of the landscape my parents had chosen: uneasy, not a level place of right angles. Owens Valley clutches four little towns that line a single highway. With a population of about twelve thousand, sprawl and all, Bishop is the only incorporated place in Inyo, a county larger than New Jersey. A tourism website lists Inyo County attractions: deserts, martian landscapes, mines, abandoned cemeteries. Ten thousand square miles lie mostly free of humans, because, as the historian Marc Reisner tells us, California has a desert heart.

My father's map company is just him and his friend Mike and sometimes my brother or sister or me. He merges his knowledge of the landscape with the technical skills of a cartographer. SIERRA MAPS name tag pinned to his delivery shirt—blue, button up, short sleeved with a crinkled collar—he drives his van up and down the Eastern Sierra to the places that serve the birders and climbers and skiers and hikers and campers streaming by: ranger stations and mini-marts and outdoor gear stores on a two-hundred-mile corridor from Pearsonville to Bridgeport.

His maps show mountains and a flat valley floor. They suggest the crests of the foothills, ubiquitous granite, and the pale pinkish hunks of igneous rock called Bishop Tuff, sooty with desert varnish, produced during a prehistoric eruption that determined the shape and character of this place. They can keep a tourist from succumbing to a poor sense of scale in wild country. Spread on a table or over a lap, my father's map of the Eastern Sierra quilts together wilderness, national park, national forest. At the northeastern corner, black dashes form the state line, dividing Esmeralda and Mono Counties, where the Boundary Peak Wilderness of Nevada gives way to the White Mountains Wilderness of California. Near this border lies Mono Lake, Paoha and Negit Islands afloat in the big blue round.

The names of the streams and peaks call to be arranged into stanzas, full of rhyme and alliteration: Sand Canyon, Cardinal Pinnacle, Cottonwood Creek, Blind Springs Hill, Sherwin Crest, Round Valley, Onion Valley, Bear Creek Spire, Mount Starr. There are first names for these places, too. The Owens Valley Paiutes spoke a dialect used nowhere else in the country. Say it PIE-yoot, and know that these are the people indigenous to the valley, who first called themselves Nuumu. They named Mount Tom "Winuba." Many still call Owens Valley "Payahuunadu," the land of flowing water.

Places we know well get nicknames. There's Robert's Ridge, where Pop's hot air balloon snagged in pines, the basket swinging over the ground, and he toted a passenger, an eighty-five-year-old woman with a pacemaker, down a steep pumicey slope. "She weighed eighty pounds," he remembers, "and I just carried her on my back like a backpack. She said it was the most excitement she'd had in twenty years." There's Mount Dave, after Pop's hot air balloon partner, where snowmobilers toss old helmets into a dead tree, and Will's Peak, nicknamed after a Swall Meadows neighbor killed in an avalanche on Mount Tom. Up a canyon to the north, he calls a meadow after Mom.

In the photo albums Pop rescued from the redwood house, Mom naps on a lakeshore while we Atleeworks cover her to the neck in sand. She holds a piñata strung from a pole, a dinosaur fluttering with strips of green. She crawls through dirt and sagebrush on all fours, teeth bared in a snarl, an earnest bear. She climbs an apple tree. She lies back on a granite slope as she might stretch on a sofa, a wadded sweatshirt pillowing her head while we sprawl around her. She puts her arms around my waist and leans into me beneath a wall of red stone. She sits behind me on a yellow plastic sled, and we careen.

She used to make a little creature with her hand, her index finger the head and the rest the legs, which scurried around, talked in a high voice, and entertained me for years past the point that this should have been embarrassing. We called the creature our Little Bug. *Oh, hello, Kendra!* Little Bug cried. *Will you be my friend? Will you take me with you on all your adventures?* And I leaned down and whispered, as if only Little Bug could hear me, yes, yes, yes.

Saturdays, chore days, when Mom did laundry—her only domestic task, being the one with the full-time job—the five of us played the clothespin game, trying to clip the back of someone's shirt without getting caught, an excellent contest for a desert family not allowed to use the dryer. Mom was the ultimate opponent: deft, coy, and fiercely competitive, if only at games. She was all about timing, subtlety, delivery. *Last night I tucked a very sweet, snuggly Kendra into her warm little bed and sang our usual quota of bedtime songs,* she wrote in a letter to Pop's mother when I was four. *She put her arms around my neck and said, "Tell me something wonderful, Mommy." I told her I loved her. "Say it longer, Mommy," she insisted. So I did. I whispered softly in her ear, "I love you, sweet girl. I will always love you. I think you are wonderful. You are precious to me, little one. I love you so much."*

"Mommy," Kendra whispered back, "you sort of stink."

She came from the pines and deep snows of Houghton, the Upper Peninsula of Michigan beside the shore of Lake Superior, the water as wide as the sea, without its smell. Once a quiet, skinny child, she played flute and wore bell bottoms and got a boyfriend who sang with a Bob Dylan rasp. She wrote poetry for an underground school paper and sketched the caterpillar from *Alice in Wonderland*, plump on top of a mushroom and clutching a bong. She smoked weed under the bleachers with her friends when she was supposed to be practicing with the marching band. She crept out at night and did not tell her parents where she was going, saying *Trust me,* until they followed her to a drug rehab facility. When they called the place, panicked, they learned that she volunteered on the late shift, answering the crisis line.

She left home, left the Midwest, lived alone in a cabin deep in the pleated Sierra Nevada. In winter she tunneled from her doorway back to air. That town was a place of snow and pine cones, her first home in California. She commuted on cross-country skis and taught middle school and coached the girls' basketball team, though she never quite learned the rules and could only shout to the players, *Run! Shoot the ball! Good job!*

A few snows fell and thawed, and something known only to her led her across to the east side of the Sierra, to the near-empty lanes of Highway 395 that carried her past alfalfa and sagebrush and the little red sign for the Marine Corps Mountain Warfare Training Center, past the stone monument for Dog Town diggings, the turnoff to a ghost town called Bodie where wind shrieks in winter, and finally to a summit, a bend in the road where she must have looked over salty Mono Lake and two islands heaped in stone—Negit black, Paoha white, adrift like a mirage.

Mono Lake, sixty miles north of Bishop at the base of the same line of mountains, is ancient and skittering with alkali flies, its banks a moonscape turreted with pale tufa towers. She ran on this shore between mineral sculptures taller than she was, formed under salty water. The movement of centuries and drought and an aqueduct running 380 miles south to Los Angeles drove the lake's surface down, exposing what was hidden, thrusting towers that once flickered aquamarine into daylight.

Was it an interview for the teaching job open in Lee Vining, a town of three hundred with a high school of thirty, that brought her across? And when she saw the place we call the East Side, so different from the west or the middle of the mountains or any other part of California, what did she know?

At first she saw what the tourists see: barren, brush-covered country. She saw desolation. Did she imagine the batholith fractured by fault lines, Earth's crust separating, dropping into valleys, the layers of history buried beneath her? I don't know the season or the weather or the time of day at which she first saw home—whether she knew, as my father knew, that this was the place for her life.

THE WRITER JOAN Didion describes the times she has "'come back,' flown west, followed the sun, each time experiencing a lightening of spirit as the land below opened up, the checkerboards of the midwestern plains giving way to the vast empty reach between the Rockies and the Sierra Nevada; then *home, there, where I was from, me*, California."

Wallace Stegner once told us to get over the color green, but some of us grew up without much need for it. I spend cross-country flights from Minneapolis to Los Angeles nose to window, waiting for the moment, two hours in, when my plane crosses gristle. From thirty-five thousand feet the weathering of canyons mirrors bronchi branching in lungs. Veins bifurcate, muscles striate, arroyos jag like wrinkles in the brain.

On one diagram of precipitation, Owens Valley is colored red, the shade used by the Western Regional Climate Center to indicate zero to ten annual average inches of precipitation. Owens Valley sits at the western edge of the Great Basin Desert, an arid expanse that includes parts of California, Utah, Idaho, Oregon, and most of Nevada. The Great Basin Desert exists because the Sierra Nevada and the Cascade ranges squeeze most of the moisture out of storms that sail inland off the Pacific, leaving the land to the east of these mountains dry for hundreds of miles. This phenomenon is called a rain shadow and it defines our lives.

The year I was born, it rained four times in Owens Valley. In my first five years of life, less than twelve inches of precipitation fell. Here, rainfall in a good year is equal to apocalyptic drought east of the hundredth meridian. Dry wind crisped the wave out of Mom's hair, and as a child, I didn't know what it was to sweat. Our noses bled perpetually, and the skin split over our knuckles.

But Payahuunadu, this country of flowing water, was not named by the Paiutes as metaphor but as literal description of the land before it was visited by outside forces. The valley was desert only when judged by rainfall: scarce precipitation yet so much water, water that used to be snow, flooding out of the mountains, softening the rain shadow.

In 1927 a Paiute man called Hoavadunuki—his English name Jack Stewart—told what his life had been in Payahuunadu. He was past one hundred when he told his story; he had come of age before the whites showed up. "When I was still a young man, I saw Birch Mountain in a dream." Birch Mountain, Pa'o'karanwa, is a peak visible from Big Pine, standing over thirteen thousand feet. "It said to me:

'You will always be well and strong. Nothing can hurt you and you will live to an old age.' After this Birch Mountain came and spoke to me whenever I was in trouble and told me that I would be all right."

Birch Mountain watched over Hoavadunuki, held him in conversation. The same brown land hunted Mary Austin down and kept her. She wrote of this country that the "people who found themselves enmeshed in it sometimes cursed as they curse the beauty of women." Austin herself left the verdant Middle West as a young woman and crossed the Great Plains for California, then followed her husband to the Eastern Sierra and took a teaching job. Not too far from Birch Mountain, in her little brown house beneath willows, she wrote *The Land of Little Rain*. "This is the sense of the desert hills," Austin tells us, "that there is room enough and time enough."

Inside the cover of her autobiography, she gazes from beneath the brim of a hat clearly intended for sun protection over fashion, its crown lumped over her slit eyes and square jaw, her gaze so sharp she seems to catch you by the collar, eighty years after her death. Perhaps the apparent emptiness of country that isn't empty at all guided her writing. She seemed to understand the lingering kind of absence. Mary Austin had a father who died in great pain when she was ten years old and a little sister who died two months later from a diphtheria infection that Mary had brought home. She had a slightly older brother with whom she clashed on spiritual and intellectual terms and never shared her grief. She read as she drank water, as she breathed.

"She was smart," said the women who knew her in the valley. "But yet it took a lot to understand her."

"The things that she did, they were extreme, you know."

"Such a queer woman."

"Very peculiar."

"Dreamy."

"Very odd."

"Her mind was somewhere else all the time."

The immensity of the world Austin perceived around her wrenched her from her husband; her horizon was too big and blue to fit inside a nineteenth-century marriage. When she was young, an etiquette manual advised her in conversing with gentlemen. According to the manual, Austin recalled, she ought to "lead the conversation along genteel bypaths of literary and musical comment, affording ample opportunity for His Whiskers to display for her benefit those gems of wisdom which only gentlemen could produce." She was to suggest topics of conversation without expressing an opinion, as gentlemen would tell a lady what to think.

"Not Mary, they wouldn't!" Austin wrote. "They would have to be spry about it or Mary would end by telling them."

Here was a woman booted from the Methodist church in the town of Independence for her insistence on closely reading scripture without the approval of the pastor. Disinvited by the Methodists, she befriended Nuumu healers. You might say she went West to disobey. The desert, she wrote, gave her "the courage to sheer off what is not worthwhile."

What draws a woman to a moon bowl, a bare basin dissolved beneath the teeth of mountains? Something about a space at once open and walled off from the world eliminates the rules of elsewhere about how a person might live, what she might write, where she might climb.

MY PARENTS MET in the Eastern Sierra Symphony where she played the flute, he the trombone. "She was the only member who would walk around the Catholic church during orchestra practice barefoot," Pop says, and laughs.

She from the wooded shores of Lake Superior, he from the golden California coast. He remembers an early date: "She said, 'Do you want to go on a hike this morning?' And I said, 'Sure!'" They grabbed backpacks and sandwiches and nine miles later reached the lake she wanted him to see. And then they turned around. "I was thinking, Eighteen miles, that's a little long, that's a little grueling! I don't even remember where we went, we went so far. I was just hiking, hiking, hiking, hiking, hiking." He had entered the life she built before him, her miles dictated by daylight alone.

Ninety years earlier, Mary Austin walked in the desert with coyotes and pocket hunters. She outwalked a husband who required a version of womanhood she could not abide, and she learned to love what was not palpably fertile. After the end of her marriage, she wrote, "I am often asked by women how I would go about to pray myself a husband, and I have to answer that I have never wanted one badly enough to work that out." She recognized, it seems, true love in the land and the creatures upon the land, human and not human—a love not conscripted to family or nation or a lucid conception of God.

As far as I know, my mother never read Mary Austin. Across the decades they were never introduced. But something makes certain people at home in a moon basin. As a child, Austin believed her dreams really happened. It was not until she related them to other children that she learned to separate internal life from reality. She dreamed a language spoken only by animals. At age ten she stared out a classroom window and imagined herself slipping into sky, where she saw "white clouds against the blue, and mysterious trepidation going on in all the upper rooms of the trees." I read this and remember dreams of drifting through my bedroom window beneath Tom and Wheeler, floating above roofs as neighbors slept, to stray with the movement of air over chutes in stone too steep for me to climb.

AUSTIN OFTEN WROTE about herself in the third person, not as "I" but as "Mary." An understanding of herself as singular and contained, a version of herself who transcends the worries of ordinary life to commune with something larger—a self she called "I-Mary"—came to Austin when she was four years old. "There was the familiar room, the flurry of snow outside," she wrote, "Mama kneading bread . . . Mary in her flannel frock and blue chambray pinafore. . . . And inside her, I-Mary, looking on." Imagine I-Mary grown up and in the desert, the chatter of the schoolhouse, of her own mind, suffused by something beyond sound. She wrote in her autobiography: "In the wide, dry washes and along the edge of the chaparral, Mary was beset with the need of being alone with this insistent experiential pang . . . beauty-in-the-wild, yearning to be made human."

My mother must have understood the way certain places protect and enlarge. Mary Austin called this dry side of California "a big mysterious land, a lonely, inhospitable land, beautiful, terrible." It was with a mixture of insularity and permeability, peppered with the holes the desert carves, that Austin, and perhaps my mother, too, met what Austin called mystery. "It was in her mind," she wrote of this country, "that all she needed was to be alone with it for uninterrupted occasions, in which they might come to terms."

Coaching me through interminable shyness, a thing she understood, Mom told me: *You just have to say something.* A classmate had caught me in the hall to ask, "Aren't you the girl who can't talk?"

Say something, anything, even if it's just "You have nice teeth."

Certain places let you quit complimenting teeth for a while and walk under the sky, alone but not really, exposed but unafraid, the rules of human and woman cast aside.

BEFORE SHE HAD any of us, my mother had the Sierra. Here, a bear smashed her car's window and shredded the seat in search of spilled peanuts. She named her gray cat Serendipity. She chopped wood to heat a rented cabin and got her water from a pipe that ran out back into a spring. When her tap stopped in winter she went into the woods and smashed the water's frozen surface.

Here was a woman on a rock face, on a lakeshore, the mountains ringed around her like the backs of dinosaurs. When storms closed the highway, she skied seventeen miles through a canyon over fresh avalanche debris to feed the class hamsters. She made a friend, who taught her to rock climb, and another, who played flute duets with her outside in the desert, and a group of friends with whom she started a square-dance band and yet another group with whom she fought the city to the south to keep water in Mono Lake so coyotes could not walk onto Negit and Paoha and gorge themselves on the eggs of California gulls. Sometimes she walked alone, but when she wanted company, these people walked beside her, more or less in stride.

My mother joined the search-and-rescue team and sought the victims of the unexpected, sought to bring them home. People who love solitude must understand what it can cost. I believe she joined because she knew she could be the one in need of rescue. Because she wanted to live in the kind of place where people go into the storm after the lost.

One rescue she remembered: a flight gone wrong, a plane down in the Sierra, the pilot dead on impact, his passenger alive. It was my mother's job to climb inside the crunched cockpit and wrap her arms around the pilot's shoulders and hold his body back against the seat so the others could drag the living man from the plane. The impact of the crash made the pilot's eyeballs bulge from his skull. My mother remembered that he wore a wedding ring.

Not long after, she took an eighteen-mile hike with a man who liked to loop over the land in a little silver plane he built himself. Her early knowledge of home was flight and its swift snip. She knew that beauty in the wild might manifest as solitude without end.

Its antidote might be found in the others who scattered themselves across a desert caldera. All the parts of life— lonely, beautiful, terrible—mixed up in the right combination and lodged between these mountains. She married the pilot, my father. In a training session for the search-and-rescue team, she volunteered to be buried in the snow with a breathing apparatus while the others scavenged the avalanche field with dogs and poles.

I have seen sunlight filtered through snow, leached of color and warmth yet somehow made brighter. I imagine her waiting, listening to the muffled sounds of the searchers or listening to nothing, all noises absorbed, her hands freezing inside her gloves. I do not believe that bed of snow felt like a grave. Perhaps sunlight through snow resembled some sort of hereafter, beauty in the wild, dispersed and cold.

This was the beginning of the ways she found to risk herself, as if she declared to those little towns, to the sky that swallowed sound, You are worth this life, this much.

This, then, was the place to stay. She put her arms around death in the cockpit and then she went home and ran beside a lake as strange as the moon, where nests speckled a dark dome. She waited under snow until she caught the barking of dogs, saw the shadows of footprints, heard voices calling her name.

3. Whiskey's for Drinking

IN PAYAHUUNADU, SNOW MELTS out of the mountains and runs toward a single river flowing south. On my father's maps Owens River is a thin blue groove at the bottom of the gorge, thickening briefly at Pleasant Valley Reservoir, then curving past the Bishop airport, around town. Even on paper the river seems ancient, immovable. It has washed through the valley since the Pleistocene. But there's another line on this map: gray, almost graceful, dipping in and out of sight.

The pipeline.

When I was hardly taller than the sill, I used to look out the windows of the redwood house and watch heat waves rise and trace the pipeline and its attendant canals until they disappeared south between the Whites and the Sierra. I can't remember a time when I didn't understand the movement of water in this valley: always south, always away.

"The aqueduct is like a gun," Pop says. It begins as a concrete-lined channel in the Mono Basin sixty miles north of Bishop, at the saline lake where Mom once ran. In 1944 Los Angeles added this northern extension to its original aqueduct, collecting water that would otherwise fill Mono Lake.

The channel funnels creeks away from the lake and into a tunnel—"like a gun barrel," Pop says. The tunnel runs south to Grant Lake and farther south to Crowley, both reservoirs dug and dammed by Los Angeles, then on to Owens River Gorge. Deep in that shadow, visible from our windows in Swall Meadows, water falls over turbines at three power plants, spitting over the tuff canyon walls. Still southbound, the water fills the original bed of the river, snaking past Bishop and Big Pine, the flow fattened by tributary streams and wells that pump up groundwater. For a while water remains in Owens River for fishing, floating, dropping off a rope swing, until twenty miles south of Bishop that water enters another reservoir, then abandons the original path of the river and flows into a canal that charges south, bypassing the now dry bed of Owens Lake.

"Then the water enters double barrels," Pop tells me. Past a final reservoir at the south end of the valley, the river fills two pipelines, one added in 1970 and the original, ten feet in diameter, pimply with rivets, a serpent of rusted steel, finished in 1913. Together these barrels escort the water south with the conviction of gravity. In the end snowmelt from the Eastern Sierra travels 380 miles, a six-hour drive through the desert, to Los Angeles.

The river once emptied into Owens Lake, which was deep enough to ferry steamboats to silver mines on its shores. After Los Angeles finished draining the lake in 1926, particles of arsenic and desiccated mining chemicals billowed from the bed. The wind in our valley has kicked up some of the most hazardous dust storms in the world.

This used to be farming country, first irrigated by the Paiutes and "the finest watered portion of the lower half of the state," according to a military scout in 1859, but after the city began piping water away in 1913, most of the crops died. Many of those who could afford to leave left. Some of the wealthiest people in Los Angeles got richer off development as land in Southern California became arable and desert was displaced to the north. On a smaller scale, Owens Valley ranchers still graze cattle and grow alfalfa on land leased from the Los Angeles Department of Water and Power, known locally as DWP. The water local ranchers use—water that, unobstructed, would cover this valley in green—is metered by the city hundreds of miles to the south. In dry years Los Angeles cuts the ranchers off altogether.

Call us the city's big backyard. CITY OF LOS ANGELES, read signs in the desert, in vacant lots in town. PRIVATE PROPERTY. In 1927, the year the valley's economy completed its collapse, someone put up a sign just north of Bishop: LOS ANGELES CITY LIMITS. Poplars, planted as windbreaks, died when Los Angeles dropped the water table below their roots. Now they lie silvery on the valley floor. They might remain for centuries in this place bathed only by fire.

WILLIAM MULHOLLAND LOVED Shakespeare—we share *Hamlet* as a favorite—and the opera, and baseball. He said, "Damn a man that doesn't read books." He raised saplings in empty salmon tins before planting them outside—palm, eucalyptus, willow, and oak. You can see them grown tall in a park in Los Angeles on the site of his old wooden shack. Growing up poor in Dublin, he did not finish high school. His father blackened his eyes over poor grades, and at fourteen he ran away, joined the British Merchant Navy, and came to America. Working in a logging camp in Michigan, Mulholland sliced open his leg. The leg became infected, and when he overheard the camp doctor say it should probably come off, he escaped from his infirmary bed and hobbled into the woods. The leg healed, and Mulholland stowed away on a ship bound for Los Angeles.

He stepped onto California soil for the first time in 1877 and got a job digging artesian wells. He was twenty-two and he went by Bill. The year he arrived Los Angeles was a pueblo of nine thousand, called a "starving cow town" by one historian and a "vile little dump" by a newcomer. But Bill Mulholland was smitten. "It at once became something about which my whole scheme of life was woven, I loved it so much," he said of the unruly Los Angeles River, which ran through the pueblo and fed into the sea. In a scrubby field he watched a horse pace in circles, guiding a drill bit into the clay of the Los Angeles Basin, turning dust onto his shoes.

Did Mulholland understand that the place he loved was a near desert? In the same decade the one-armed geologist John Wesley Powell completed scientific expeditions down the Colorado River and advised the government that cities and economies similar to those of the East could not be sustained in the West. Developers poised to profit from the transfer of goods and people west on the newly completed Transcontinental Railroad accused Powell of fraud. The boosters enticed settlers with cries of "Rain follows the plow!"—and rain did happen to increase for a while in the late nineteenth century after migrants settled on the plains of Montana, Colorado, Oregon, Washington, and in the valleys of California.

Mulholland looked around him at the gamblers and highwaymen that filled his city and envisioned what he could conjure with enough water. One year after his arrival, he got a job tending irrigation ditches in Los Angeles, just as my father, more than one hundred years later, earned his keep clearing ponds and streams at his first home in the Eastern Sierra. Mulholland lived in a shack with a smoky stove and dragged a rake across the bottoms of canals, earning ten dollars a week to keep water flowing in what he called "a beautiful, limpid little stream, with willows on its banks."

Like my father, he knew the feel of a shovel breaking earth. When Mulholland moved to clear a trench, he flung dirt with such intensity that a man passing on horseback one afternoon paused to watch him work.

The man asked what he was doing.

"None of your goddamned business," Mulholland said over a shoulder. Later, when he learned the man was William Perry, president of the water company and his employer, Bill Mulholland gathered his things and went to the office to collect his final pay. Perry promoted him to foreman.

In young Mulholland's California, water fell under his control only as far as he could bank the earth and guide it with a shovel. The Los Angeles River fed into a channel called the Zanja Madre, the Mother Ditch, and from there into smaller streams and trenches. The river and its ditches dried up in drought and roared with winter rain, tumbling boulders through streets, washing out train tracks and bridges, overflowing sewers, bursting reservoirs, collapsing houses, and drowning or crushing Angelenos. When it wasn't trouncing the city, the Los Angeles River delivered water that newspapers called "slimy" and "so offensive to the taste and smell, as to be not only undrinkable, but positively nauseating." Waterborne illness flared. Fish and rotting plants flopped out of the pipes, "enough to drive every temperance man to drinking beer or whiskey straight." Stories circulated of a bloated man and a mule floating in a reservoir.

By the 1890s Los Angeles had a major newspaper, public transportation, and a burgeoning clutch of white midwestern Protestants. The new citizens built Victorian houses with shaded porches. They had not gotten over the color green; they did not find brown country beautiful and they planted lawns, which California's dry summers promptly killed.

Promoted to superintendent of the city water company by 1886, Mulholland was responsible for bringing the bursting population more clean water than the Los Angeles Basin could provide. He suggested to the city commissioner, half in jest, that the need for water might be checked by shooting the spokesman for the chamber of commerce—the man who advertised sunshine all over the country. But the booster lived on, Eastern newspapers touted California an eternal summerland, and newcomers gushed west on the rails.

As it turned out, Mulholland loved the dirty little town enough to engineer an aqueduct the world called impossible, delivering the elixir that helped Los Angeles multiply fourteen hundredfold. He advanced from ditchdigger to superintendent in eight years. Twenty-seven years later, in 1913, the completion of the aqueduct branded him a celebrity engineer, one of the most powerful men in the West. He was called a modern caesar, a genius, and a superman in the same headline. All his life he'd followed his culture's utilitarian code, chasing the greatest good for the greatest number. The thirty-nine hundred workers and thirteen hundred mules that built his aqueduct finished under budget and ahead of schedule. What the president of the water company saw when he interrupted a young Mulholland at work, be it simmered strength or a ruthless sense of possession, a confused sense of belonging to the soil or a sense that the soil belonged to him, I don't know—but I can bet it was that spark, a little frightening and wild, that made Mulholland the father of the second-largest city in the country, the thirteenth in the world.

In Hollywood's not-factual version of the story, I recognize Mulholland as split between two men, one benevolent and one rotten. The latter is puffy eyed and loose jowled, chasing an infinite California, and it is this Mulholland that triumphs in the film, drowning his moderate alter ego. I never watched *Chinatown* in childhood. I didn't need to. It was Mulholland-as-villain that I imagined into history, and I hated his abstraction, the shadow I perceived he left over the land.

MY FRIEND ELIZABETH and I are out of high school for the summer, flying through night air. Elizabeth drives. In Bishop, Main Street blazes, but the stores are closed, all except Kmart and Vons grocery, set side by side behind a too-big parking lot, over which the sky appears very black. We are sixteen. Elizabeth is tall like me, and her fingers are long and thin. When she was little, she cut the heads off dead ravens and speared them on sticks and drilled the sticks into the dirt at the side of the highway. She hangs a rubber shrunken head from her rearview mirror and burps like a baritone saxophone. She loves this valley, but even so, she used to run away from home.

Tonight we are just off the closing shift at the burger joint where we jot orders, balance hot plates and coffee mugs, and gather the money of people from somewhere else. Every summer, fishermen and hikers throng north on Highway 395, and every winter tourists swish on skis over Mammoth Mountain. In the town of Mammoth hotels loom, their lobbies crowded with enormous Christmas trees. From Los Angeles you have to drive through Bishop to reach those ski resorts. Some of the tourists stop in Bishop and stay for a weekend; others blast by, pausing for fast food on Main. Oh, they cry, just look at the mountains! And the sky, deeper blue with the altitude, the thin air so bracing. To slide down the side of a rambling lava cone—but do the visitors know Mammoth Mountain is an active volcano?

We pass the restaurant where the waitress calls Elizabeth mijita and she knows she can get margaritas without being carded, where I drink tamarind sodas at her side because I am not adventurous in the same ways. Then we're into the desert, where cottonwoods stand in ghostly clusters along the river, alone in this valley of brush. On a dirt road the car chatters over washboard, music loud—acoustic guitar, Tracy Chapman pining to leave home. We put our hands out the windows into night air and let our hair fly with the dust.

On the outskirts of Bishop, the Owens River swells with spring snowmelt, and tall grasses grow around its banks. Here, the air has the clean smell of mud and the rotten smell of reeds mulching in the shallows. Cattle wade, and cottonwoods sink their roots. Years before, my parents loaded inner tubes and the five of us jumped eight feet off the bridge on Warm Springs Road. We floated south as the rubber smudged our skin, passing deflated tubes that lolled in low branches. Pop called us back when we drifted too close to the snarl at the river's edge. "Stay out of the willows! Don't get popped!" We broke cattails apart, and the fluffy seeds stuck to our skin like fur. Floating on our backs, we glimpsed miles of brush beyond the banks. All the time we could see mountains to the east and west, standing guard.

The river turns and doubles back as if it will never end, but it does end, and we know it. Elizabeth parks the car at the water's edge, leaving the doors open so we can still hear music, and we jump in and float in darkness. Our campfire spreads gold scraps over the water. The cold of the river unclenches the knots in our feet, wind stirs the cottonwoods, and between the leaves we see stars. Here, we drift until after midnight.

And here, we make a point to pee in the river.

"Take that, LA," Elizabeth says. "How do you like our water now?"

• • •

MARY AUSTIN CAME to Owens Valley fourteen years before construction began on Mulholland's aqueduct. She saw the way scant water defined life between the mountains. In a 1905 newspaper article she accused Los Angeles of buying land and obtaining water rights from valley dwellers without admitting plans to carry that water away. Owens Valley ranchers believed they were selling to an irrigation project launched by the Department of Reclamation to boost agriculture in arid lands. President Teddy Roosevelt dealt a death blow to the land of flowing water, subscribing to the line of the day: the greatest good for the greatest number, *good* perhaps only ever a subjective term.

"It is the mistake of cities to assume that everything in the world is run upon what is called a 'business basis,'" Mary Austin wrote, "which is to say that money is the end and aim of every operation. Is all this worthwhile in order that Los Angeles should be just so big?"

She may have seen the future: two girls reeling in a river, in a plain of the lost and all that cannot be undone. Floating in southbound water, Elizabeth and I missed a thing that had never been a part of our lives. We did not understand the full nature of what had been taken. We could not remember, nor had we even seen pictures of, this valley covered by green.

STILL, A LOSS lingers, like humidity in damper places. Near midnight in September of 1976, two boys from Owens Valley used a crowbar to break into a shed containing equipment for the maintenance of wilderness trails. From the shed they took two cases of dynamite, blasting caps, and twenty feet of fuse.

Surely the boys knew the tradition of Owens Valley ranchers who attacked the pipeline nine times between 1924 and 1927, placing dynamite by moonlight at crucial junctures. In November 1924 hundreds of valley folks camped for five days by a set of steel doors embedded in the aqueduct, called the Alabama Gates. The gates sit next to the Alabama Hills, beside the empty, salty body of Owens Lake. Nearby, the Alabamas are more rock garden than foothill, half-buried boulders worn oblong by blowing dust. They stand upright, pronged like fingers. Some are fifty feet tall, others small enough to step over. From here, skirted in brown, the Sierra appears perfectly vertical.

The Alabama Gates keep water from returning to the lake bed and control the flow in the aqueduct. In 1924 seven hundred people gathered at the gates. Darkened storefronts in Bishop were hung with signs: IF I AM NOT ON THE JOB, YOU CAN FIND ME AT THE AQUEDUCT. A group of men from Owens Valley turned the wheels that opened the gates while everyone else threw hats in the air and the water coursed back to its old home.

Perhaps that water was a wall. Maybe it roared, splattered, and rushed out of the spillway, soaking the men standing by, cold water, icy, but they couldn't step away. They saw the dust of the valley covered up with the glint of a new river.

"I know there are at least one hundred sawed off shotguns in this territory," said the Inyo County sheriff, by way of explaining why he could not disperse the crowd. The valley people, he said, "feel they are fighting for their homes, and they are of the stock that fights."

"Inyo county is in a state of anarchy," the *Los Angeles Times* declared. "Guerrilla warfare is a possibility. . . . Appalling loss of lives and property seems certain. . . . Women as well as men are ready to shoot in defense of their homes."

While waiting for the city to agree to further negotiations, the valley people set up camp and threw a party. A barbecue pit. Tents and bedrolls and kids kicking up dust. One man sent word to friends camped at the gates that his cattle grazed "just north of you across the ditch. Tell Jim to collect the fattest ones for your barbecue. You are welcome as long as they last."

A half century later two boys found the Alabama Gates in darkness.

They ran before they heard the explosion.

The boys were kids, really, one seventeen, and I believe they resembled Elizabeth and me, angry at something they couldn't catch or see or understand. People from else-where—1.3 million in winter, 1.5 million in summer—flow through our towns. They scale our tuff boulders, take selfies, buy T-shirts, and drink in our bars. They make our economy viable, leaving money on the gummy tables of the old cafe and cheeseburger cartons by the highway, which Pop and I gather, our neon safety vests flapping, on the stretch adopted by Sierra Maps.

After the boys made their escape that September, the sheriff found a crowd gathered beside the Alabama Gates, cheering. Often in Payahuunadü the moon shines so brightly it throws shadows. That night in 1976 it rose waning gibbous yet huge over the mountains, and the sheriff saw water, a million gallons flowing from the aqueduct, wetting the long-dry lake bed.

"We'd all thought about doing something like that, but they actually hauled off and did it," a woman who worked in a local gas station told the *Los Angeles Times*. "So we gave them rousing shoulder punches and clinked beer bottles in their honor." The father of one of the boys is alleged to have told a neighbor, before he learned the culprit was his son, "If I ever find out who bombed the gates, I'll buy him a steak dinner."

The writer Ellen Meloy once visited a dam on the Colorado River. She walked into a visitor center and immediately alarmed the receptionist. "What would this river look like without the dam?" Meloy asked, her hair wind-wild, as if she could see the river freed—not *did*, she asked, but *would*—and the receptionist excused himself quickly behind an office door. Meloy got gone before a security guard could answer her question. "I felt the River's pressure," she wrote, "the lurking power of the outlaw."

How must the water have looked on any of those nights, forty years ago, or ninety, dampening the desert floor, flooding the dens of burrowing owls? It's something Elizabeth and I imagined as the current tangled our hair, the river not yet a penned and caught thing. Always, we felt, the landscape was on our side, drenched by loss as much as the people left behind.

AND SO WE grew up knowing: water runs until it doesn't. "Desert is the fossil of water," the writer Richard Rodriguez tells us. Near Jerusalem, a guide showed him "striations in mesas and the caverns water has bored through mountains of salt." The gorge, the cliffs and canyons and dry washes that cut this country, dry country, wilderness—these are water's opposite. And so my home is fossil. The water goes, but we remain.

WE LIVE BESIDE absence. What does it mean to be left behind with the dust or, in the case of many people in the Eastern Sierra, to follow the compulsion to make a pillaged place a home?

It was evening, Pop tells me, when his well went dry. Mid-November deep in drought and Mom eight years gone, the winter before Swall Meadows burned, the days growing shorter without losing the heat of early fall. In his house in Bishop, Pop put a glass under the faucet and flicked the handle. First, nothing. Then a choking noise from the pipes beneath the sink while outside in the backyard, forty feet below the roots of the dead lawn, the electric pump at the bottom of the well began to drag at the air. Without water to cool its moving parts, a pump burns up in sixty seconds. My father grabbed at the breaker box on the wall in the hallway. He saved the pump, but after that the house was without water, at least in the way we are used to having water. A little trickled from the aquifer if he waited, and water ran from a faucet for two minutes at a time before the pump threatened to burn up again. Thus began months of showering in increments, turning off the water to lather, washing dishes fork by fork.

A well, once run dry, cannot be deepened and restored. In the front yard two drillers, Bill and Gunny, looked at the ground, walked in slow circles, and chose a spot for a new well beside the bare peach tree, in front of the bay window.

Bill is six foot two and muscular. Gunny is an ex-Marine built like a brick, a few teeth missing from his smile. Bill used to work for a tech company in Washington until he decided he wanted a different life. Now he surrenders his hearing incrementally to the roar by which he guides the drill, listening without earmuffs for a change in pitch, which could mean a jam. It's Bill's job to stand on the rig's operating deck while mud splashes around him. When a driller's boots freeze to the platform, he has to whack them free with a hammer. The guys earn the phrase "colder than a well-digger's ass." It comes from way back when well diggers passed their days doubled over, wrestling dirt from a deepening hole. Rigs working all over Bishop, all over California and the West, sputtering in the dark, spitting up long-buried basalt and sand and silty clay, suggest a turning over, the loss of something hard to define. Old earth makes a mire over young lawns. Dry wells slip away into silence. But we are still up here walking around, living in the only way we have been taught—and it is water we must have.

I've flown home, on break from school in Minneapolis. In Bishop, I sit at Pop's kitchen counter while he stands at the stove, browning corn tortillas in a pan. Outside, the drill rig hums as it has hummed for days, a chorus mumbling Drought, drought, no water. At the counter Pop cuts carrots, and sunshine filters over him through the skylight. I examine a postcard I got at Manor Market, along with eggs from Bishop coops and tomatoes from the Central Valley. The aisles in Manor are narrow, and teenaged girls in heavy eyeliner operate the cash registers. Shy boys push mops over the floors and help me search for vanilla extract. Outside, battered trucks fill up at the pumps. On the roof a giant plastic rooster perches.

I found the postcard in a counter rack. The picture shows two men beside a creek in a cow-spotted pasture, swinging shovels at each other's heads. The caption reads, "Discussing water rights, a western pastime."

I slide the postcard across the counter to Pop, and he turns from the stove and smiles. "Whiskey's for drinking. Water's for fighting over."

This is a western adage I have heard many times. The contest over water passes between generations like a sodden torch. Bishop folks dam the shallow tributaries that pass through town, flooding their own yards and cutting off those below. Once, in summer, Pop passed a neighbor's house and noticed that the pond in his yard was full, a rare sight during the drought. The neighbor, Ole, an old Swede with a crew cut, had diverted the barely dribbling stream that crossed his property until water darkened his garden.

"Ole, your neighbors downstream are drying up," Pop said with a smile. "Just making an observation," he told me later, but Ole scowled.

"Those goddamned people," he said. "Let them come. I've got a shotgun."

That autumn, Pop and his neighbor Philip saw that the stream had stopped running through their own yards. Someone had dammed it higher on its course, where it spilled across a vegetable garden.

They returned after dark. "We wore black," Pop told me, "and climbed the fence." My father searched for the obstruction while Philip directed the beam of a flashlight onto the glitter of water. When he flashed the light toward neighboring houses, Pop growled, "*Philip*, knock it off, point your light at the ground, you're gonna get us shot." Pop found plywood and rocks and plastic blocking the stream and wrenched the mess free.

We fight with dynamite, we fight with newsprint. In 1905, when the city's seizure of Owens River loomed, Mary Austin wrote an article informing Angelenos what exactly they were about to consume. "Pigs wallow in it," she wrote of the river. Of the proposed site for a reservoir: "Cattle that died of anthrax still lie on the ground." After the aqueduct's completion, the *Owens Valley Herald* reported a mountain lion and deer drowned in the canal, along with a man whose body was not recovered for five days. "Los Angeles people should relish the thought that the water they are supposed to be drinking often times contains dead bodies before it reaches them," the *Herald* proffered—"a kind of cannibal soup, flavored with the carcasses of the lower animals."

How do you like our water now? In 1976, the day after the boys blasted the Alabama Gates, someone shot an arrow strapped with a stick of dynamite into the William Mulholland Memorial Fountain, a concrete and turquoise structure in a park between Hollywood and Glendale that spurts immense and sparkling, even in drought. Whoever launched the dynamite was never caught. It might as well have been any person in that midnight crowd. It might as well have been Elizabeth or me at sixteen.

Or anybody whose well has run dry in the valley of once flowing waters. Our wells fail because of drought—and because, during drought, DWP continues routing streams into the aqueduct. The groundwater beneath Owens Valley is not replenished, so its levels drop. Meadows die. Trees die. Invasive yellow grasses take over. DWP cuts the flow of the river so low that if you tried to float our old inner-tube route, Pop says, "you'd scrape your bottom."

In local newspapers, after the water left, Mulholland became the King of the Home Destroyers. Around Owens Valley I've heard him called a "lying thief." His successors at DWP are "LA slimes." On internet forums people suggest that the engineer should have been tarred and feathered, that California would be better off if Los Angeles were subsumed by a colossal flood. A member of a local group that monitors DWP activity calls the city's behavior "colonial rule" and "exploitation as usual."

Water's for fighting over. The local air pollution control district negotiates constantly with the city regarding the dust that billows from the lake bed. As a result, the bed is now an industrial zone devoted to dust mitigation. DWP trucks haul giant coils of plastic piping across the salt flats. The city covers swaths with broken rock to keep dirt from blowing. Paiute tribal monitors patrol the treatment of accidentally exhumed burial sites and teach DWP workers how to reinstate native vegetation, which keeps the soil in place. In some areas the city pumps shallow water back onto the bed it has drained, where curlews and gulls and tiger beetles and brine flies skitter. Signs invite visitors to watch for migrating waterfowl and walk through giant rusted tunnels: disembodied slices of the aqueduct. But though tourists swarm our towns and the mountains, visitors in this place of dust and heat and sulfur are rare. The lake bed is beautiful and weird, a reminder to everyone who drives past its white expanse that Los Angeles is still taking water from Owens Valley, just as it did one hundred years ago, as it would like to be doing one hundred years from today.

The tug-of-war between the city and Owens Valley is far from over, but Los Angeles was not the first entity to change this place. Here at the eastern base of the Sierra Nevada, deposits of sediment and earth splay from the mouths of canyons across the valley floor. These are called alluvial fans, flat and well watered by snowmelt from the mountains and good for farming. I've walked the outskirts of Bishop with a Paiute historian, Harry Williams, who studies the irrigation ditches his ancestors dug with a long stick made from mountain mahogany, called a pavado. With the ditches, the Nuumu watered nahavita and other seed grasses on the valley floor. Women harvested the seeds of the grasses. When spring came each year, the people got together for a feast and elected a head irrigator, called tuvaiju, for the summer.

Then white ranchers set dynamite to deepen the Paiute's irrigation ditches and planted different crops. The seed grasses once cultivated disappeared. When nahavita was no more, women took domestic work in white households. Men worked on ranches for wages. Some Paiutes owned homesteads, around which Los Angeles prowled.

Western water rights are often based on the concept of "first in time, first in right." In other words, whoever was using water first retains a right to that water. Before 1871 many tribes in the United States made treaties with the federal government in which they exchanged swaths of land for the freedom to govern themselves and use certain areas according to tradition. In California, between 1851 and 1852, eighteen treaties of "friendship and peace" were negotiated but never ratified. Then, in 1871, Congress put a stop to treaty making, and so the Paiutes drifted in limbo, without clear land and water rights, first use forgotten. DWP lurked close to the ear of the federal government, whispering, Put them here, not here, and not here.

"It is suggested that the Indians be moved from Owens Valley to new locations," DWP wrote in a report in 1933. Their homes "should be abandoned for reasons of conservation of water . . . and particularly to prevent contamination of water supplies."

An attorney for the secretary of the Interior Department visited Owens Valley in May 1932 and referenced the city's "program of destruction" in the valley. Sometimes, the attorney wrote, the Paiutes received "not over one-half or even one-fourth" of what a white counterpart got for comparable property. Of the Paiutes' relationship to their newest landlord, he added, "I am impressed as to the apparent lack of interest by Los Angeles in their welfare."

Around the same time, Owens Valley Paiutes formed a committee and wrote to the mayor of Los Angeles, noting that the city had rendered the valley "a barren waste" and requesting involvement in future water decisions. Meanwhile, Los Angeles urged the federal government to add big chunks of Owens Valley to the public trust and thus keep the land free from settlement. DWP sought the consolidation of the Paiute people so that their needs for water might infringe less on what the city intended to remove. In 1932 Paiute lands around Bishop were reduced from 67,000 to 875 acres.

These days tribal members are still taking Los Angeles and the federal government to court over water rights that were stripped and never restored. As lawsuits swirl in the bureaucratic drain, folks drive five hours south to DWP headquarters— on Hope Street, in downtown Los Angeles, once a plane of chaparral, now surrounded by pools reflecting skyscrapers—to request, then to demand, and sometimes finally to plead for water for their farms and gardens. In much of the literature written about the aqueduct, the Paiutes are not mentioned.

When I walked with Harry in the valley, he pointed to a depression in the brush that I could've mistaken for a jeep road or a dry wash. Picture it full of water, tended by the tuvaiju, the land all around us growing green, a busy Nuumu village. On that day the only moisture visible danced miles away at the foot of the White Mountains, a mirage. "I stand here sometimes," Harry said, "and I think, Can you imagine?"

SITTING AT POP'S counter, I hear a screech and a muffled curse, and the rig falls silent. My father turns from the stove and is gone out the back door. In the yard Gunny swears and spits and kicks the tires, and Bill stands with arms folded, his sweatshirt and jeans coated in sludge.

The rig's hose has ruptured. The hose is supposed to pump mud into the deepening well, washing out crushed rock and lubricating the bit. Now it lies on the ground like a run-over snake, the black rubber torn. Bill has wrapped the hose in duct tape, but tape can't hold back another fist of frigid mud. The mud pumped into the well applies hundreds of pounds of pressure to the soil walls, preventing collapse, and "when the hose blows," Pop says, "it blows spectacularly." The peach tree and the window drip a slick gray slurry.

The drillers put their hands under their armpits and shiver. Pop offers to run downtown to the hardware store for a hose clamp while the men change into dry clothes. "Just a half-hour delay," he says, hope in his eyes. "With any luck, we'll have water before dark."

My father spent the autumn digging trenches, tearing up the rocky yard, making way for the new well. Sometimes my brother and sister worked beside him, each of them calmed, momentarily, in the chaos of their lives, Kaela too skinny to be of much use, Anthony solid muscle, his dark hair gathered in a braid at the nape of his neck. Pop worked fastest, hurling dirt over his shoulder with ruthless concentration, an efficient strength that seemed to come from somewhere other than his thin body.

Weeks before I came home to listen to the rig roar in the yard, when the trenches for the new well were half dug, my father hoisted a jackhammer and attacked the soil. A rare rain had fallen in the night, and the soaked earth froze harder than concrete. Frozen dirt has a little give, just enough spring to resist the point of a jackhammer, and so my father bore down with his scant weight and precarious height. A jack-hammer is fifty pounds of steel, almost a third of his body, and with it, he split the ground. Twenty years ago he lost some of the vision in his left eye to a virus but not, as might be expected, to the shards of metal and rock that have flown into his face over the years.

William Mulholland designed water systems without blueprints or charts. The veins of his city existed as maps only in his mind, and I can't help but think of my father's map business, his haphazard, hand-scrawled invoices, his life in the mountains planned around no proven model but some inclination snatched from the belly of a lenticular cloud. Mulholland must have known the risks demanded by the California sky. Where else to run your life on intuition, to fly by the seat of your pants, but in a place of dreams, of long shots and plane wrecks?

When my father digs trenches in the backyard, that is all he is doing. Try to talk to him and he doesn't hear. The shovel fills and dirt flies. At work in LA ditches, Mulholland knew the same quieting, the distillation of everything to the task at hand—but more than that, he labored with a goal greater than a dug trench or a clear stream, greater than money or social position. Something else pushed that shovel, something the president of the water company must have seen as he passed. For Mulholland, the core of that concentration was his version of the greatest good. The core was water and all it could mean for his city. For my father it is the gossamer earth of this valley, transformed by another man's great ambition.

UNTIL 1926 BISHOP's Main Street was a dusty, unpaved ribbon with a white flag pole planted in the middle and posts for hitching horses studding the sides. Downtown had a general store and a market, a law office, a jewelry shop. Farm families came to town to buy flour and sugar, to do their banking, to eat ice cream cones at the Clark Hotel. The men had names like Dick, Will, Oliver, and Ross, and the women were Fanny, Grace, Vivian, Ada. The farmers planted rows of cottonwoods to block the gusts of the Sierra Wave. They sent their children to Bishop Union through the eighth grade, dressed a calf in a Red Cross sash to fund-raise for the poor, gathered their fattest pumpkins for the Tri-County Fair, and marched for the ban of alcohol.

In 1906, just before construction began on the aqueduct, Mary Austin sold her house and told Owens Valley goodbye. She wrote, "She knew that the land of Inyo would be desolated, and the cruelty and deception smote her beyond belief."

Be here for a moment now. Evening settles as we head downtown for the hose clamp. Pop drives while I ride in the passenger's seat, windows open to the dull chill of this drought January, catching the scent of dry pasture. Bishop is the self-proclaimed "Mule Capital of the World" and every May hosts a week of mule shows, a parade, and lots of line dancing. In the metal filing cabinets of the Eastern California Museum, blocks from Mary Austin's barely changed house, I have often flipped through folders in the archives, their titles painting a portrait: bats, barbed wire, deer, fossils, fire protection, guns, ghost towns, hantavirus, sheep, saddles. I've found four fat folders labeled "Mule Days," six labeled "Packers and Pack Outfits," three "Aircraft Wreck," five "Earthquake," and more stamped "Water Rights" than I have time to count.

The police blotter in the *Inyo Register* recounts: "6:11 p.m., report from South Main Street business that a raccoon dropped out of the A/C unit. Raccoon released in the field." On Line Street, a motel advertises CONTL BREAKFAST on one side of the marquee and INENTAL B EAKFAST on the other. Downtown features four stoplights, a few antiques shops, a camera store, a bookstore, a bakery, and two coffee shops. Wander past Rosie's Palm Reading, Hi-Sierra Crafter's Mall, Taylor's Family Shoes, Joseph's Bi-Rite Market, all hunched together Wild West style. Wilson's Eastside Sports, big and brightly lit, puts fleeces, jackets, and merino base layers on sale every spring. In Dusty's Pets, an immense blonde woman frowns as a bell jingles on the door. A clutch of teenagers saunters, Wranglered and Stetsoned, in town for the rodeo state finals. Tourists eat enchiladas and gaze through restaurant windows at the town going by.

This place can feel like a sieve, punched full of holes by the headlights that stream through, the drivers resentful of the little valley towns they have to pass before reaching ski resorts, this mandatory slowing down. Those watching from the sidewalk stumble backward in the gust of a passing semi. They have the job of retaining the character of the place against a tide of movement. Dwellers of tourist towns live in the history, the seasons, the drama and gossip of a place, while the drivers of sports cars jitter at the stoplight, look down at their phones, refresh the weather forecast for tomorrow and tomorrow. A tourist is a bug on a dead thing, according to David Foster Wallace, but I disagree—a tourist is a bug on a thing being kept alive by the people who stay.

Listen to the clatter of horse trailers, RVs, Harleys, high-way patrol. At the open mic in the Black Sheep coffee shop, a spectacled man sings, "Country roads, take me home," and the sunburned staff behind the counter belts loudly along. In 1924 a doctor interviewed at the occupation of the Alabama Gates said, "This is the only place on Earth I can live in and I'm going to remain living here until I die a natural death. They can't drive me out."

"I know this people," Mary Austin wrote in 1905. "Breed of the desert they are . . . and I promise you there will be entered against the city of Los Angeles incalculable forces, intangible and immeasurable by any standard known to them, maddening meekness which seems to surrender and rises up over night."

It has been argued more than once that the people who fought the city one hundred years ago were happy someone wanted to buy them out of difficult country—that in light-ing dynamite, they hoped only to drive up the price of their land and get rich before leaving. Being of this country, I don't believe the story is that easy.

Pop turns onto Main against a stream of tourist traffic. We park at High Country Lumber, and I follow him among stacks of garden tools. A popcorn machine hums in the cor-ner, and shoppers dribble yellow crumbs.

My father can build bathrooms, walls, roofs; repair burst pipes; and muck out plugged sewers. If my car doesn't start, I call him, mimic the noise it's making, and I'm on the road in fifteen minutes. He knows his way around the aisles of every hardware store in town. On birthdays and Christmas he passed out wrench sets and screwdrivers, wrapped (wadded) economically in newspaper. For a long time, I thought a hammer was a toy. Now he finds the hose clamp quickly; he doesn't browse.

Two local kids, James and Heather, stand at the registers. Heather has long platinum hair, but Pop mixes her up with a brunette named Paige. Once, he asked Paige to tell him about some of her favorite books, "so I can remember that Paige is a reader." The kids at High Country Lumber are used to my father, who's known around town by his height and his friendliness. He says, "This is my daughter," and pats me on the shoulder. He's thinking about the well waiting in the yard, perhaps filling slowly with water and perhaps not. But you can't get anything done quickly in a town this small, a town this busted, this pretty.

Today he gets Heather's name right and jokes with James as he rings up the hose clamp. James has the deepest voice I've ever heard and he reads ads for KIBS, the local country-western station. Maybe someone from the station heard him counting change here in High Country Lumber, and now his baritone punctuates ballads by Merle Haggard and Garth Brooks, promoting Manor Market gift certificates and specials at Perry Motors. Talent in Bishop is communal. Pop plays trombone enthusiastically in the local orchestra, and my allergy doctor sings in the accompanying choir. In the ways small towns share what's good and what isn't, ours hasn't changed too much from the start of the twentieth century when Mary Austin wrote of a collectively owned hat: "*the* hat; this was a high silk topper which had been brought into the Valley by a young Jew, who had bought it for his wedding and afterward had no use for it. It was always produced for important funerals."

It must have been city shock that led my father, when my sister and I moved to Los Angeles after high school and he came to visit, to act slightly insane. He doesn't understand what it means to spend most of the day indoors. "So many people," he'd say, baffled by a jammed freeway. "Where do they all go? What do they all do?"

In Los Angeles once, a man boarded an elevator with us, rode a few floors, and stepped off without saying hello. "Did you see that guy?" Pop said, hurt. "No interaction at all; no eye contact!" And I had to explain that probably this man was not a nasty person, that this was a cultural thing.

In 1888, two years after Mulholland became the water company's superintendent, Mary Austin was "daunted by the wrack of the lately 'busted' boom" of Los Angeles. Of the "evidences of planlessness, the unimaginative economic greed, the idiot excitation of mere bigness, the strange shapeless ugliness," Austin wrote that she was frightened. "What have I come to? What if this thing should catch me?"

When Pop talks about water and Los Angeles, he uses the word *unethical*.

"Swimming pools," he says. "Tropical gardens in a desert."

The city poses a threat to a certain way of inhabiting the world. When I help my father send late notices to the tenants of the storage units he owns, he won't let me use full names. "That's too formal!" he says. "Just write, 'Hi, Jim.'" The place he loves, the only one he understands, is a place where your neighbors walk up the drive and tattle when they see your son chasing deer on his mountain bike or smoking on the porch. Where anyone's snowplow becomes communal property after a blizzard.

"I think my grandfather—his vision—was a city like Dublin, which was the city of his childhood," Mulholland's granddaughter said. "And it was a vision I think of a nineteenth-century city, where people ambled on streets and knew one another."

The historian David Carle wrote to ask what the granddaughter thought Mulholland would make of Los Angeles in the year 2000. "I don't have to speculate," she wrote back. "He wouldn't like it."

It is fair to say Mulholland created a city unlike other cities, a city beneath seemingly eternal sun, the light diluted slightly as nitrogen dioxide mixes with atmospheric water vapor to produce a haze visible from the tops of mountains, which we call smog. This man made enemies of prominent Angelenos, installing meters to stop them from overwatering their lawns. Did he imagine Hollywood? A march of identical noses? Bastions of wealth set off against tenements, apartment fires, beaches that charge admission, concrete covering the banks of his beloved Los Angeles River?

One of the boys who blasted the Alabama Gates in 1976 spent a month in juvie, likely in Owens Valley, in rooms my brother came to know, wracked as he was by his own desire to devour and destroy. That final dynamiter went away for a while, came home to Owens Valley, and got a job as an aqueduct and reservoir keeper with DWP.

"This is the most beautiful place I know on Earth," the teenaged bomber, now in middle age, said to a reporter from the *Los Angeles Times* who tracked him down after four decades and took his picture, his back to the camera as he looked over dry land. When the story of home was still simple for him, he could only articulate his love with violence.

Now he believes Los Angeles is to thank for saving Owens Valley. When the water went away, growth occurred some-place else.

Certain historians agree. They suggest that with water, Owens Valley might not be the country that drew my par-ents together for love of its strangeness. As it is, Bishop can't grow much larger, can't sprawl much farther into the desert, because the economy is limited, because 1 percent of lands in Inyo County are privately owned while more than 90 percent are controlled by federal agencies.

In 1906 chief forester Gifford Pinchot created a protected federal forest in Owens Valley. When prodded later about this decision, the forester wrote that he did what he could "to prevent the people of Los Angeles from being held up by a handful of people—and a very small handful of people—liv-ing along the line of the proposed canal. . . . I used the power that lay in me for the greatest good of the greatest number . . . the results have abundantly justified my action. I would do the same again." The forester did not intend to guard the desert for the desert's sake; the thought of a protected forest with few trees was ludicrous. As he saw it—as plenty see it now—there was nothing in the desert to preserve. And yet he preserved desert. The Inyo National Forest, which wraps Owens Valley in wilderness, was created because Los Angeles had a need to keep the land undeveloped and its water unclaimed. We will never know what might have existed, what kind of world this valley might have been, if Mulholland had known a version of good not wedded to growth, had lived by a different code.

When I swim with Elizabeth, when I listen to the drill rig guzzle in Pop's yard, anxious at the sputtering tap, feeling all around me the absent and the sparse, am I mourning what I believe to be mine? What would it mean to claim this history and its results? The bitter self that climbs from Elizabeth's car at the water's edge knows little of the past, knows only that something is gone. The story of water in Owens Valley, as I first understood it, was a sad story of wrong done, a near tall tale with a suit-coated villain and cowboy heroes. The legend of a loss, its familiar, abstract pain, accompanied me when I had to go away. What was missing became its own force. We felt it like skin scraped off bone. But that story was incomplete.

For one, the story of my home, as I first learned it, was missing half. It was missing what happened before the farmers showed up to have their water taken away. Hoavadunuki, the Paiute man from Big Pine, said this about his life: "I learned to hunt when I was just a young boy. I made all my own bows and arrows, and hunted in the valley for rabbits and ducks." He played a hoop and pole game. He hunted a mountain sheep with a musket given to him by his future father-in-law, to impress his wife's family. When he killed a deer, he said: "I remained overnight on the mountain and treated myself to a feast of deer meat. The next day I returned to the valley.

I distributed the meat to my people and sold the upper part, which belongs to the hunter."

"Now, what is it you own?" a judge asked the Los Angeles City Council in 1892. "Water in the river was never owned by anybody. You can't get a title to water as it flows in the river. It is like the wild animal. It has to be captured."

Hoavadunuki's deer was divided between hunter and tribe. To whom does water belong? To its harvester? To all who need it? When water is taken, who inherits the loss? A Bishop man whose grandparents sold land to Los Angeles in the wake of the aqueduct wrote to the *Inyo Register* that "multiple 'truths' exist about what occurred in the valley in the early 1900s." The lake bed billows. We find old foundations, the trunks of fallen cottonwoods, ancient ditches, and we wonder how best to carry on.

Water from the aqueduct first poured down a hillside near Los Angeles on the fifth of November in 1913. A woman sang "California, Hail the Waters!" and Mulholland addressed a crowd of forty thousand from a makeshift stage. Amid cheering, cannon fire, and the detonation of aerial bombs, Mulholland threw a hand toward the cascade and spoke immortal words. "There it is," he said. "Take it."

All his life he kept a vial of Owens River water, collected from that first gush.

I can almost picture Mulholland's younger hands on a shovel. He is eighty years gone now, gone since the decade of my grandparents' birth, though he doesn't feel so far away. I find a picture taken at the end of his long career. In old age Mulholland sits before the photographer, no longer measuring, in his mind, the distance between a city and a river, and all I can do is note the darkness of his jacket, the weariness in his eyes.

When he was a ditchdigger and the aqueduct not even a dream, Mulholland rescued a three-inch oak from the blade of his shovel and planted it nearby. He returned to the tree not long before his death and laid a hand on its trunk.

"I saved its life once," he said. "I wonder if it is conscious of my presence today."

THE SUN SETS over Bishop. Leafless red-barked willows line the river, and the valley turns to copper. The sky is yellow, the sky is magenta. In Pop's yard beside the peach tree, the drill rig rests, quiet, the rusted trunk retracted and collapsed above the mess of coils. The long black hose wears the clamp my father bought, a silver band in the place it's torn. Mud that spewed over the rig's yellow paint has dried to a dusty skin. Someone has halfheartedly wiped the slurry from a window, and the glass is streaky and bright in the day's last light.

Bill and Gunny kneel around a fresh hole. The new well is a tube six inches across, rising to knee level and dropping two hundred feet into the ground. It is possible, even after so much mud and hope and toil, that the soil at the bottom will prove parched.

Pop and I linger in the yard. If there's water here, the old well will be allowed to slip into darkness. It's up to my father to sever its lines. Once he makes the cut, sand will work into the tubes and the plastic will grow brittle.

Already Bill and Gunny have lowered a test pump to the bottom. When they turn it on, water will spray, or the pump will choke on air. My father calls this *the moment of truth*.

There it is. Take it. The bare branches of the peach tree rustle, and twilight comes moonless. Soon stars will appear, and wind will cool the valley floor. For now, though, the night is warm for January.

Okay, my father says. Bill flicks the switch, and water rises from the ground.

4. Flight Plan

MY FATHER HAS WHITE hair and wind-cured skin, and sometimes his knees bother him. He is late in his fifties. "Weird!" he says when I ask him what that's like, yet he heaves enormous pieces of furniture into truck beds while I trail uselessly behind. He wears glasses and occasionally wakes at night and cannot go back to sleep. Beyond this, he is not much changed from the young man caught in a photograph on a hike to Coyote Flats three decades ago. In midleap he hovers at the center of the frame, between granite and blue sky, the white tops of the Sierra flung up in the background. His back arches, his head tips, and sun fills his face. His shirt flies behind him. His arms stretch, wing-like. It does not seem possible that he will return to the ground.

I have often wondered how he came to stay here, but never why.

Some morning thirty years ago, he makes the short climb up a hillside of tawny boulders, where orbs of granite lean in piles like dinosaur eggs. Pinyon pines scatter. He pauses for water, pauses to look over the valley floor and Bishop, a small plot of green amid brown. The river gorge cuts a shadow. He screws the cap onto his water bottle. Wind buoys the brim of his canvas hat. A hawk catches a gust and he watches it rise, then drops his pack and runs downhill, long legs pounding dirt heels first. He runs until he turns weightless, body ahead of feet, feet skimming rock, looking up to see the hawk pitch and turn, the valley beneath him deep and wide.

AT TWENTY-FOUR MY father left his first home for a new one. He left the central coast of California where he lived with his father and mother and sister in the town of San Luis Obispo, among low mountains, strawberry fields, oak trees, and hills that rolled to the sea. Later he brought Kaela and Anthony and me to visit San Luis Obispo so we could know his parents as Nana and Fafa and learn to hack the seeds out of pomegranates and slide down dunes.

"The mountains to the north were covered with clouds at their summits," a traveler from New England recalled of San Luis Obispo, early in the spring of 1861: "Their green sides, the great green plain to the south and west at our feet, the curious old town, the rugged buttes rising from this plain, the winding streams . . . the ocean beyond, covered with a fog near its surface, white, and tossed by the wind into huge billows." California, this windy place that seems to be on fire half the time, can be many things, can be soft and green. Among these hills and plains, not far from the tossed billows, Fafa made a bench from a fence post to mark my father's birth, the wood polished by the flanks of cows who rested there for a century. My father and his sister trained a chestnut gelding called Chico. They raised a sheep and jogged with her through the neighborhood. In summer the sun shone and yellowed the grass on the hills. In winter rain wet the pasture. My father's brown hair curled; he looked like his mother. He raced bicycles and taught himself to fix popped tires and loose chains. At the little airport two miles from his house, he watched planes lift off the runway. To him, riding felt like flying.

I can imagine him, skin sun browned and not yet weathered, seeing the place that became his home for the first time, on a high school trip to the Sierra Nevada. "I just remember how big the mountains were," he says. The students walked over snowfields. "And I had the lightest pack and the biggest feet, and everybody else punched through, while I stayed on top of the snow crust and had a great time!" He jumped from forty-foot cliffs into a frigid lake and camped in three inches of September snow. He passed six diamondback rattlers basking on a hiking trail and listened to the whirring of rattles around his tent in the night. All this sold him on the place. He left San Luis Obispo and drove through the San Joaquin Valley, around the southern tail of the Sierra Nevada and north along the mountains' east side—all so he could fly.

IN THE MONTHS after he arrived, my father woke in the night with snowflakes falling in his face. Wind crawled through a hole in the roof of an abandoned restaurant, his first Owens Valley home. He wrapped a worn down jacket around his shoulders and lay awake, listening to the whining needles of the blue spruce.

The burned husk of the Rocking K restaurant, gutted by fire years before, sat in a little neighborhood five miles west of Bishop, divided from town by desert. The pipes and the plumbing had frozen and burst, and the beams that supported the roof stood blackened and coated in ice. The owner let my father stay rent-free if he cleaned the little pond and the streams that ran around the neighboring houses. He repaired the restaurant's charred roof with a staple gun and a blue plastic tarp. When the wind ripped the tarp from the hole, my father climbed a ladder in the dark, hands freezing, headlamp strapped to his forehead, to tamp it back down.

To "fly by the seat of one's pants" is an aviation term from the 1930s that means going into the sky without much in the way of a plan or helpful instruments, to rely on intuition, to hope for luck. Climbing the power pole with an electrician's manual and a pair of pliers, he bootlegged his electricity—"Sort of a miracle I didn't fry!"

A four-inch hole remained in the ground where the toilet used to be before half the building was bulldozed. "I had an open sewer, is what I had." Pop laughs. When it rained he set buckets around the dining room; if he forgot, a river ran out the back door. He stood under an old metal showerhead and hopped and whistled in the cold spray.

He rode his bike to his job at the Bishop airport winter mornings when his little green car wouldn't start in the cold. Winter nights the walk-in freezer stayed a snug forty degrees while the dining room, where his cot lay, dropped to twenty. There, a dark stone fireplace loomed, and a row of broken six-foot windows overlooked the valley, the glass blown out by fire. When the wind snuck inside, he dragged his cot to the freezer.

At the Bishop dump, from a sprawl of twisted metal, he rescued two stainless-steel sinks, a stove, and a washing machine. He learned to sweat copper fittings and buffed the granite of the fireplace, stoked it with pine and pinyon, and sanded ash from the beams that raised the roof, exposing redwood. You could say he made his first home out of fire.

THE COUNTY-OPERATED BISHOP airport sits at an elevation of four thousand feet, closer to the White Mountains than the Sierra Nevada but well in view of both. The airport is a clump of hangars, an empty control tower, three runways, and a terminal converted from an army barracks. In the fall of 1982 when my father first saw the terminal, it was sided in olive-green asbestos. Inside was a lobby with chairs, a few benches and couches, and a back room where pilots could spread maps on a table and chart flight plans. Planes came in for fuel or to tether for the night, each a blur of white, lights at the wingtips and tails flashing pink and yellow after sunset, snub-nosed Cessnas and Beechcrafts with red-banded wings. The planes waited on the tarmac, their dark windows gazing over miles of brush. My father had the job of climbing onto the wings with a hose and filling the fuel tanks and cleaning the bathroom and checking long fences along the runway for holes that might let cattle through. At day's end he walked across the tarmac and secured the tie-down chains that hooked wings to the earth. If a windstorm rose in the night, an untethered plane could rise up and fly away.

The writer Ellen Meloy once called the Sierra Nevada "the land's attempt at flight." My father built his own slick silver airplane, an RV-4 he named Zippy, and as he looped through the sky, he learned the way peaks shrink and swell, pines become green points, lakes appear in beds of granite in the hidden parts of the mountains. All this made sense. It still does. He is Robert Atlee: even his name suggests his place at the leeward base of mountains. As a child, I watched him leap off granite cliffs into frigid Mack Lake, tumbling with long legs pulled to his chest, and I could not imagine him anyplace else.

I have flown in small planes with my father, and I have run behind him down a mountainside, leaping over brush, sliding in loose soil, as if we could lift off into the very cobalt sky. Risk is omnipresent, but most days in the mountains remind him of his first trip in a glider: the plane looped, and my father, eleven years old and seat belted behind his pilot uncle, felt his body go weightless as he peered through the clear canopy and saw ground where once was sky.

"Here—here's his place," the poet Robert Browning wrote in 1855, "where meteors shoot, clouds form, / Lightnings are loosened, / Stars come and go! Let joy break with the storm." Many times in those early days in Bishop, my father took off in the RV-4 after dark, here in the high desert, where the sky moves closer. "I just drifted," he remembers. "Like an astronaut." He flew until the peaks shrank to shadows, the air clear, nothing but plexiglass between him and the stars.

SOMETIMES, IN SPRING or late winter, a strong west wind crests the Sierra Nevada and throws lenticular clouds into the sky. Remember the wind that fanned flames into Swall Meadows. The clouds that accompany the wind we call the Sierra Wave look like enormous stacked pillows, hovering stationary over Owens Valley for hours.

The Wave rises forty thousand feet above the valley floor. Below the wind's crest, the air churns in a horizontal vortex called a rotor—an F3 tornado turned on its side. Through updraft and downdraft, the Wave snaps the wings off planes, shreds cabins, and drops pilots through miles of open air. The Wave also provides incredible lift, a sensation of swinging over the earth. Pilots who know what they're dealing with catch its updrafts like hawks and set altitude records. Over Owens Valley, small planes called gliders—engineless, their cabins often without pressure control—climb ten thousand feet above the cruising altitude of passenger jets. At such elevations the fluid inside veins bubbles, and skin crawls with the ghost-legs of a million insects. When outside air temperature reaches seventy below, tears freeze at the corners of the eyes. Frostbite blanches toes. If an oxygen system malfunctions at altitude, a pilot loses consciousness in fifteen seconds.

From his post at the airport, my father often watched the Wave cloud line up along the Sierra and warned the pilots who came into the terminal not to take off. The ones who tried anyway came back with windows smashed and seats soaked in urine. Engineers, meteorologists, and daredevil pilots had been studying the Wave phenomenon long enough to nickname it "the Monster." In 1952 a pilot named Larry Edgar rode the Sierra Wave deliberately for eight vertical miles in a Pratt-Read glider, setting a world record for altitude and landing safely. Three years later, as Edgar descended toward Bishop, he hit the Wave gusting at 185 miles per hour and his wings shattered, the glass of his cabin shattered. Feet trapped in the rudder pedals of the maimed Pratt-Read, he plummeted, temporarily blind.

"It may sound a little funny to some and inadequate to others," Edgar recalled, "but at that time I exclaimed aloud, '*Darn!*'"

His parachute engaged and his boots slipped off. Larry Edgar landed alive in a gravel quarry while construction workers watched the scraps of his glider swirl in the sky.

My father flew the Wave before he knew better. He warned the passenger of his RV-4, a man who needed a ride to Mojave, that the sky, clear except for a stack of lenticular clouds, raged wild. How wild, he didn't understand. He flew below the level of power lines to stay clear of the churning rotor and could see, in detail, clumps of sagebrush and rabbitbrush on the ground. When they rose too high, wind grabbed the wings and wrenched the plane halfway upside down.

On another flight he remembers descending the Wave's crest, plummeting toward the valley floor, the airplane momentarily out of his control.

ONE AFTERNOON WHEN I was eight years old—a warm Halloween, Wheeler Crest still bare of snow—Pop and I followed a deer trail until we reached the wreckage of a plane, crumpled above our house against the oldest granite in the Sierra. Soft gray seats, belts still dangling. Scraps of plastic, a notebook that belonged to the pilot, scattered in the sagebrush—the fuselage already lifted out by helicopter but these remnants left to the mountain. A year earlier two men and a woman boarded the Beechcraft in Los Angeles and flew north into a snowstorm. The granite face in front of them was invisible, swallowed by cloud.

That October afternoon I picked up the silver Beechcraft logo that had fallen from the side of the plane and carried it home.

Not long after the crash, I remember a helicopter landing on a patch of dirt near the corner where the school bus left Kaela and Anthony and me. We watched two sheriff's deputies unload three long, zipped bags of gray plastic and stack them in an ambulance.

"We should be prepared for the possibility . . . that the terror of the universe has not yet fossilized and the universe has not run out of blowups," Norman Maclean wrote about a great fire in Montana in 1949 that killed thirteen firefighters. "When last seen," Maclean wrote of the smoke that merged with the jet stream, "the tri-visual figure had stretched out and was on its way, far, far, far away, looking like death and looking back at its dead and looking forward to its dead yet to come. Perhaps it could see all of us."

If the universe has not run out of blowups, if the smoke of every great fire can see us all, that billow must resemble a Wave cloud, and what kid can look up from the bottom and not wonder?

Austin called this country empty of most things but beauty, madness, death, and God. But no god of human definition is taller than the Wave, can clout the tops of the mountains. No answers and only questions for those of us living below. That afternoon at the bus stop, before the sheriffs unloaded the helicopter,

I remember standing on the bodies in their bags. I remember climbing into the cockpit, being shown the instruments of control by the pilot, all the while standing on bodies in my light-up tennis shoes. I remember the softness under my feet.

"No way," Pop says now. "That was another day, another time, that you got to climb inside a cockpit. We didn't let you stand on bodies." But death and flight and mountains and the desert below are mixed up in my history.

AFTER AN ILLNESS Hoavadunuki remembered, "I died and my soul started southward. . . . While I was traveling, I looked down and my soul saw a stick in the ground not quite as tall as a man." This was the soul stick, muguvada. "I seized the stick and looked back toward my mountain. . . . I knew then that I would be all right and live forever, for whenever a soul going south sees the soul stick, it knows that it will come back."

Hoavadunuki greets his death flying. But something in the valley below tethers him. The landscape, his Birch Mountain, talks to him out of the mystery of wind and weather and death, bringing him down to the earth again. You will live forever, that mystery tells him, in your relation to this place.

I grew up watching Wave clouds pile above the mountains, listening to my father talk about the wind the way other men might talk about God. In flight logs, pilots describe nosing an aircraft down at the base of those lenticular clouds—"I felt like an ant looking up a wall of the Grand Canyon"—or riding the wind eight miles into the sky—"It's like God holding you up in His hands."

Mary Austin said that weather is "the visible manifestation of the Spirit moving itself in the void." If God is ever present, if God can get in through the frames of our doors and the pores in our skin, then on this obsidian edge of California, God is the wind and the dust it carries.

Before the plane hit the mountain, before I imagined that I stood on bodies, our little pug dog, Ricky, got into the garage and chased my pet rabbit until she curled in a pile of Pop's ski equipment and her heart stopped beating from pure fear. I don't remember if the Wave cloud filled the sky, but it could have hovered above us, a shifting being. My mother helped me scoop the stiff little body into a shoebox. I stood on our porch with the box in my arms and asked her where the breathing, nose-twitching part of my rabbit had gone, and she said, *I don't know, sweetie, I don't know.* I remember her tears. I had seen mule deer crumpled on the roadside, and our neighbor, a bearded man called Whispering Jim who gave us bananas whenever we stopped by his cabin, had vanished from our lives after catching hantavirus from the mice beneath his floors. But as I held the rabbit, I was, for the first time, considering death as a state separate from life.

As a child, I went willingly into the First United Methodist Church and sat on the red velvet pews and looked up at the wooden cross above the altar, at the stained-glass windows, the rose and dove, and listened to Caddy, a stout and smiling man with white hair and a round belly, who declared he might as well have been born Buddhist, Jewish, whatever— he answered to the presence of God as love, and in this way, he was Mom's kind of pastor. Caddy sat with us on red

carpeted steps beside the pulpit and gave the children's lesson. We answered earnestly when he asked each kid to name
her favorite flower—in my case, the Venus flytrap—before
sending us off for Mom's Sunday school class, which was
usually about sharing and never about dodging hell or getting
yourself to heaven, whatever that was.

It was my job to carry the light of Christ into the church
at the beginning of the service, quivering at the tip of a long
brass pole, and back out at the end. And I was happy to be
complicit in this idea, even if, in my child eyes, what poured
over us at this high elevation was only sunlight, and sunlight
alone was just fine.

On the afternoon I stood with the rabbit in my arms, I
asked my father, Where is she? Where has she gone? And he
told me, gently, the valley stretching behind him, that as far
as he understood, life was consciousness, and consciousness
was synapses firing in the brain. Once those synapses stopped
firing, that consciousness was gone—not gone somewhere
else, but *gone*, as if before birth. Years later, soon after college and newly flung into the world, I met Pop and my siblings
at Nana and Fafa's house on the coast, that place of tossed
billows. Here in my father's childhood bedroom, I woke with
a fear of nothingness, of what it means to not exist—a need
for light, a panic I could not push aside. And then I woke
Pop; I stood in the doorway of the room where he slept on a
futon on the floor. He lifted his head from the pillow. In the
dark I could not see his face. He did not seem surprised to see
me there long after midnight. He told me something about
how many billions of lives have passed before us, about the

futility of railing against what you are powerless to change or understand. A shrug, a surrender to the unknown. This was not salvation, but it was a way to go back to sleep and live the next day.

I accepted this, accepted life and its absence without inherent meaning. How could I believe in a presence my father did not see rolling over the mountains with the wind?

TERRY TEMPEST WILLIAMS, a Mormon: "It's strange how deserts turn us into believers. . . . I am brought down to my knees by its beauty. . . . I will have no other gods before me."

Richard Rodriguez, a Catholic: "God is a desert God who comes in the middle of a desert winter. . . . I kneel to the desert God."

"Whenever I dream," said Hoavadunuki of his life in the desert, "especially if it is a bad dream which means trouble, I talk to something in the darkness. I talk to my power. . . . I talk to the night."

"The desert," according to California author Rebecca Solnit, "is the best place to hear the voice of the whirlwind." In the thirteenth century, the mystic Meister Eckhart wrote of the "still desert . . . where there is no one at home, yet where the spark of the soul is more at peace than in itself." Eckhart christened his god "Nameless Nothing," and the mystic Boehme wrote in the seventeenth century of the love of something vast that "may fitly be compared to Nothing, for it is deeper than any Thing, and is as nothing with respect to all things, forasmuch as it is not comprehensible by any of them. And because it is nothing respectively, it is therefore free from all things."

Those of us who know desert know it to be at once empty and full, know the way water's fossil remains, know the response that sometimes comes from the night. "Dazzling obscurity," the mystics wrote. "Whispering silence; teeming desert." Any mystery fit for this place must exist laden with contradictions.

So many times Pop has told us this story: "We would sit out there in the little terminal and have discussions about this and that, and one time I was just playing devil's advocate in a discussion with a Christian lady who worked for the rental car company. She was talking about God's existence, and I told her I didn't disagree with what she said, but if we were in a philosophy class, this is what the philosophers would say if they believed and followed the philosophy of Nietzsche."

Even now he dregs up Nietzsche, arguing gently with his Jehovah's Witness friend about whether she should disown her daughter, who doesn't believe. "Nietzsche said that you could justify the death of God," he explained to the rental car lady. "Since he interprets God as a belief, then as long as people believe in God, God exists. But if nobody believes in God, then God is dead. And that's a very simplified version."

The rental car lady did not appreciate hearing that her god was dead—even if, as Pop pointed out, this was "just a philosophy. That if you don't believe in it, it doesn't exist."

My father was fired from the Bishop airport on a warm morning in fall, one year before he met my mother, five years before I was born. Pop had forgotten Nietzsche's angst over God's loss, which the philosopher sees as humanity's loss of a moral compass. In my reading, Nietzsche didn't fear the absence of a concrete deity in the lives of the people. He feared the absence of meaning, of mystery and love.

Pop was awkward during communion at First United Methodist the few times he came along, but he has never needed any god to give him a compass. He once took an eager family for a hot-air-balloon ride when he was miserable with the flu because they wanted so badly to be up in the air. He forgot, in his sickness, to collect the check, and when he wrote to them later, they never paid. He rents the cabin he used to live in with my mother to a new tenant without doing a credit check and lowers the man's rent when the economy is bad in town. He'll lend money to anyone, once.

"Anyway," he says, "she complained to the director of public works, who was Mormon, that I was an atheist and I was talking on public time and arguing with people, and I got fired. Mike had to fire me because on county time I was not supposed to be expressing political or philosophical opinions. I was just supposed to be doing my job and keeping quiet."

I can imagine him telling the rental car lady that her god was dead, not in anger or jealousy or fear but in the way he once told me to get a shovel from below the porch to dig a rabbit's grave in the apple orchard. Saying to both of us, in his way, Look, this life is your own, all you have. And if you can live your life here, rooted in such a home, what use is heaven? What more could you ask from the universe? On that fall morning he walked out of the airport under a sky that, to him, held no promise beyond the lift he could catch in the RV-4 and was no less beautiful for it.

MY FATHER LOVES to fly kites on Pismo Beach, not far from his childhood home. He doesn't know that the writer Frederick Buechner calls kite-flying "fishing for God."

Other writers have spoken with my father's version of mystery. They call it the sublime. "Whatever is fitted in any sort to excite the ideas of pain, and danger, that is to say, whatever is in any sort terrible, or is conversant about terrible objects, or operates in a manner analogous to terror, is a source of the sublime," the Irish philosopher Edmund Burke wrote in 1757. How many times, looking up at the stars from the old hot tub beyond the redwood porch, did my father remind us of our smallness, the limits of what we could chronicle or understand?

Though Burke named the sublime in a time before flight, it is this power of earth and wind and wings that he described, and this my father taught us to revere. When I was a toddler, I dragged around a plastic toy airplane on a string. I dragged it over the tarmac at the Bishop airport, and Pop lifted me into Zippy's cockpit for just a moment. I loved the book *West with the Night* in elementary school, written by Beryl Markham, a woman bush pilot in Africa. I made an old-fashioned flight helmet out of brown felt and carried around a pamphlet Pop gave me called "The Principles of Flight," from which I learned about lift, how a decrease in pressure over curved wings allows a plane to rise. On commercial flights across the country, he offered his thumb, a pretend yoke, and let me direct the jet as it cruised, pulling back the moment the wheels left the asphalt.

At home I sat with him on the mountainside as he launched remote control gliders, and in our driveway we stood and watched hawks ride thermals. The hawks hovered, balancing their bodies, wings still, held in place by anabatic wind that rose as it hit the mountain, and he said he'd like to be rehatched as a hawk so he too could ride thermals over Owens Valley.

I realize I have known it, this whispering silence, this answer in the night, since before I had any need—before I held the rabbit in the shoebox, before the long, gray bags, since the days when Mom came home from work on winter evenings and sat with us in front of the woodstove—before I knew to fear anything at all.

When I was seven and my sister six, we roamed with Pop through the meadows beyond Swall, past the snowmelt creek and the Fairy Glen, until we came to the foundation of a burned house sunk among willows and rose hips. The pit dropped six feet below the ground, its walls made of pinkish cinder block, charred boards piled in the corner. We didn't know when or how the house burned, or who it once belonged to. My father lowered my sister and me into the foundation, our gangly legs and floppy hats, and from the bottom I looked up and saw a blue square of sky and the wall of Wheeler. We were lizards in a burrow, all that elevation above us.

Pop stood at the edge. His face hovered against the mountain. "What if a bad guy threw you down there? How would you get out? How would you get home?"

Then he disappeared.

My father has never heard of the sublime, of Edmund Burke or the writers who stir the philosopher's ideas. He knows his place among what is larger and older than he, and it is knowledge of this role, of a human as something brief and potentially joyful, that he passes to his children, the way another father might pass on a prayer. It occurs to me, two decades later, that some children might have been scared. I leaned a few burned beams against the western wall. Charcoal dusted my hands and nails jabbed from the boards as I helped Kaela balance before climbing out after her. And there crouched our father, hiding in the brush nearby, cheering as his daughters emerged from that hole in the ground.

DROP YOUR CHILDREN in a pit, and they will figure out how to take care of themselves and each other. They will participate in their own rescue, because they are equally alone—or not alone—out here as any western fence lizard. The sky above our heads might have been a void, but in this moment we began to understand, began to learn to talk with immensity. Wallace Stegner claimed he never understood identity problems. "I knew well enough who, or *what*, I was," he wrote of his childhood on the western plains, "even if I didn't matter. As surely as any pullet in the yard, I was a target, and I had better respect what had me in its sights."

Pop learned the hard way about rescue and just about missed the chance to pass the lesson on.

A June morning before sunrise. My father, though he is no one's father yet, lifts a tourist family—three generations: grandpa, father, son—over Mammoth Meadow in a hot air balloon. The balloon belongs to my father and his pilot partner, Dave, and it hovers green, blue, maroon in the pale sky.

Below, saltgrass meadows are silent except for the mooing of cattle. Mountains rise in a jagged ring.

Early morning is the best time to fly. The anabatic winds that race up the mountain in the heat of the day are not yet awake, and the night winds that dash down from the high country to tousle the valley floor are still asleep. Dawn is gray and silent until the burner blasts, and the radio at my father's hip crackles. In the basket the tourist family cover their ears. They peer over brush and meadows as the balloon's shadow ripples, and cattle and mule deer run in panic. A blue suburban kicks up dust as the chase crew follows.

"Close your eyes," my father says. "You won't even know you're flying."

The balloon moves through the air at twenty miles per hour, but without tracking its progress over the earth, without watching the trailer parked at the launch site recede, this motion is imperceptible. From two thousand feet in the sky, the ground appears soft. It seems impossible that the balloon might fall, that this flight might be disrupted.

My father spots a landing site, a meadow. Hop a set of power lines and he can bring the basket to rest, let the nylon lean into the ground, a room of filtered light, colored as if by stained glass. With his thumb and forefinger he pulls a brass valve over his head. The burner roars.

But the balloon is wrenched from his control, to drift, as if drawn by unseen hands, toward the Mammoth Pacific geothermal plant.

The spaces belowground are lively in the Eastern Sierra— after all, Mammoth Mountain is a volcano. At the geothermal plant, magma heats vapor that spins turbines, now directly beneath my father's balloon, which pauses in the warm current rising from the plant and bobs, Pop says, "like a Ping-Pong ball caught over a hair dryer." He looks down at a mesh of power lines. He cannot move twenty feet to the right or left; he cannot drop a rope to Dave and the chase crew, who stand on the ground, necks craning, for fear of striking a line. His propane tanks hold fifteen minutes of fuel. When that is gone, the balloon will descend, slowly, onto the network of wires.

Pressed together, power lines release a crooked bolt called an electric arc, so bright it hurts to look at even in a photograph. An electric arc is five times hotter than the surface of the sun. It sizzles through the air for a few seconds before the lines die and in these seconds can cleave steel cables and drop a balloon's basket 150 feet to the ground. It can slice propane tanks like zucchini and set flame-retardant nylon ablaze. It can engulf a wicker basket in a flash of charring energy so ferocious one survivor of such a collision felt as if he were inside a firework.

In this moment, my father is still a young pilot. He has not met my mother at the first summer rehearsal of the Eastern Sierra Symphony, has not danced with her barefoot in the grass. He does not know that on a cold March day, seventeen years and nine months after they are married, he will kneel at the side of a creek, open a jar, and let her ashes be carried downstream. He does know what will happen to him, and the old man, and the younger man, and the boy in the basket, if the balloon comes to rest on the wires.

The passengers don't know anything. The morning is sunny and calm, perfect for flight, and they are pointing at

hawks gliding by, hoping for a glimpse of the pale head of a
bald eagle. They are not afraid, and this is because my father
is a calm man.

I've seen him in the state he calls *worried*, what other
people might call terrified, only twice: on a night black with
smoke when I was twelve years old and a wildfire glowed
orange and clawed toward Swall Meadows, and again on a
hike that took us up a near-vertical heap of rock, when slate
daggers began to rocket over our heads. He clenches his jaw,
squints, concentrates. The night of that first fire, he prowled
our dusty acre with a hose, keeping watch for drifting
embers. That day on the crumbling mountainside, he showed
me how to flatten myself, to use the wall of the mountain
as protection, and after the rocks stopped sliding, he chose
a safe course down. I wonder how many times, caught in a
thunderstorm on Mount Starr or packing the car with pets
and photo albums to flee avalanche warning, my father's calm
belied real danger, whether I've been just as close to vanishing
as he was that morning, bobbing over live wires.

I ask him what he was thinking as the balloon hovered.

"Well," he says. "This is not good."

Beneath him the power lines seem to diverge in twenty
directions. He radios Dave on the ground, wondering if the
plant can be shut down. It can't—that would take days.

"Dave said his mouth went completely dry. He thought we
were gonna have a big accident, hit power lines, kill people.
You know."

For the longest time I believed my father indestructible. I
might still. He is a man of wild plans and long shots and so he

pulls the burner and with the last of his fuel rises one thousand feet. At this higher altitude, still caught in the column of air, he tugs a line that opens a vent at the top of the balloon and releases heat. He hopes this will allow the balloon to drop with enough momentum to break free of the column—that the balloon will jaunt sideways and diverge from the mesh of wires.

He tugs, and it works. The basket lowers, shifting away from the plant and slipping through a V in the power lines.

"We came in and just drilled the ground. We hit at a pretty good speed. I told everybody, 'Bend your knees, hold on to the side of the basket.' Even the older guy. I told everybody, 'We're gonna hit and we're gonna bounce.'"

The crew comes running toward the balloon, and he shouts to them: "The second we hit the ground, get your weight on the basket so I don't recoil back up into this column of air!"

He was so relieved to hit the ground that he opened the top of the balloon, he remembers. "And I shouldn't have. The burners were still hot, and the balloon started to come down around us. I wanted to be landed, with no chance of taking off again, so I pulled the top out the second we hit the ground and ended up melting a little bit of nylon and doing about five hundred dollars' worth of damage. But that was nothing compared to what could have happened."

Then the passengers are back on the grass of Mammoth Meadow, and the chase crew cheers, and this is all an adventure, a sunny morning in the mountains, a story to tell a daughter in thirty years.

What's the best way to greet a mystery, an unknowable future? When Pop and I climb mountains, we leave the trail and scramble. We make our own rules: do all you can to ensure that things work out. And then hope, when hope is all that's left, that the next day will bring sun in a clear sky. In drought that the next day will bring rain.

Years later, walking in the desert with my father, I recognize the lesson he learned above the geothermal plant and handed down to me at the bottom of that burned foundation. I follow Pop twelve hundred feet to the top of Tungsten Peak, a quick scamper around boulders, marked at the summit with a single stunted pine that hikers sustain with the dregs of their water bottles. We hike in a wind so strong we can barely stand, and I cannot hear Pop's voice ten paces ahead. My hat flies off and cartwheels over the sagebrush, and as I chase after it, I remember that square of sky; the wind skips my hat farther, and I feel comforted by the knowledge that I can be obliterated by this country and safe because the same knowledge can protect me, can make me careful.

"For all the toll the desert takes of a man it gives compensations," Mary Austin wrote, "deep breaths, deep sleep, and the communion of the stars . . . wheeling to their stations in the sky, they make the poor world-fret of no account. Of no account you who lie out there watching, nor the lean coyote that stands off in the scrub from you and howls and howls." To be like the lean coyote is a comfort beneath a sky that is full of fog or full of sunlight and either way impenetrable. Such comfort is not a reason for carelessness. Precisely because you might not know everything—because the night answers but not with words you can understand, and the stars swing above you, moving, as Austin tells us, as if "on some stately service not needful to declare," you must accept certain responsibilities—among them the task of taking care.

Care is a thing you learn, Pop says, this man who has nearly fallen from the sky a handful of times, after watching enough blustery days turn to storms and enough storms turn to blizzards. "A perfect day can turn marginal, and you can usually survive marginal. A marginal day can turn catastrophic."

He knows that if he rides his mountain bike ten miles into the backcountry and breaks a leg, his aloneness becomes dangerous, and so he takes precautions. He calls this "filing a flight plan," which means telling people where you're going so if you don't come back, they come looking. Once, he filed flight plans with my mother. Then he filed them with his friend Mike. Then he filed them with me. He isn't motivated by fear but by an understanding of the shared steps in rescue, how easily a crumpled bike and an injured man might disappear in wilderness.

"There's bold pilots and old pilots, but there's no old bold pilots." Pop laughs.

To my father the fact of all the many pilots who have died in the mountains is not a deterrent from the life he pursues but a set of instructions in which the wind and the rocks are sometimes your adversaries, sometimes your partners, always a reason to fly. To file a flight plan is to buy time in your home, when time and a home are all you have. Often the people who die or almost die in the wilderness do not have a friend who can identify the canyon among a thousand canyons chosen for that afternoon's bike or hike or climb. People lost to loneliness in the city have the same problem, maybe. They forget the care of others; they forget the first step in rescue. The man who sawed through his forearm with a pocketknife when a boulder fell and trapped him in a Utah arroyo hadn't told a soul where he was going. When Pop comes home, he hangs his bike in the garage and drops his pack on the kitchen floor. Then he calls Mike. Closing flight plan.

To be made careful is to be made grateful. Loss highlights all you have, just as absence in the desert highlights presence, until what little water we harbor glows. Sitting on a rock slope on one of my visits home, eating apples, our little pug, Ricky, scampering in the dust around us, Pop says, "If something happened to me, you kids would be all right. You wouldn't be devastated."

I couldn't explain to him how when one parent is lost, the other is clung to with twice the fierceness.

When something goes wrong, he says softly, with great gentleness, "Darn."

He pats your back. He sits with you in silence.

I wonder, sometimes, if Mike waits for the day that he doesn't get a call. As do I, despite the care my father takes, despite how well I have learned to trust him. For now, he makes it home every time. "Closing flight plan," he says. Don't come looking for me today.

Pop and I are walking around the block in Swall Meadows, following the incline of Mountain View Drive, when I ask him how Mom felt about flying.

"She flew once in the RV-4 with me," he says. "I took her for a really smooth early-morning flight. I think she was three or four months pregnant, with you. I flew her from Bishop, up over June Lake, then out over Mono Lake, and we were just looking at the islands and cruising along, nice smooth flight." Wind rustles the poplars; the road up Wheeler is steep. "And then suddenly I look out and there's a whole flock of seagulls right in front of us. And I'd never seen this—I mean, birds are a danger for pilots, you've gotta keep your eyes open!—and the birds, when they feel like they're being threatened (here comes this airplane at two hundred miles an hour, you know), the birds, they fold, they just fold their wings and they drop out of the sky like rocks. Like an eagle is coming after them. That's their self-preservation, just to drop like a rock. So all these birds are going *tchew! tchew! tchew!* like darts. There's a big group right in front of us, and so I kind of swerve the airplane, turn it way over on its side, and Mom gives a little yelp."

And then they were through the birds, and it was okay.

So why her, Pop? Why that woman with the flute and the bangs and the cross-country skis and the gray cat called Seren for short?

"She was cute," he says, "and she was really really nice to me!" What more could a guy want? She filed one flight plan before they were married, maybe before she even knew the term. He was cavorting around Europe on a bicycle and she stayed home to teach. A friend invited her to climb Half Dome in Yosemite.

I feel like I should sit at home and knit a something, instead of going climbing, to reduce the odds of one of us not having a safe return, she wrote to him in a letter. *But I don't even know how to knit and I know I can't sit.*

I might as well get really weird in case I don't come back tomorrow. She would leave the letter on her bed in an envelope with his name. She just wanted him to know (*in case I don't get to tell you, in case you don't get to ask . . .*) that she wanted to be with him forever *and ever and ever. So now, off I go to climb. If I come back safely—and you do, too—you can forget this paragraph if you like.*

They married in view of Mammoth Mountain, tiny doll people at the foot of the volcano. She was barefoot in the videos I have seen of the wedding reception, dress dusty, dancing in the grass.

PART 2

WILDFLOWERS

5. Lupine Land

M Y MOTHER MADE A place called Lupine Land and gave it to Kaela and Anthony and me when we were small. In her story three children hold purple marbles in their palms and find themselves transported to Lupine Land, a world where wands of purple wildflowers walk and talk and grow as tall as people, a place to which they can travel whenever they need.

One day when the children are playing in a meadow, the marbles in their pockets begin to glow. There is trouble in Lupine Land. The Lupine People are calling, and it's time to go.

If I could draw a map of Lupine Land—or hand you my father's map, maybe—if I could mark the places that contained us when we were whole, I would track the highway as it meanders through the valley. Seven miles south of Bishop, a tendril of road breaks west of 395 toward the rattlesnake foothills and ends in the dirt parking lot of Keough's Hot Springs. You say it KEY-yos, and I can't remember a time before knowing this wedge of warmth in the chilled winter valley, the water smelling slightly of sulfur. Keough's pools, one large for swimming, another smaller and hot for soaking, lie hemmed by a concrete path and four wooden walls—a roofless room, open to the sky. The walls that border the pools wear a pale mint green, and the gaps between the boards are rounded by many coats of paint. Curtains printed with tropical fish hang over two showers, and the clocks on the walls, once set to Pacific standard, read three different times. The dressing rooms are without lockers; leave your car keys in your shoe and your clothes in a white plastic bin; catch yourself, warped slightly, in the long mirror.

Over the larger pool, droplets spray from a rigged waterfall suspended fifteen feet in the air, cooling as they fall. Some days wind whips the waterfall restless, and in the pool faces at arm's length vanish. Watch a crescent moon in cobalt dusk, and then the sky turns black and the mist stands out whitely. The pale concrete floor beneath the water is riddled with cracks like fault lines.

An old woman reads a battered paperback in the shallows. A pregnant woman perches on the side of the hot tub and pulls up a black T-shirt to rub her belly. She looks like Mary Austin—square face, strong chin, downturned mouth. Austin left Owens Valley in 1906, thirteen years before Keough's came to be, but she described its patrons when she wrote of "old miners drifting about the desert edges, weathered into the semblance of the tawny hills." Men and women a few steps removed from dust tip their heads back in the water and sigh. Here is a place of water in the desert, of screaming children, of life and its slow fade. As it was a century in the past, so it is today.

A Paiute man, Sam Newland, grew up in Pitana Patu, the name for Bishop before the whites came. He remembered hunting rabbits at what became Keough's. He remembered dancing for five days and five nights with people from all over the valley at the annual festival. The men from Independence, he said, were known to be good dancers, and they did the totso'ho, wearing eagle down skirts and feathers. He remembered a fishing party to Owens River, remembered damming the stream and tossing in leaves from the plant tu'un'wava, or slim solomon, which when smashed with a rock released a toxin that stunned the fish and made them easy to scoop. Remembered going to the sloughs, pulling tules, and eating their roots with salt. Crossing the Sierra to trade salt for shell money with the people on the other side. Stealing horses and eating them, too. Remembered finding a porcupine up in a tree, "which my companion killed by clubbing it on the nose. . . . The next morning the porcupine was cooked and we had a fine breakfast." Remembered hunting up Bishop Creek, past what I know as Lake Sabrina, lighting a fire, flushing deer toward the hunters below.

Such was life—before life was interrupted. In the valley of flowing water, in the summer of 1861, a band of cattle ranchers found what they needed after a long, dry journey—water they could hardly believe, which must have seemed like a mirage. The party had crossed two hundred miles of desert. Their leader, Samuel Addison Bishop, dressed in Mexican spurs and buckskin leggings. He weighed three hundred pounds and wore his hair swept back, his mustache waxed into points, his goatee hanging like a squirrel's tail over three soft chins. Like most white men in nineteenth-century California, he carried a revolver.

Bishop was a Virginian, a prospector, a fighter of the Ahwahneechee and the Chowchilla in the western Sierra foothills. Rumor has it that in 1853 he provided a ten-gallon bucket of whiskey for the preservation of a severed head carried by a band of soldiers who swore it belonged to the near-mythical Mexican bandit, Joaquín Murrieta. That summer of 1861 Samuel Bishop drove some five hundred head of cattle and fifty horses north, planning to sell beef to silver miners in Aurora, Nevada.

The route to Aurora took Bishop through Payahuunadu, at that time empty of whites besides scattered prospectors and a couple of drifters patching together stone cabins. Trappers and surveyors and military scouts had passed through before, bringing back reports of a fertile valley irrigated by its original inhabitants, but few white folks had tried to make the place a home. In the summer of 1859, one army captain, sent to look for stolen stock and finding none, informed the Paiutes that he had "reason to believe that their Country was set apart by the Government—exempt from settlement—for their use."

Two years after that promise, on the afternoon of August 22, Bishop's party paused beside a full creek. Bishop must have noticed that the creek was banked and built and dammed, the place already a home to someone. Water fanned across the meadows, and fields of wild rye and love grass grew lush, as if—and could it be that they were?—irrigated. Well, never mind. On the first morning he might have ridden toward the Sierra and found Jeffrey pines too large for his arms to encircle. Perhaps he saw purple lupine and wild iris in the meadows. His men built two wooden cabins beside what they began to call Bishop Creek.

No doubt this was very near Pitana Patu, home to the largest Nuumu population in the valley.

Bishop named his settlement San Francis Ranch, after his wife. Soon others came driving cattle: Van Fleet, Bodle, Kisport, Keough, McGee. "Wherever water touches it, it produces abundantly," wrote a military scout of Owens Valley soil in 1859. The ranchers had found water in the desert, a place of safety and rest, and so they stayed.

THE EASTERN SIERRA contains two climate extremes: Owens Valley, though whipped by windstorms, gets little snow or rain, while in the town of Mammoth Lakes, forty miles northwest and almost four thousand feet above Bishop, cars are often buried by blizzards until spring. Around rain-shadowed Bishop, rattlesnakes, horned lizards, and burrowing owls hunker beneath volcanic dust. Mammoth, meanwhile, sits at eight thousand feet in elevation, among the peaks of the Sierra. Bears sleep in the woods as tourists stand in line for chairlifts. Strands of skiers move across the flank of Mammoth Mountain, the dozing volcano.

In Swall Meadows, lodged against the Sierra and overlooking Owens Valley, we became intimate with both desert and storm. People from Swall are supposed to go to school in Bishop, but our house was too remote for any school bus to collect us. And so we enrolled in Mammoth, where Mom already drove to her job with the school district. Each morning we traveled thirty minutes through the gorge and deeper into the mountains, watching alpine and desert climes collide, a tournament of extremes.

Pop the pilot did his best to explain our wild weather: "When you get atmospheric pressure differential, that's what creates wind. Because the air's all trying to equalize pressure. Where you have mountains, they disrupt the upper-level airflow and it causes turbulence. The winds break over the Sierra and tumble and curl, instead of being a smooth, moving mass."

As moisture from the Pacific moves east on prevailing winds, it condenses while ascending the western, windward slope of the Sierra Nevada. Rain falls on the western foothills, snow buries summits, and the storms dissipate before they reach us here at the lee. The Sierra presents a four-hundred-mile rampart that keeps water out of the Great Basin Desert, out of Owens Valley. But now and then, storms creep more than eleven thousand feet over Wheeler Crest and blizzards pile onto Swall. Then the highway patrol warns everyone to stay home for fear of being lost.

What could smother us could also insulate us from the world, bundling our lives together. This was a strange sort of safety. In our living room, fire simmered through the night, contained and benevolent in its hearth, and heat rose upstairs where the five of us slept, each beneath a window so that at any moment we could roll in our beds and face the stars. Maybe that house in a blizzard reminded Mom of the moments she spent beneath the snow, buried so that others could save her for practice, certain that rescue was on its way.

Warmth in winter, water in the desert. Once, Mom soaked at Keough's while threads of elastic frayed from her purple one-piece, and Pop butterflied in a lap lane, and we three Atleeworks submarined in goggles and smacked each other over the head with foam paddle boards until everyone climbed onto deck chairs, sun-dizzy. See us as we were, a family caped in faded beach towels. Kaela and Anthony and I stood in the steam of the waterfall and watched one another dissolve and reappear. This was Lupine Land, a place of beauty and trouble, the story smudging the edges of the real.

In one chapter of Mom's story, the children are called to help defend Lupine Land from the Weed People, green villains with spiky arms and legs. The Weed People catch the children and throw them in jail. If they want to save Lupine Land, the children must escape.

Of course, the Lupine People come to the rescue, and peace and justice are restored. In our lives, Lupine Land was ritual as much as place. Mom tied my hair in two red braids as I sat at the window. Sometimes the White Mountains beyond were blue like the sky, and the crest, dusted in snow, seemed to float. Other times a storm gathered. We sat, and she sang, *Where have all the flowers gone?* She sang, *I've looked at clouds from both sides now.* Then she kissed Pop on her way out the door and ferried us to school along the lip of the gorge.

We were never quite safe; we were never quite in danger. She drove too fast, this careful woman. Defensive posture, shoulders clenched, back straight behind the wheel. Driving never came naturally to her—too much speed and machine. How many times she smashed the porcelain house numbers marking the start of our driveway, pulling in after work, worn out and distracted.

Here we are on our way to school one October a couple years before she got really sick. We are late, as usual. She drives, Kaela next to her, me and Anthony and my friend Elizabeth in the back. It's chilly in the car, the windows cracked so they don't steam up from our breathing, the sun not yet risen over the Whites, our headlights beaming through dawn as Mom all but floors it, when a mule deer, brown blur, rockets across the road in front of us. Mom slams the brakes. The doe freezes on the far side of the road, looks back, glares, and disappears over the sagebrush.

I tell Mom, Good grief, slow down, and I'm sneering through my lip gloss, newly aware of what might be her flaws. Elizabeth remembered years later: "She laughed! She laughed when you said that. And she didn't slow down."

In a blizzard before I was born, a car went off the road we traveled on our way to school, soaring into the gorge and killing the two children in the backseat. I remember the morning she hit a rock and tore out our transmission, there at the bottom of the gorge as she drove us to school, my oatmeal, which I had been eating in the passenger's seat to save time, flying all over the dash. Lower Rock Creek Road became icy in winter and I could almost imagine us aloft over the cliff's edge, plummeting toward the creek and the mountain bike trail below. She dropped us off at school, peeled out of the parking lot, and raced through the doors of the county office of education in her hand-me-down dresses, past the desks of the receptionists for whom she found little gifts on work trips. We were known around town as the late Atleeworks, but she kept us out of the gorge.

In winter storms Pop taught us to keep the stove roaring. "If you've got a cold house, you need one good spot where you can get really warm." On the sheepskin after school, I sat beside my brother until the skin on our backs reddened and itched; we did homework, read and reread Calvin and Hobbes cartoon anthologies, turning the pages as a boy and a tiger flew on a wagon through the woods. The fire flared, then faded, and we knew to gather logs from under the porch before it died.

Remember Pop explaining our skies: "Just think of a wave breaking. The air falls. But then it rolls." While the reason for wind and storms and the Wave could be had, reason was not control. The wind rolls, the world rolls. And a boy who became a brother because of tragedy and accident was nothing unusual. It could have been another kid my mother brought to Lupine Land, just as it could have been a different creek or valley that persuaded the ranchers to stay. But Samuel Bishop got this desert, and we all got Anthony.

ANTHONY THE CHILD had a way of listening, a sense for what another person needed him to say or not say, an intuitive courtesy and restraint that made him a good companion even for a sister five years older. In the quiet redwood house after school, he boiled water and brought me bowls of

ramen, and we ate together in front of the fire. On Monday
nights, while Kaela was in town doing some extracurricu-
lar, Anthony and I went to Bishop with Pop, just the two
of us. Pop practiced with the community jazz band while I
guarded our allotted ten-dollar bill, and we shared enchiladas at Amigos on Main, sitting together on one side of the
booth with a street view, his little sneakers bopping against
my legs. And then we walked to the cemetery outside the
hospital where I was born. In the shadows between elms and
headstones, we became velociraptors, grew claws and tails,
and roared at the stars.

THE STATE OF California plucked my brother from
birth parents who hit each other and perhaps hit him. The
extent to which this particular kind of theft was wrong, and
what spurred the violence that enabled it, I do not know
exactly. I have never met those first parents, and both of them
are dead now. I can guess, though, that this mother and father
did not want to hurt their son or each other as they passed
forward what they themselves had received.

We first saw his picture in an adoption catalog, small
and blurry, one among pages of little faces in our bright
kitchen light. These children were California born, not
babies, wrapped in the long arms of the state. It was Mom
who pointed to Anthony. A brown face, nose arched slightly,
cheekbones high, hair capering in soft little spikes. Long gone
now, but I can still call it up as if it sits on my table, the very
first image I had of my brother. He held a macaroni necklace
to his mouth and smiled.

In an exceptional instance of autocorrect, the description beneath his photo called him "neurotic," meaning mentally ill, disturbed, unstable, unbalanced, maladjusted, psychopathic—when it should, we learned upon inquiring, have read "enuretic": a bed wetter.

When Anthony was four years old and I was nine, I met him in Northern California, in the driveway of a foster mom he called Auntie Rita. By age four he had spent half his life with various Auntie Ritas. We shot a basketball together, and he rode in circles on a tiny red bike, of which he was proud. Since it was almost Halloween, we carved pumpkins on the concrete.

A few weeks later Anthony spent his first night with us, his new family, and in the morning he woke up screaming.

HERE'S ANTHONY PLAYING horse with me in the driveway, chasing the basketball down the mountainside. Here he is hauling Mom, who had a liberal definition of dignity, in circles in a wagon, Anthony with a shiny black bowl cut, Mom in her old jeans, feet hanging off the wagon's front, Ricky panting happily in her lap.

Here he is swaddled up as a sheep to my shepherd at the Methodist church; crying because he hates tomatoes and has to eat them anyway; cocking a hip on the staircase in red lipstick and a purple velvet gown, letting us call him Antoinette, while Kaela and I howl. Here he is lying on the couch next to Mom before a game night, the tops of their heads pressed together, both of them going *bzzzzzzzz*. *We're merging our brains for Pictionary*, Mom says.

His bedroom shared a thin wall with mine, and we sat together beneath my window overlooking Wheeler Crest and played with Pokémon cards. Because I met my brother four years after the beginning of his life, I have spent a lot of time imagining him in reverse—as if I sensed the importance of looking backward, were I to understand the many people he might become. What did mornings feel like in Northern California, in the city of his birth? What made him laugh when he was a baby? To conceive of him before was to enter the slanted world of someone else's dream. His memories bubbled and mixed with the snow that fell around us, with the stories I told him when we roamed Wheeler Crest or played on the neighbor's swing set, which sat bolted to the mountainside. Months after he moved into the bedroom next to mine, I wrote in a diary:

> *Anthony said, "I had another mommy and daddy, older than the pine cones."*
> *He said, "My daddy said to my mommy,* I'm going to kill you, you know. I'll kill you. *My daddy said* bitch."
> *I told Anthony what* bitch *meant. A female dog. We laughed.*

If Anthony cried in the night, I heard through our shared wall and came to his door. The skunks with red eyes stalked his bedside, he said, as Mom and I knelt near him in the dark. She told me, *That means fear is beside him.* She looked backward so we might see ahead. She knew that violence survived in baby years can return.

In the wake of the 1906 earthquake and fires, which killed about three thousand people in San Francisco, hundreds lived in tents, fearful of returning to indoor life as aftershocks rippled the city. Those early days for my brother in our house must have harbored a stability terrible because it could not be trusted. Until, after a while, the woman with cold, thin fingers and an eagerness to get down and play with him in the dirt—who, during that time of nightmares, slept on a futon a few feet from his door—didn't go away.

WHEN MY BROTHER is six years old, Pop rides with him down a hill on a skateboard, Anthony's feet positioned between Pop's size 16 sneakers on the deck of the board and his small brown arms raised, one hand in each of his father's. Anthony looks ahead and feels himself whisk through air. Here is a kid inclined toward speed and quickly losing his imagination for disaster, companion in training to a father who has calloused hands the size of baseball mitts and sees a broken shoulder here and there as fair tax to join the wind. Pop laughs as the board gains speed, then holds the small hands tighter, then murmurs *uh-oh* as the hill swoops into sand.

"That's when we got speed wobbles," Pop says—and down they go. Airborne, is my brother afraid? Does his trust, still fragile, falter? Does he blame the man whose hands he holds, whose hands then slip from his? Anthony hits the ground first and Pop lands on top of him. They bounce. Pop says: "Bam! If it had been one of you girls, you'd be squished." Anthony cries, curling inward, and Pop rolls over in the gravel to pat his son's back, smiling his "oops" smile, his "I hope the kid is okay this time" smile—don't we all know it well. Anthony came with a sturdy rib cage instead of his sisters' bird bones. He might have been bruised, but he had started to feel safe on unsteady ground. He had begun to know Lupine Land. Within an hour he clambered up a tree trunk and leaped from the top of a boulder.

MY MOTHER WAS once principal at a school for delinquent boys. In boxy temporary buildings on a plain of sagebrush just south of Mammoth, she wrangled children determined to burn themselves out rather than carry heavy histories. They came to the school because of violence at home and violence that ruled within their minds. Parents and social workers threw up their hands and sent them to Mom. Fix them. Make them whole. Heal them from their inheritance. One kid flipped my mother's desk on top of her a few months before I was born. A student twice her size struck the chalkboard with such force he crumbled the bones in his hand.

Here's a true story: One February morning when I was six months old, the counselors at the school took the students on a field trip to Convict Lake. It was Presidents' Day, and Mom was at home. Convict lies in a bowl cupped by mountains, and in autumn the canyon walls blaze yellow with changing aspen leaves. I have paddled a canoe with my family to picnic on the southern shore. I have stood on the beach before a thunderstorm and watched the sun vanish.

That morning in February, Convict lay in ludicrous clarity, frozen and brushed white, as it might have looked to the Bishop party in those early days, unmarked by what was to come. The boys from Mom's school were laughing at their lives, deaf to the crackling as they walked, four of them, over the water.

One dragged himself out and used the rough fabric of his gloves to grip the ice and scoot, belly down, toward shore.

Four men went after the others. Paralysis of hands and feet, then arms and legs, occurs in icy water after five to fifteen minutes. Witnesses on shore reported seven heads bobbing above the surface until, one by one, they disappeared.

We heard the story of the boys' disappearance more than once. It was a part of our history as intimate as the memory of the birth of four kittens in our dark living room one April night. I was twelve, Kaela ten, Anthony seven. I remember the wooden floor hard beneath my knees and Mom at my side. I wrote in the diary:

> *Susan is having her kittens! Right now! It is 10:25 p.m. and we are all (including Anthony, woken up) huddled around her box. She has been crying out for some time. She isn't mewing; she is yelling. We see a tail (black) and a little bit of blood.*

Ice was melting off the mountains and rumbling in the streams. There was spring warmth in night air, the moon new and the sky wet with stars as Mom switched on a lamp, shed light on the prone cat who met our eyes, who must have taken some comfort from the presence of the woman who snipped hairballs from her fur, gathered her in skinny arms, placed a hand on the gray back now while we watched, hushed.

Then, all of a sudden, we see feet! Blackish-pinkish feet with little white nails. She licked him off for a long time.

The cat ate the afterbirth and cut the umbilical cord with her teeth. And with me again is the smell of my mother, not of perfume but of her particular skin, the faint detergent of an old T-shirt printed with wildflowers. She sits on the floor with legs folded, feet calloused, bare nails nipped short. The words she might have said are lost, but what I remember, what I recorded in green pen over many pages, was her desire that we witness, and not only witness but celebrate, and not only celebrate but take into the center of ourselves.

"There was something else there besides what you find in the books," Mary Austin wrote of the California desert, "a lurking, evasive Something, wistful, cruel, ardent." Was Lupine Land our mother's answer to the story of a place shaped by blunder, by one man's dream of endless water, by a band of tired ranchers who paused beside a creek? Above her moved a spirit in the void or nothing at all. She lived on a darkling plain in an unruly body. Perhaps back then, in the early days of her diagnosis, she needed to tell a story of safety, of rescue and wildflowers and children who return.

We grew up gripped by blood on blankets, by the memory of boys drowned in the desert, of water frozen to false stability. A moment marks the crack. Once, we skated together on a Bishop pond. The bare cottonwoods, the rope swing that launched us into the same water in summer, shone back from beneath our skates, from a plane of ice so solid and bright we forgot what stirred beneath. When a pond freezes you may walk or run or skate or slide or dance across its surface in moonlight. The ice holds beneath your skates until it doesn't.

But Lupine Land, remember, is a place you can never really lose. The purple marbles glow and the children heed the call. I remember Monday nights in summer in the Bishop park, the community band playing "Pink Panther" in the gazebo, Pop's head and trombone bobbing over the rest, Anthony trampling the blankets of old couples, trucks grumbling by on Main, the creek ambling at our backs. We paused in our running, climbing, skidding over the grass to kneel on the blanket where Mom sat listening. She walked with us the few blocks to Baskin-Robbins for ice cream, holding Anthony's hand. When a family of ducks wandered from the park and huddled in the lot behind Schat's bakery, we herded them back down the sidewalk, toward the creek.

Once, in a blue stroller, I sailed down a hill when Mom accidentally let go, my descent a joy in contrast to her terror so that after she picked me up and dusted me off I remembered more the flight than the crash into bitterbrush. And I remember climbing—pine trunks, our corrugated metal roof, piles of pitted rock that roughened our palms. While Mom went to work for the schools in Mammoth and Pop repaired the porch or cooked dinner, we three Atleeworks ranged, caught rock and slid, arms and legs working out a system beyond thought that buoyed us up the biggest boulders into the branches of Jeffrey pines, believing, for a while, that the world was not flat or fenced and held no danger beyond mountain lions and hantavirus and earthquakes and blizzards and Weed People—a fair trade for all the dried jack-rabbit droppings you could gather in the brush. The drowned boys were a story of tragedy but also of love, of almost rescue and men who risked themselves, and there was beauty in that, a reason to dash out into the world with open arms, a reason to climb and to fall. Every cat we fed died wild between the teeth of coyotes or mountain lions or the talons of the great horned owl, none lasting long enough to meet old age. We took this as a given, for who were we to deny our animals the mountainside? We buried the birds, bats, and mice left limp at the front door, then noted when the hunters failed to come home. That gray mother cat vanished tooth and fur and claw, but something remains.

In a dangerous world, the sustained desire of our mother's life was a bag of marbles she could hand to lost boys, to her son and daughters—to impart to us some design that might teach us care and yet let joy master fear. Those marbles were, all along, a token meant to tell us we could always come home.

In kindergarten, Anthony caught the school bus by mistake on a day he was supposed to go to soccer practice. He got off at the usual stop in a neighborhood called Sunny Slopes, separated from our house by seven miles of wilderness and gorge, since the school bus went only partway to Swall. He waited around and concluded that no one was there to meet him. Highway patrol collected a child, tufts of black hair fluttering, backpack strapped to his shoulders, walking resolutely at the side of Highway 395. He didn't know how many miles lay between him and Mountain View Drive, but he knew where he needed to go.

6. Miracle Country

THERE IS A STORY Mom tells, not for the first time, at the Fairy Glen when I am a kid, her voice muffled by water. Naked to the waist and mud smeared, I tie dandelions together in a crown. Mom lies back on the grass in old shorts and a T-shirt from an eighties music festival, hair stuffed in a ponytail. Sap drips from the Jeffrey pines on the hill, and the jays go mad in the trees. Tonight Pop will grill trout, and we'll eat on the porch and get splinters in our feet and watch the long day fade, but for now I've got dirt under my fingernails and two braids dipped in snowmelt and I'm keeping an eye out for grains of gold pyrite as they rise from the creek bed and race downstream. Kaela and Anthony crash around in the meadows nearby, accumulating ticks, and we are alone together, Mom and I. She tells the story. *I remember when you were about two weeks old, you and I went to a gathering—a "crossing of the bridge ceremony" for Margaret, who was about to have her first kid. She's always been into symbolic rituals, the goddess, drumming, all that.* I lay the dandelion crown on her head. Mud flecks her hair. *I had already crossed that bridge a few months before and I cried for the pure joy of holding you.* Our backs on the grass, we watch the shiver of the leaf ceiling. *Standing shoulder to shoulder, babies in arms, or not born, the moms sang and chanted to our children:*

Listen, listen, listen to my heart's song
I will not forget you
I will not forsake you
Listen, listen, listen to my heart's song.

She chants, and I listen, and water runs. Willows scatter sun. Sound of wind in pines.

The light lingered late in those days as we cut watermelon on the porch and watched the shadows of Wheeler and Tom cover the valley. But every summer ends. One rainy December night a decade later, we drove to Bishop, just the two of us again. Mom had three months left to live. We drove to Bishop because I had begged to get my belly button pierced, and she shocked me by saying yes. The light inside the salon on West Line Street was golden against the storm.

We realized later that the woman who led us into a peach-colored room with a padded table in the center had never pierced anything but ears, and while I lay on my back and looked up at the ceiling, the woman rammed the needle through three times.

Mom sat in a chair against the wall and gritted her teeth.

After, we waited in the car—was it the drive-through line at the taco shop?—and rain rolled down the windshield, a cold rain in the desert, painting our brush plains unfamiliar.

Christmas garlands wrapped the streetlights and Main flashed with headlights, the cars of tourists moving north. The storm pattered the roof of the car. "Under Pressure" played on the stereo, and I told Mom how beautiful I found the song, a prayer for what David Bowie and Queen called the people on the edge of the night.

She turned to me. How thin her shoulders. How tired she looked, finally, this woman who went with Pop into the mountains in an old brown tent for her honeymoon, who once ran on a saline lakeshore. She said to me, *I'm on the edge of the night.*

I heard this, and I did not know how to reply. I asked her why she had agreed to let me get the piercing, and she surprised me again. She looked at the water running down the windshield and she said, *So you'll remember me,* and for just that moment I saw her fear, saw behind the peace she tried to radiate, saw the future as it must have seemed to her: murky with everything she would not see. I saw her desire to stay, to sear herself into my skin. With her blessing and under her gaze, the amateur aesthetician marked the place that had once fed between us, and my skin burned.

Then she hugged me across the center console, her seat belt stretching as far as it would go, and held on.

A JANUARY MORNING and I walk toward my locker in the junior hallway of Mammoth High, the hall empty because I am late, when the boy comes out of a classroom. My locker door is beige except where black drips from the vents. With Elizabeth I spray-painted the inside of the locker one day after school, shaking cans and blackening our fingertips, running before the office ladies chased the smell down the hall. Outside, clouds hover over pines. Most days Mammoth is a sunny town. But the hallway has no windows, and the ceiling caves in the same spot each winter under the weight of snow. This is no place for miracles.

My mother is no longer driving us to school or herself to work. With great effort, she is able to meet us at the door in the evenings. She has been sick two months and she will be sick two more. Of this I have been informed. The boy who catches me in the hall is Taylor, scruffy bearded and pale, hair pushed into his eyes beneath a beanie, hackysack in hand. Does he hug me without warning? Does he place hands on my shoulders and seek my eyes while I look down at the dirty carpet?

"I have something to tell you." He says my name, and I reel backward, pull away my headphones. Is he going to invite me to the Mardi Gras dance? I stand before Taylor in my black sweatshirt unzipped to show a bald, two-headed doll with buttons for eyes and grinning stitched mouths. I am our high school's resident corpse bride. I paint the skin around my eyes the color of dried blood. With Elizabeth I skip class and sit in the dim hallway by the band room, throwing a sticky eyeball at the wall and watching it roll to the floor.

An invitation to any dance is unlikely. I think of the physics book inside my locker and the class on the far end of the school, probably halfway through a quiz. "I have the best news," Taylor says, and his voice overflows—with what?

With hope unknowable to me in this moment. "Your mom," he says. "She's going to get better." He beams. He and Casey have been praying. The Lord told them it was so.

"Oh," I say to Taylor. "That's good."

In this moment I remember the smell of snow, the taste of it, as I once brought handfuls into the old hot tub outside our house to cool the water. We leaped, under moonlight, into the fresh bank at the tub's edge on Pop's dare, tingling feet and fingers, Anthony squealing that he didn't want to be next. In warm water that snow expanded to fog, broke apart, disappeared.

Weeks before Taylor's ambush, I slept a few nights on his sister's bedroom floor. I did not know Taylor or his sister well. A storm closed the highway between Mammoth and Swall as the three of us lingered around a pool table in a bar that tolerated teenagers, sharing a chocolate shake. I went because those two liked the same squalling music as I did, ugly music that articulated this dream, which could not be life. At home in the dream, an oxygen tank rasped into the night, and Mom woke covered in a full-body rash, her wrists and ankles thinner than I believed wrists and ankles could become. At school the dream was dances to which I was not invited and adults who patrolled the halls and forced a baggy gym shirt over my elegant Halloween gown, which was somehow in violation of the dress code. That world grew empty in a way that childhood, full of rocks and lizards, never was.

At a pool table in the thick of winter, I did not yet know that Taylor believed himself saved from any advancing blizzard by means inaccessible to me. I sensed, in him, a friend. When the bar closed, we crammed in the front seat of his truck and crept down Old Mammoth Road as snow gathered on the windshield faster than the wipers could brush it away. The highway stayed closed and that night I could not go home. From the sister's bedroom carpet I watched as white obscured the window, lights blinked from a stereo, the shadow of a mouse crossed the floor.

School shut down. Stores shut down. Cars and shorter pines disappeared. The highway remained impassable, and we played a card game with one rule: no one could explain the rules. The rules were invented by the players; they changed with every game. I understood, vaguely, that I had to follow suit; that I should avoid penalties; that bizarre actions must accompany each card.

In the winter of 1861–62, the first winter Bishop and the other ranchers spent in Owens Valley, a storm hit California. The stock they set to pasture in summer had devoured rye and love grass planted by the Paiutes, and when the snow did not stop falling, the First People began to starve.

Try to find a marble beneath deep snow, long after summer's lupine is gone. Snow as heavy as earth blocked doors, snapped the heads off shovels, and gathered in the maw of the plow that rasped along Old Mammoth Road to blacken in berms twice as tall as Pop. The storm kept me away from home for days. I collected a penalty card at Taylor's coffee table and watched streamers of white pass the windows.

Did I try, amid that storm, to fathom the heft of snow, the force of a drop of water multiplied? Years before, I met Elizabeth with sleds in the middle of Mountain View Drive. Mount Tom shone in a sheet of white fire, almost too bright to comprehend. We flung ourselves off the porch ten feet into the air and landed in softness. Mountains look beautiful a moment before the avalanche. Mountains look beautiful on fire.

Taylor dropped a seven of hearts faceup. "Have a nice day." His sister dropped a four of hearts and rapped her knuckles on the table. I played a queen and was silent.

"Penalty," Taylor said. He played a jack, stood up, and spun in a circle. We saw then that the snow had stopped falling.

I will not forget you. I will not forsake you. Mary Austin wrote about a flash flood in a canyon and afterward "a bobcat mother mouthing her drowned kittens in the ruined lair built in the wash, far above the limit of accustomed waters, but not far enough for the unexpected." There are forces from which we cannot protect ourselves or each other.

I do not remember disentangling myself from Taylor in the junior hall.

"Your mother is going to get well," he says. "Thank the Lord." Then he walks, luminous, back to his classroom.

PURPLE MARBLES SPILL across the floor, and we lose them, let them gather dust beneath the stove. The desert that once teemed is only empty.

In 1871 Frederick Loring, an explorer from the East, described a desert valley near Owens as "white and poisonous . . . a lifeless mass of still white soil." This man said of the desert: "Its beauty is evil."

Rebecca Solnit tells us that the desert is the best place to hear the whirlwind. But what if the whirlwind has nothing to say?

"What would an ocean be without a monster lurking in the dark?" asks the filmmaker Werner Herzog. "It would be like sleep without dreams."

Like sleep without dreams. How could this desert have once been full when empty is the origin of the word? *Desert*: Middle English, via Old French, from late Latin *desertum*: something left waste; past participle of *deserere*: leave, forsake. Whatever illusion held my childhood aloft had spooked, taken flight, vanished faster than a spirit with wings. "It may well be that the voice of the Almighty speaks most profoundly in such beings as lives in silence themselves," says an ex-priest to a wayward boy in a desert camp, in a Cormac McCarthy novel about death and violence in the West. Theirs is a world of monotonous cruelty, not a place one expects to find miracles or any trace of mystery.

"For let it go how it will," the ex-priest says to the kid. "God speaks in the least of creatures. . . . No man is give leave of that voice."

The kid spits into the fire. "I ain't heard no voice."

"When it stops," says the ex-priest, "you'll know you've heard it all your life."

When I was a kid, Mom and I played flute duets at Bishop's First United Methodist. We sat in the pew with our flutes in our laps and waited for our slot in the program. Then we walked down the center aisle and stood before a black metal music stand.

I did not play in tune. Doubtless she had to listen closely in case I skipped a measure, wandered off the page a little before she found me, led me back to the verse, up and down the chorus, our sound sliding to the ceiling and swirling through the stained glass. In later years doing anything in front of a room full of people made me want to pull the fire alarm. But there in front of the congregation, I tried to stand the way I'd seen her stand when she practiced her flute on weekend mornings, dipping and swaying with each fall and climb. When I told her that she swayed when she played, she was embarrassed—*I had no idea!*—but when I watched her I thought of lupine in the wind. She dipped for the low notes. Her breath traced fog across the metal, her fingers clicked the keys, her freckled shoulders tensed and relaxed beneath the straps of her sundress. She looked at me, and lines gathered at her eyes. She smiled without dropping her embouchure, her foot tapping in an old leather sandal smudged with river mud. We counted out the rest and then began.

She taught me how to hit the high notes, how to listen and watch, how to be a shy person in a noisy classroom, how to walk in the desert, alone or with someone else. And so I was her shadow, for a while.

I USED TO love First United Methodist because I loved Bishop, loved seeing Mount Tom from another angle, loved riding bikes halfway there, following Pop down the old Sherwin Grade, whipping behind him between mounds of sagebrush that once served as deer-hunting blinds for the Paiutes, as Mom followed in the van. That world still exists somewhere, and sometimes its mood or melody settles over me like pollen, like dust. We sat in the sanctuary beside Mom in her bright cotton dresses, always a little loose on her skinny frame, the nylons she wore to hide her never-shaved legs. She dressed up a little on Sundays in tiny hoop earrings, a thin leather watch, a tarnished silver necklace etched with a rising moon.

I loved the church sanctuary and its name, a word made for a room of wood and white walls and red velvet. I loved church for its aesthetics and not for the promise of a tangible God.

My mother transcribed one of our conversations in a letter to Nana when I was three years old.

> Mommy, why do we get sick?
> *There are bad germs . . . blah, blah, blah . . .*
> Does God make us get sick?
> *No, sometimes we can be careful and not get sick by eating healthy food and . . . blah blah blah . . .*
> Does God get sick?
> *No, God doesn't have a body to get sick—*
> You mean he's just a head!?

I could never quite pin it down, that god others seemed to believe in, not exactly a disembodied head but something no adult could explain to me. I didn't need to see the hands of somebody else's god stirring my life. I didn't need divine help passing a math test. I needed the mountains to remain in their positions, east and west; needed the sun and then the moon to draw the line between. My problem arose when other people tried to cram an expanse into words. They gestured at something; they frowned when I did not see.

When I was fourteen one of our mother's friends, a counselor, agreed to talk with Kaela and me about our inability to share a motel bed without inciting a roiling brawl over who had more of the sheet. We are not twins; we exchanged no cells in the womb—yet it seemed we each held monopolies, an overabundance of traits the other lacked almost altogether and therefore could not understand. In the wood-chipped yard of our preschool, Kaela followed me, and I pretended I couldn't see her, even when she cried. Her hair was a short blonde bob, her eyes fixed on me, her skin so soft it felt slippery. As I sensed how easily she could be torn, I became brittle. How invaded I felt when she learned to open doors.

We met the counselor after sunset on an evening when a storm grumbled in the Sierra. Toys lay scattered on the carpet of her living room, her curls backlit as she sat across from us and asked us how we thought God liked the way we treated each other.

Kaela, chastened, lowered her eyes. And I bridled, looking into the woman's face while thunder gathered force. How dare she invoke this imaginary judge? How dare she presume her fantasy controlled *me*, a pilot's daughter who answered to the power of storms? Later Mom told me the counselor made a mistake. Mom had suggested before the meeting that the mention of divine expectation might be a good way to reach Kaela but was best left out of the conversation with me.

Kaela took belief into her life with a willingness and ease I could only watch from the periphery of the Sunday school classroom, muttering along while the group sang "Nobody Loves You Like Jesus." And all this was okay, because sanctuary extended beyond the doors of the church and into our world between mountains—until it didn't any longer, and it occurred to me to wonder: who looked over those blue-lipped boys in frozen water?

I WAS HER shadow—until she became mine. In a dream Mom appears at the top of a grassy hill and calls out to me where I stand at the bottom. She runs toward me with open arms, quickly over the grass, and I run, too. The dream ends before we reach each other.

Adrift from the meaning of his life and work, Tolstoy asked, "Why? Wherefore? What for?" and received no answer.

"The world now looks remote, strange, sinister, uncanny," an asylum patient reported in 1900. "Its color is gone, its breath is cold, there is no speculation in the eyes it glares with."

"I see everything through a cloud," said another. "Things are not as they were, and I am changed."

A few years after she slipped into my shadow, I blew dust off the VCR and played the old family videos.

Once again, flickering but in full color, Mom crawls in the dirt with a purple leash around her neck and three-year-old Kaela clinging to her back while I wallow in the sagebrush nearby. Pop holds the camera. *Tell who you're riding, Kaela*, Mom says from hands and knees, and Kaela hollers, "The kitty!"

Meow! says the kitty in her old green jacket and sunglasses. She crawls around in the dust for a while until it's time to drive to the city for a work conference, then sits up gently, Kaela sliding down her back.

Into what shadows had the purple marbles rolled?

When Los Angeles took the water and the farmers moved away from Owens Valley, an old woman convinced a neighbor to chloroform her big yellow cat, her "constant companion for a number of years." She didn't know where she was going and she would not leave him "to make a doubtful livelihood among other abandoned cats." The valley was growing empty as the farmers had never seen, though the people who came before them likely witnessed something they recognized. "Many of the old roads, and, one time, shady lanes of the little valley have been abandoned and closed," a woman wrote before she, too, went away. "There is no longer any use for them. They lead nowhere, except to scenes of desolation best left unvisited."

As the farmers left, did the place that had been their home lose its meaning? If you stop believing in something, does it die? Flee? Fade back into dust?

Amid their dancing gods, the ancient Greeks wrote of "nothing and nothingness." Oedipus in 406 BC: "How can I learn aught when naught I know? Being naught I came to life: once more shall I be what I was."

Shakespeare in 1603: "And yet, to me, what is this quintessence of dust?"

Matthew Arnold, 1850: "We are here as on a darkling plain."

William James, 1902: "Something bitter rises up . . . the buzz of life ceases . . . as a piano-string stops sounding when the damper falls."

An empty beauty becomes evil. The absence that visits the

little valley is terrible because of what has gone before, what has been abandoned or killed or stolen or chased off.

The big yellow cat lies in the dry ground, sleeping its sleep without dreams. In Owens Valley, a departing woman passed a hanging gate and thought of the many gates that now opened to nowhere. "I asked the sage lands and the old mountains, 'What is the answer?'" she wrote. "The wind moved the sage a little, but the mountains were mute."

IN THE NEXT video clip, a car stops halfway down the dirt driveway, the door opens, and Mom hops out of the driver's seat. In baggy spring jackets, Kaela and I totter around her. Snow patches the ground. Mom gets down on her knees. Kaela clings. I display a piece of shoelace for Mom's admiration. In Pop's hands, the camera cuts wildly to the woodpile, then back, as Mom stands and combs fingers through our hair. *Now Mommy has to go.* Her voice is sorry. *But I'll be back before you know it.*

Then it's just Kaela and me, grainy in the frame.

7. Last Days of the Good Girls

AT THE HOUSE OF some friends in Southern California, Mom and I shared a room. Her illness felt commonplace, not yet cancer, just a reason to make occasional trips to city doctors who said everything was fine, more or less. On this night I was barely a teenager, scrawny and morbidly shy. I had recently put the soft frog Mom had given me in a box in the attic and closed the lid on its glass eyes. In school my friends were invited to dances, on dates. And here I was expected to sleep in a bed with my mother.

I had entered that era of late childhood when a parent turns into an embarrassing rash. I wanted to sleep in my own bed and mope over my unrequited crush on the bass player in the school jazz band. My mother came out of the bathroom and climbed under the covers and yawned and patted the place beside her. *Ready for bed, sweetie?*

In tents and motel rooms all through my childhood, we traded back rubs. I drew her hair out of the way and reached under her baggy flannel pajama top and found the knots between her shoulders and spine. She liked you to push hard, really dig your thumbs in, and you knew she'd return the favor, that you'd flip on your side and she'd trace your ribs, and these were the best nights, free from dreams of burned things or ghosts or stalking mountain lions.

I was newly measuring myself against my peers—a measure that wouldn't matter long, and she knew it. This was just a wrinkle, a moment when distance between us seemed desirable. I believe now she understood, logically, and had our lives together been longer, I might have forgotten this night. But there on a bed at our friends' house, I did not want to rub my mother's back. I was beginning to sense the oddness of the world I had been given, a world of purple flowers. I wanted to be like our city friend's daughter, with her pink hair and bedroom full of music posters. I lay stiffly on top of the covers, closed my eyes, and reached for my headphones. And when I turned to look at Mom, she was crying.

SHE WAS A woman with an understanding of time and consequence, cause and effect. She wanted to control things, all things—our lives, her life, the drivers on the highway, the pilot's hand on the yoke. She might have made subtle adjustments to the drifting of the continents. She resisted that urge to control, mostly. In the years our mom had with us, we Atleeworks were not made overly neurotic about grade-point averages. We did not aspire to huge salaries or fame, were not expected to be piano prodigies, though we did run our scales after school, just as we spent hours in the dirt. We could quit, we could fail—but we had to own it. When at age eight I decided I could no longer handle the intense social experience that was Girl Scouts, I had to call the troop leader and explain this. When I quit Little League, sick of getting socked in the chin with the ball, I had to reimburse Mom for the sign-up fees by cleaning the garage and washing dishes for three dollars an hour until I cleared my account.

I knew well the serious set of her mouth in disappointment. Maybe I was flippant about a bombed math test or I'd griped through a family hike. Then came the long exhale through the nose, the blue eyes fixed on me, a little cold.

Our mother invited solitary alcoholics from church on our family outings in case they were lonely—then got rejected for jury duty because, she admitted, she had little mercy for drunk drivers. Consequence was meted out by Mom, and we couldn't ask Pop if Mom already said no. It was too easy to negotiate with Pop, until a punishment was whittled down to nothing. Mom identified the problematic behavior and required restitution: *Apologize to your sister, give your sister back her toy.* Then, in the absence of compliance, the counting began. *One.* Her voice deadly serious. *Two.* You felt compelled to meet her eyes as she lowered her chin and grew frown lines. *Three!* At three she sprang up, firm hands on your back and elbow, and escorted you not quite gently to the mudroom to sit among shoes and jackets and cultivate your remorse. A child who wailed through time-out (Kaela) or vindictively tied her mother's shoelaces in many tight knots (me) got bounced to the front porch to repent alongside the mountain lions.

At seven Anthony was deeply conscious of fashion. The collars of his little striped T-shirts had to pop just so. His shoes had to be fat, loose-laced Vans. Once or twice, Mom caught him playing an off-limits video game in which trolls struck one another with clubs. Once or twice, he lost his temper and walloped a kid at school. In both instances she sent him to the mudroom for hours of remorseful meditation and the next day confiscated his favorite jeans and took him to school with a pink satin bow bouncing effervescently from his backpack. She did not enjoy driving to town with her small son sullen and puffy eyed in the backseat. She told him, *You've got to be kind to be cool.*

We were expected to maintain certain standards of conduct, never mind the social consequences. At twelve I diverged from the music she chose for me—traces of her hippie past, mandolin, veiled references to psychedelic drugs—and brought home a pop CD I'd borrowed from a friend. The singer squatted on the cover in a white bikini, knees apart.

Hmm, Mom said when she saw it, lounging by the fire after work while I read the liner notes. *I wonder why she dresses like that on the cover. If the music is really good, do you think she'd need to be naked for people to buy it?*

This was enough for me to return the CD to my friend the next day.

At fourteen, the year I will not share a bed with my mother, I am a redheaded, nearsighted scarecrow in children's clothes. My only desire is for the delinquent bass player to notice me in band, to be like the girls who know how to use blow-dryers. Those girls do not have a hairy-legged mother who climbs rocks and sings *I am woman, hear me roar!*

Nothing can be done to improve me; apathy is the only thing, I've decided, that looks halfway good. Elizabeth at the same age is beautiful and womanly, but she is also weird and irreverent and angry at everything, and this bonds us nicely. At school we are ignored. And for denying us access, the populars must be punished, so on Valentine's Day each receives an envelope stuffed with unmentionables scrounged from Elizabeth's floor. Dirty Q-tips, toenail clippings, litter from the cat's box. Roses are red, violets are blue. We sign each note the Cat Litter Pirates. Before school, when I am supposed to be playing flute in zero-period band, we slip them through slats in locker doors.

Ms. Belkin says you're moving toward an A, Mom told me hopefully in those days, and I said, Ms. Belkin can stick it where the sun doesn't shine. It wasn't so much mediocre grades that hurt my mother but the insult of not caring, when I let my gaze slack and slide off whatever was beautiful about the day, the future she imagined. She, who we teased and called a workaholic after long hours at the county office, could not abide apathy. The more she cared, the less I wanted to. This is called being fourteen and afflicted with the desire to be left alone to wait out the painful days of growing into yourself. But she didn't have it in her to let me drift away.

I GET MY first boyfriend two months before she dies. He's a kid with skin the color of skim milk, who combs his bottle-black hair into his eyes and wears a belt studded with metal spikes. He listens to the music I love—ugly on purpose, screamed instead of sung, verses full of toppled angels. He is older, out of high school, and rarely steps outside. The fact that he chooses me to watch him play video games is a pure and holy miracle.

In Mammoth, I sit on a living room floor with this boy and his black-clad friends after school. Afternoon leaks into chilled evening as the boys fire bullets on the screen. Then my cell phone rings, and I am summoned to the driveway.

Bring him with you, sweetie, please, Mom says. *I want to meet him.*

The headlights burn. The boyfriend's complexion turns, unbelievably, even more curdled. Mom sits in the passenger's seat beside Pop, her face thin and yellowish, her nose sharp, her wrists bony. She looks at us through the car's open window, and I cringe at her grimace of a smile.

This trip to town is an effort, and to get out of the car and stand would be double that. Maybe she fears her knees buckling, fears clutching the side of the car in front of her dead-eyed daughter. She unfastens her seat belt and extends her hand.

I want to hide her from him. I just want her to cooperate. But this is my mother in the end. She doesn't know this boy and can only imagine what I will navigate alone. And so she is compelled to communicate: My daughter has been taught to file flight plans. Someone will be waiting to close them.

Her eyes say, I'm here, I'm in the world, I'm watching.

She says, *I'm Jan. Kendra's mother.*

She says, *It's nice to meet you.*

The boyfriend scurries back inside. And I remain standing on ice, Mom waiting for me to open the door and climb into the car behind her. But I am singed. Her desire to be present in our lives, to protect us from the despair creeping in around the edges, is hotter and brighter than the thing that is taking her away, and it scares me. It is something I am not ready to see.

The boyfriend broke up with me over text message a week later, and I sulked and scowled and banged the door of my bedroom on what I sensed was her last Valentine's Day with Pop. It was easy to blame her. She frightened my few friends with her oxygen tank, her conversation, her sharp interest in their lives. She asked them questions as she lay withering beneath blankets on the couch, and they shifted and stared out the window.

Every night in those last days, before she went to sleep, Mom asked Pop to bring us to her, one at a time. Would we have come if we hadn't been called? Already we sensed the weird energy that seemed to fill the spaces where her body should have been as she grew smaller, as she stopped riding in the passenger's seat to town, stopped climbing the stairs, stopped knocking softly on my bedroom door and sitting beside me on the floor.

I come when my father calls.

Here are her many pillows—her teddy pillows, she calls them, piled around her to prop up this or that limb; the little squirt bottle of water on the bedside table, since she can no longer sit up; the pain pills she doesn't take before bed, so she can be with us. *Hi, sweetie.* I bend to hug her and then I climb in. The bed is big and soft and not much used since she and Pop spent so many nights on a futon upstairs between our three rooms, happier in our orbit.

Will you tell me about school?

My face is on her pillow, my arm across her chest. I am careful not to press where it hurts, which is everywhere, and now there are no more back rubs. The tumor, I have heard her say, makes her look five months pregnant, but not really. She weighs eighty pounds. She is a scary doll in her pajamas, soft and dotted with little blue roses. I don't want to talk about school.

You are my firstborn, she says softly. *I count on you. How desperately I wanted you in my life. I practically strangled the other little mothers with their cute strollers with who knows what inside.*

Sorry you got me, then, Mom.

Hush. Babies always screamed when I held them, until you. You liked me. (Thanks.)

When I kiss her, her forehead leaves salt on my lips. The room is cool, but she blazes. I think it is the mystery, the thing she is going into, but I cannot get close to that fire yet. I can only lie beside her here and wait for moonrise. Out the window across from her bed, the mountains are a few shades darker than the sky, almost invisible, but I can sense them, blackest black without shadow or reflection.

My mother has crept one hand out from under the covers. The other is holding mine. She raises a finger on the free hand. The rest of the fingers are legs. They skitter feebly on the blanket. Oh, Mom.

Do you want to talk to our Little Bug?. . . Sorry. Maybe save him for later.

POP WAITED UNTIL dark the last day, then led Kaela and Anthony and me up the road that climbs Wheeler. The land drops away steeply, and the neighborhood fans out below. The row of Jeffrey pines stood at our backs, and from here we watched a full moon rise.

Now when I am far from home, Pop sends me text messages

every so often. "Full moon tonight," he says. What he means: Think of Mom.

A friend in my high school, whose parents, she told me, had been saved from alcohol and violence by God, asked what I believed, and I couldn't answer. I couldn't explain that though no god has ever lived in my father or me, that even though the mountain is a mountain and granite is old stone, the moon—etched on the necklace my mother wore, as the silver darkened—the moon, when it shines so brightly it casts shadows, when it rises over desert and mottles the clouds, makes both of us remember.

THE DAY AFTER she died, Kaela's ninth grade theater troupe performed a musical based on the books of Dr. Seuss. Kaela played the youngest Who in Whoville, whose village is caught on a dust speck and blowing toward oblivion. In the high school cafeteria—site of the horror of choosing a lunch table, of grapes thrown into the principal's eye—Kaela stood on the stage and sang her big solo. *I'm alone in the universe,* the chorus repeated.

Mary Austin wrote of stars wheeling to their stations, while below, the poor world frets of no account. The lean coyote and the woman in her tent howl and howl. Maybe it was the size of our sky that made the whole of our family such a crucial point of reference, a key on a map. No matter how far I roamed before Pop blew a conch shell calling us home for dinner, there was this certainty: if I went looking, I would find her. These few humans made the stars a little less distant. We filled up the world.

Mom felt it, too. When I was thirteen, I went on a long trip with my grandparents. Mom cried when we said goodbye in the airport, and of course I was embarrassed. After I came home she told me, *While you were gone I just sat on the floor of your bedroom every once in a while.* Pale purple walls, rusty redwood ceiling, dust bolts in the sun. *And I just looked at the mountains and missed you.*

The strange culture of our family broke, dissolved, like the icicles that trailed from our roof, then fell and shattered on the deck. The three of us were beginning to understand that someday no one will meet you at the bus stop, that you can't really walk home. Those days add themselves to memory like ice on your boots. The person who carries the memory grows heavier for it.

I used to dream that she returned, though her return was never joyful. I understood that her presence was temporary, that she was on loan from somewhere else. She spent a few days, fitful because they were short, and I counted them down. Always she was haggard. In one of these dreams we drove—her at the wheel, me in the passenger's seat, though I was no longer a child—south from Mammoth toward Swall Meadows, past the saltgrass meadows where Pop launched his balloon, and as she drove, she cried.

I'm so tired, she said. *So tired.* I asked her why.

Passing back and forth, she told me. *Coming home, then leaving.* I turned to ask her where she goes when she leaves us. Before she could answer, I woke.

In real life, after she died, I drove alone seven miles through the gorge most evenings, tied an apron around my waist, and with Elizabeth took orders for beer and cheese-burgers at the old greasy spoon, halfway between Swall and Mammoth, that drew tourists off 395.

In this cafe—mariachi music oompahing from the kitchen, deer heads on the walls, croutons lost forever beneath the freezer—a kind waitress with graying blonde hair taught us to slather butter across English muffins. She called Elizabeth "Little-Bit" and laughed hoarsely. From her we learned to dodge the LA fishermen who tugged us to sit at their tables, who called us honey and tried to guess our age. At school I ate lunch in my car, skulked around in T-shirts printed with blood-spattered roses, and inoculated myself against conversation, hiding headphones from teachers beneath a black hood.

Anthony shut the door to his bedroom while Kaela sat on the floor of the shower and sobbed. Pop puttered in the kitchen, cooking dinner, which we carried upstairs to our rooms. Before school he put bags of nuts and dried fruit on the counter for us to take for lunch, which we ignored. Beneath magnets on the refrigerator, he hung scrawled reminders: *Keys, wallet! Call Mike!* When mice invaded and he needed to set traps: *Mouse highway!* Sometimes moral guidelines appeared for his children: *Look before you leap! It takes two to tango!*

Anthony peeled Pop's suggestions off the fridge and tore them into pieces. We no longer went to church or to Keough's or to the Bishop park. We abandoned Pop to eat by himself and clean up our messes. In the kitchen before school, we passed one another without looking up. We no longer did homework in front of the fire, could not sit shoulder to shoulder on the rug, as if, placed together, we might burn.

Whatever took place in the private worlds of my brother and sister, they expressed through property damage and an accumulation of interesting scars. Anthony had not yet discovered jail, but he knew juvie. When my brother stayed with friends on the Paiute reservation in Bishop, the house on Mountain View Drive was silent. When he was at home, the walls ricocheted with his shouts as he refused Pop's attempts to do the work of two parents. Pop made Anthony type letters of apology, print them, edit them, print them again. There was a truck stolen and crashed in the desert, a field burned. "I'm sorry for my behavior," my brother wrote to the Mormon minister, after his crew spray-painted KILL on the church walls. "I am working hard to get my behavior under control."

Kaela shoplifted from lingerie stores in Mammoth that catered to tourists and drove in the woods with boys. She and Anthony listened with resignation to the howling of the stereo as I drove us to school every morning. I controlled the wheel, I controlled the music. We arrived late for first period, always. In the back, Anthony was silent. Kaela sat in the passenger's seat with bangs pinned in a bouffant, and we traded words like thorns. She played volleyball and sunbathed in the driveway. Fresh ridges of tissue appeared on her body in places where clefts and gashes had little reason to be. She loved a band called the Pussycat Dolls and hung sparkly puffball ornaments from the rearview mirror, which I yanked off and threw on the floor.

Kaela's nickname, coined by her classmates, was Plan B. She explained: "If you wanted to hook up with somebody and it didn't work out, there was always Plan B." When parents left town, kids threw benders with guest lists and guarded the doors with sheets of notebook paper. Kaela made it onto those lists, though not under her own name. Plan B was always welcome at the party.

Across the heat of a bonfire, she saw a boy she had been dating kiss another girl.

She went over and asked the boy if he had a pocketknife, because she needed to cut a strap in her car so she could recline the seat and go to sleep.

She took the knife and walked into the woods and cut at the skin on her arm. She was trying, she said, to erase how badly it hurt not to be loved. After that, if she didn't have a knife, she used a nail file. She took paper clips, bent them into shapes, held a lighter to the metal, and batiked her arms with stars. She sat on the bank of Crowley Lake, in the pine woods, in the brush and pinyon plains along the Owens River Gorge, beneath the void, and she noted the different layers of her skin.

KAELA HID HER scabs under terry-cloth wristbands.

She remembers the night she and her friends Sadie and Ellie decided to try drinking for the first time. Out in the middle of the desert, no boys. These were the last days of the good girls—a junior now, Kaela was still an honors student, still going weekly with her friends to lunchtime youth group. She and Sadie and Ellie drove a couple of hours to Death Valley and hiked out to the dunes, where they drank an entire handle of raspberry vodka. Sadie passed out. Ellie started twitching and vomiting all over the back of Sadie's sweatshirt. Kaela walked to the car to get water, and when she came back, the girls were gone. They'd run into the desert. So Kaela drove through seven sets of wooden fences in order to find them, drove the Subaru onto the dunes. It got stuck in the sand, sunk in, and she got out to dig under the tires.

She left the car with the headlights on to illuminate the desert and went on foot after the girls. She found Ellie, but she couldn't find Sadie. Kaela tried to get Ellie into the car, and first Ellie punched her in the face. There was vomit all over everyone's clothing, and it was freezing, and all the windows were down, and by this point the car's battery had died. The two of them curled up in the backseat under an aluminum emergency blanket while clouds settled and snow filtered through the open windows.

It is hard to know how to fix a smashed world at sixteen, at fourteen, at eleven. At first light, Kaela climbed to the top of the tallest dune and screamed for Sadie. She could see a speck, far out in the desert.

When Sadie reached her, she said the night had seemed endless; that she wasn't sure the sun would ever rise; that she thought her life might forever be the strange dance that carried her through the hours, walking until she grew too tired, huddling in the sand until she grew too cold.

FROM HER BEDROOM window Kaela could see the line of the Sierra as it disappeared north toward Mammoth, while I parted curtains printed with calico cats and faded by a decade of cloudlessness to look over Tom and the sheer wall of Wheeler, sopping with light, all shadows blasted by absurd mountain morning sun. In his bedroom, beneath the same view, Anthony shredded the letters our mother wrote to him when she knew she was dying and left the scraps for Pop to find and gather, to gather and deem unsalvageable and throw away.

Anthony spent most nights on couches on the Bishop Paiute Reservation—the rez, everyone calls it. Parents and grandparents looked at him with something like pity and let him stay.

My brother did not know the history that shaped the place he made his home. But I believe that the families who took him in understood loss. Their ancestors watched trouble come to the valley, a trouble that took different forms in different decades. Years before Anthony moved onto the rez, a Paiute man walked into Meadow Farms Liquor near the intersection of Main and Tu-Su Lane and shot the white clerk six times in the head, chest, and stomach. Four days later, sheets of paper blew across the reservation, printed in red ink and signed KKK.

The letters threatened to do terrible things to Paiute girls between the ages of five and nine, in retribution. They drifted across the parking lot outside the Paiute Palace Casino, fluttered around a day-care center, and spread against the backstop of the baseball field while the mountains looked on.

In Samuel Bishop's first winter in Payahuunadu, those months of flooding and deep snow, the Paiutes began killing livestock to survive. A rancher shot a Paiute as he chased away a cow, and the Paiutes killed a prospector called Yank. One day in January 1862, Bishop and the cattlemen who had followed him to the valley called a powwow with Paiute chiefs at San Francis Ranch. Fourteen men gathered. Chief George marked the ground with two lines—one rancher killed, one Paiute. Since the score fell even, the men drafted a treaty.

We the undersigned, citizens of Owens Valley, with Indian chiefs representing the different tribes and rancherias of said valley, having met together at San Francis Ranch, and after talking over all past griev- ances and disturbances that have transpired between the Indians and whites, have agreed to let what has past be buried in oblivion. . . .

And it is further agreed that the Indians are not to be molested in their daily avocations by which they gain an honest living.

And it is further agreed upon the part of the Indians that they are not to molest the property of the whites, nor to drive off or kill cattle that are running in the val- ley, and for both parties to live in peace and strive to promote amicably the general interests of both whites and Indians.

Given under our hands at San Francis Ranch this 31st day of January, A.D. 1862.

THOSE WERE THE last days of a tenuous peace. A few weeks later, on a February night, a band of Paiutes, led by a chief who did not attend that gathering, allegedly danced around Bishop's cabins. Inside, Samuel Bishop, his wife, and the ranchers must have watched through narrow windows. The Paiutes, the whites reported, waved pitch-pine torches and declared they could spit bullets from their bodies—that they could not die.

The Paiutes perhaps called on other tribes for help defend- ing the valley, and perhaps men came from Mono Lake, from

Southern California and the western foothills. By spring an army lieutenant who'd been sent to scout the valley reported between eight hundred and one thousand warriors in possession of "one hundred or more good guns." I have heard from a descendant of those warriors that the Paiutes had four guns. I have heard they dug up waterlines and melted the lead into bullets, then bought more bullets from an Aurora merchant who refused to supply the ranchers, claiming that all the whites in Payahuunadu deserved to die.

An Indian agent wrote of the Paiutes: "They will fight to the last extremity in the defense of their homes." The First People's impulse was to protect the valley as they knew it, to protect the ways they knew of living here. Early in the spring of 1862, claiming harassment, forty-two white men and a few women and children barricaded themselves inside a stone house called Putnam's Fort. The men fortified the walls with rocks and pieces of broken wagons. With rifles, shotguns, and revolvers, they kept a constant watch.

A rancher wrote in a letter that he and the others were menaced constantly. The colonel who eventually received the letter had heard of an isolated valley, where ranchers set their stock to graze irrigated fields. "It is very possible, therefore, that the whites are to blame," the colonel wrote to a colleague, "and it is also probable that in strict justice they should be compelled to move away and leave the valley to its rightful owners." Still, he sent a scouting party, which, according to white accounts, found chaos and unburied bodies. When the scouts released the people from Putnam's Fort, some say the settlers fell in gratitude to their knees.

On the Fourth of July 1862, 157 soldiers rode into Owens Valley in the belted jackets and blue canvas pants issued to the Second Cavalry California Volunteers. The men erected a fifty-foot flagpole on a bare lot to serve as a parade grounds, gave three cheers, and fired small-arm salutes. They called the place Camp Independence.

Not long before, the riders passed Owens Lake. A man stood near the water, and as he looked after the cavalry, a soldier raised his revolver. The man fell on the lakeshore, the first Paiute the California Volunteers encountered in Payahuunadu.

As a child, Anthony used to sit on Pop's lap and put his head under Pop's big T-shirt, put his face through the neckhole, and bare his teeth while Pop curled his fingers into claws, and in this way they became a two-headed monster. Then my brother's shoulders grew broad, his voice deep, and he pushed our suddenly lonesome father down the stairs, called him stupid, moron, dickhead. He looked into our faces and shut off the light in his eyes. From my bed in the dark, I could hear a ripping as he stabbed his mattress, the flick of a lighter held to the carpet. Pop gathered all the knives from the drawers, all the matches from the fireplace, and hid them in the highest cupboard.

Anthony rode his dirt bike fast and reckless on sandy trails through groves of aspen and across streams. He launched the bike over dips in back roads that cut across Wheeler Crest. Pretty lucky, Pop says now, that the two of them did not collide, so often they rode alone but at the same time. Our father must have looked to the skies where his silver RV-4 once looped and dropped and rolled. We did not often see his sadness or fear. He was not a man who allowed himself to be consumed. We did see him racing down the driveway, the bike's engine a roar, gravel spitting behind his tire.

I watched my brother's anger simmer into something frightening, something awoken or broken. After arson, theft, and juvie came a school for uncontrollable children in another desert far away. I watched my sister preside at the head of the dinner table in Pop's chair when he was out of town, the other seats filled with the red-faced youth of nowhere—watched her spin a quarter, slap it down, pour something acrid in a shot glass and swallow. After a closing shift at the greasy spoon one winter night, I climbed into my car smelling of fries, feet aching, damp wads of fives and ones rolled in a back pocket. It made sense to drive Lower Rock Creek Road with the headlights off, and I passed no one as the gorge cut sheer to my left, dark pines and creek at its base, canyon walls reaching to a channel of sky. White faces of mule deer turned and froze. In the full moon I drifted and for a moment knew only adrenaline and peace.

I turned off the car and stepped into dark and snow. The dirt of our driveway lay frozen beneath my tires. In moonlight I could see the bent basketball hoop, its tattered net hanging, the boards Pop nailed over holes bored by woodpeckers. Roses leaned bare in their beds and weed-like along the redwood walls. The chilled branches of the apple tree rustled. Inside, I knew, Pop slept. Anthony's room was empty. Kaela stayed with one friend or another in town. The fire Pop built every morning still flickered. The shadows between the rafters stretched empty, but Pop never did let the fire go out.

PART 3

RIVERS

8. The Indestructibles

WHEN ELIZABETH AND I weren't shuttling baskets of fries and feeding tourists a fake age, fake name, fake history, we fled Swall Meadows and drove to Bishop in her Oldsmobile and sat in pink vinyl booths in an ice cream parlor until it shut down. In Kmart I pushed her around in a shopping cart filled with pillows while she brandished a fishing net at shoppers. Outside in the parking lot we chased a piece of cottonwood fluff struck white by floodlights against a dark sky. We gazed up until our necks hurt.

We stood on Main and watched traffic chug, watched trucks hauling hay from Nevada, and considered leaping onto the bails at a red light so we, too, could ride away—our one wish in those days, to go away—certain, without proof, that away was better.

Los Angeles waited. The drawers of the history museum in Owens Valley are filled with folders on bats and mules and barbed wire, but there are no universities in our county and not many jobs. My high school class, numbering fifty, scattered after graduation. The mountains that had cradled us in childhood conjured loneliness, hiding whatever lay beyond.

We were born sutured to the city. And so I turned eighteen and quit my job at the greasy spoon, went to Kmart and bought myself a red bath towel and a little wire caddy for the showers in the dorm, and packed my old bedroom into the back of Pop's map delivery van.

"MAKE YOUR MIND Up to Wind Up in Sunny California" was a ragtime song popular in 1930. On March 15 of the same year, a tornado struck near downtown Los Angeles. "The wind became playful," the *Examiner* reported. "It scooped up many rabbits and chickens and carried them out of the town." Later "glass flew like paper through the streets, more chickens and rabbits were caught in the funnel, and roofs were torn from hundreds of homes." The tornado lifted a freight train from the tracks and threw it against a barn. Walls and porches were "torn off and shot like arrows across space." The twister whisked away garages, then hoisted a house and set it down in the street while "several persons were picked up bodily and hurled a distance of fifty to one hundred feet."

A half century later the LA area experienced two tornadoes, mudslides, and an earthquake more or less simultaneously. The tornadoes wrecked more than 120 buildings and made so much noise Angelenos feared a plane crash or an atomic bomb. In close to a century LA tornadoes have destroyed about sixty major buildings, damaged around fifteen hundred houses and businesses, and wounded close to two hundred people.

A "tornado alley" exists in downtown Los Angeles, a result of the meeting of cold air, a curved coast, and mountains.

Here, tornadoes strike with a frequency comparable to the Midwest. Los Angeles is not proud of its wild side. An 1876 poster heralds California as the "Cornucopia of the World," the words printed over a tumble of grapes, bananas, and pineapples. "Private Land for a Million Farmers," the poster declares. "A Climate for Health and Wealth without Cyclones or Blizzards." An F2 tornado struck Pasadena late in January 1918, shredding streets and walloping a woman in the back with a rafter. The next day the *Times* and *Examiner* were scheduled to publish booster editions coinciding with blizzards elsewhere. "Big Drifts Bury East," the *Times* warned. "Come to California, land of beauty, flowers, and sunshine . . . Southland's arms are outstretched in cordial invitation to the East!"

The papers did not report on the tornado that destroyed two churches and uprooted a grove of orange trees. Instead the *Times* referred to the "tail end of a wind storm" that entertained Angelenos by "playfully picking up stray pieces of paper." Many folks in neighboring parts of the city never knew the tempest occurred.

To forget the past, writes the Californian Rebecca Solnit, is to forgo your sense of loss, and at the same time to lose "a set of clues to navigate the present by." The void that was suddenly my home screamed to be muffled by noise. Where else to go but the city to the south, poster child of California, shielded from the world's dangers by denial? How easy it is, when faced with eternal night, to run toward neon and a billboard sun. Historian Kevin Starr describes the galvanizing feature of early California, gold rush California, as a "psychology of expectation." Room enough, Mary Austin tells us, and time enough in these desert hills. But Los Angeles offered more than room and time—it beckoned with the promise and dreams of a certain kind of future, bright and untainted by the past.

Our state could easily contain ten European countries. It has redwoods and fog and snow, dolphins and pine martens and antelope. It has libertarians and hippies. It is a home to immigrants from everywhere. Yet all its many pieces share this in common: ours is a state thus far defined by growth. Growth demands optimism. At its best, optimism demands resilience. At its worst, optimism demands forgetfulness. And these can be difficult to distinguish.

Where did my brother, snatched from tragedy, learn to hoist himself from the pavement after that crash on the skateboard, half-crushed by Pop and smiling? Where but from his father, who came from a long line of indestructibles? Is my father's family resilient or just forgetful? Are we forever hopeful, or have we failed to learn the lessons of the past? All I can say for sure is that California seemed built for the Atlees. Nana marched with Mothers for Peace and Beyond War, then sat at the kitchen table, her hair a white halo, and informed us that all men suffered from castration anxiety. She believed the word *fuck* should be reclaimed, she told all the neighbors, "because sex isn't dirty!" and she mortified Fafa by announcing, at a dinner with my aunt's family, her plan to write a book called *Sex after Seventy*.

"Fafa smacked the table," my cousin told me, "looked at her in horror, and said, '*Susan!*'"

My father's earliest memory involves a plastic fire truck with a little hose, given to him by his parents, and a milk carton with cutout windows. Nana lit the milk carton on fire and shrieked "Save us! Save us!" while her toddler son put out the flames. At four, my father's sister treed herself at the top of a telephone pole. Later, with Nana's permission, she threw a bag of rocks over a cow's back to tame her for riding. At three, Pop crashed off his parents' California king bed and broke his collarbone. He broke the same collarbone fifty years later crashing his motorcycle and then again crashing on his skis.

Pop's optimism grew strongest when he found an exciting way to risk death. Years ago another wildfire approached Swall, the first time I saw planes dropping red powder. Mom drove home from work past a wall of flame, and all day we cleared brush away from trees and filled buckets with water. After dark, when the sheriff came around to tell everyone to evacuate, Pop wanted me to stay, to help him fight the fire. He said if we had to we could climb into the neighbor's pond and pull sheet metal over our heads. Or we could ride his motorcycle, me clinging to his back, and accelerate through the flames. I was twelve years old. Mom said *absolutely not.* He stayed by himself, patrolling with a garden hose. When I remind him of that night, Pop chuckles gleefully. "We could have gotten out of there. You'd have been fine!"

Even our animals seemed wild optimists, guided by mad instinct. The black tom, Mirage, from whose long coat Mom cut snarls, peed on Pop's ski equipment in the garage, vying for territory and persisting even after Pop plopped

Mirage down in the shower and peed on *him*. Mirage
loved Mom with dog-like devotion and mewed to her in a
high, frail voice. When Pop dropped him off on a ranch halfway to Bishop—to be a mouser, he said—Mirage walked ten
miles home.

Not much of moderation, nor a barometer for normal,
in the indestructible Atlee family. In a letter to Nana, Mom
wrote:

> *Kendra just came to visit me. She came to get me to*
> *walk her outside because she was frightened. She said,*
> *"Mom! Don't you remember when you were four and*
> *your father brought home the skull of a dead horse*
> *that had teeth and hair and put it right by the door?*
> *Remember how you were afraid to walk by it?"*
>
> *Really, that wasn't one of my memories, but then*
> *I didn't have Robert as a father—and there is a horse*
> *skull by our front door. . . .*

Mom was born in the darkest days of the year and raised
in the deep woods of Michigan. But she married a man born
in a dry summer on a golden coast, and she fledged her family in California. Once, our limbs were strong and our lungs
swelled with the thin air of high altitude. The sun shone over
our heads three hundred days a year. For all our knowledge
of rescue and caution, we were gilded. What an insult to be,
abruptly, not only breakable but broken. From my home I
learned to live afflicted half with the care of the pilot who
hopes to grow old, half with the impulse to fling myself into

the future headlong, hands scrabbling for purchase on a shifty mountainside and never mind the past. How I ran with that plastic airplane tottering behind me on its string. How we flew from the trapeze in our living room.

Nana and Fafa came to California for a honeymoon in 1951 and stayed the rest of their lives. They discovered the state during a postwar boom, after the weird chaos of the gold rush and the devastation of First Peoples and the battles that led to statehood had saturated "the alkaline dirt we call California," as Richard Rodriguez puts it, a time when a bunch of land developers and entertainment types and people from somewhere else built industries on the quicksand of history. There's more than one kind of gold to be yanked out of the ground in California. Richard Rodriguez is the child of Mexican immigrants and he writes of the ballooning Sacramento of his 1950s boyhood, of "freeways and new cities, bright plastic pennants and spinning whirligigs announcing a subdivision of houses; hundreds of houses; houses where there used to be fields."

"Better make your next location California!" went the 1930 ragtime hit. At times in the 1960s, California's population grew by fifteen hundred in a single day. How strange Rodriguez's California, the winter warmth, the press of the grinning crowd, must have seemed to Nana and Fafa for a while—the lax dress, the willingness to bare skin, against a backdrop of rabid growth. They had the prudent East for comparison, just as Rodriguez saw his Mexican parents—and the Irish Catholic nuns who taught him how to write—looking back at their history, seeing tragedy behind and tragedy ahead.

The inheritance of California is half-gorgeous, half-deadly. It is half-remembered and half-lost. It is a brother with a past like a time bomb—but let's not worry about that now. "Look to the future," Joan Didion instructs her compatriots. "The future always looks good in the golden land, because no one remembers the past."

My father has a friend who spent enough years beneath the high Sierra sun that his nose was cut off to save his face. The rubber prosthesis hurts to wear. He greets us and we see the crater, the wet cave. Still, the sun shines; we bask and forget what it can do in this place free from rust and too dry for decay.

If optimism means forgetfulness, then our optimism was necessary for a certain kind of future to occur, for growth, a certain version of the greatest good. California was home to one of the most effective advertising campaigns in history, converting not only new customers but those who had already bought the product. Remembering winter free of storms was essential to what historians call the growth machine: the developers, politicians, journalists, and newspaper owners who boosted California and in the process turned an ideal into culture. The blood of our valley supplied the state's racing heart.

IN INYO COUNTY, eighteen thousand people populate ten thousand square miles. Spread us out and you get fewer than two people per mile—we could wave to our neighbors in the distance, over mirage. Greater Los Angeles fits over thirteen million into an area half as large—that's about twenty-six hundred people per square mile. You might imagine a city where the sky hangs an infected yellow-green. Buildings cluster like bad molars. Searchlights shoot down the stars.

But I could see, for the first time, the ugliness of home, invasive tumbleweed and cheatgrass and the busted signs on Main. Fishing line snarled around lakeshores. Dead deer heaped along the highway. If country once so full could become so empty, why stay?

"Fences have been strung across these roads," a woman wrote in the local paper in the early 1930s while Owens Valley hemorrhaged. "Signs have been posted announcing, 'Road Closed,' and this is the answer to the question, 'Will you come back?'"

When the water left Owens Valley, Austin recorded, "Mary did what she could. And that was too little. The year before she had built a house—the brown house under the willow tree. She walked in the fields and considered what could be done. She called upon the Voice, and the Voice answered her—Nothing. She was told to go away."

When the eye drifts off the sparrow, when the world feels unattended, when beauty drains like water flowing south—you throw beer cans out the window. You fly away. The Owens Valley woman who watched the towns slump answered her own question: "No, you won't come back. The road is closed and the fence is up. Anyway, why concern yourself any longer with the inevitable? Fill up the radiator, pour in the gas and step on it."

9. Locals Only

POP DROPS ME IN a suburb of Los Angeles County in the brown foothills of the San Gabriel Mountains, a range obscured by smog. We've traveled here in his van, emptied of maps and packed with all my black clothes, driving by swimming pools and rows of skinny Mexican palms leaning in the direction the wind usually blew. My college did not recruit at Mammoth High, which was instead visited by a pointy-eared dog that sniffed for drugs in backpacks and lockers. I discovered the campus on a road trip, and I was here because of scholarships, the Depression-born frugality of Nana and Fafa, and Pop's offer to match the tips I'd saved for years at the greasy spoon.

Pop helps me carry boxes up two flights of stairs, takes a shower in the dorm's bathroom, and gets back on the road to beat traffic out of the city. The mustached stepfather of my New Jersey roommate drags her desk beneath the window. The parents of my Idaho roommate pull sheets over her bed. I am pale and gangly in denim shorts and velvet Mary Janes, red hair dyed almost black and chopped blunt at my ears, with no adult to override my opinion on the best location for my bookshelf. I pin music posters in the dark space beneath my lofted bed until the Idaho mother pauses in snapping a pillowcase and crosses the room to crouch at my side.

Leaves grow green year-round outside our dorm, and the noise of parties drifts through our open windows. Once, a roommate comes back early from lab and catches me sitting in the cave beneath my bed, listening to a recording of my mother's flute. I close my laptop and spring up and we go to lunch.

And what of the place I leave behind? Pop cooks dinners no one eats. Anthony decides he is a grown man.

He says to our father, "Can't I get some respect?"

He is Bishop's heartbreaker—the coffee shop seems to be staffed exclusively by girls who either dated or are currently dating my brother, and he's equally popular with the Kmart cashiers. They stitch his initials into blankets and buy him booze. They are years older than he is and always pretty.

He stays with his friends on the Bishop rez rather than returning each afternoon to a lonely mountainside. Many nights he lingers outside a McDonald's on Main, under the yellow glow of a giant *M*, smoking and eating Cheetos. He has a man's chin and jawline, a sprout of beard. He cuts the sleeves off his black T-shirts and slits the sides. Pop gives him cash for food, and Anthony uses it to buy clothes at Kmart. He and his friends box one another in the desert. They play cards and video games into the night. There are missing bicycles across town, and the sheriff looking for the swaggering shadow child, and the midnight ringing of my father's phone, and Pop no longer whistling over dishes at the kitchen sink.

• • •

SOME OF MY Angeleno classmates, learning I came from the Eastern Sierra, asked me, "People actually *live* there?"

Nothing in the strip malls and parking stalls could conjure the place I was trying to forget. I trained myself toward a new kind of beauty and in this way survived. And so I set out to make Los Angeles mine. I dated a boy whose grandparents moved to Tijuana from the deserts of Mexico, had their children in San Diego, and then bought a ranch-style house within the vast petticoats of Los Angeles. Orange trees and prickly pear cactus grew in the backyard. Portraits of Jesus and the Virgin hung in the living room. Every Sunday the abuelos juiced pomegranates and grilled carne asada and hosted family gatherings at which I received over sixty hugs. I sat at the kitchen table and ate homemade salsa and listened to talk about children's college applications and goings-on at the office and good deals on televisions and the remodeling of homes as the sun warmed my back through the window and cousins whooped outside at the basketball hoop.

My classmates sprawled on beach towels on the campus lawns, mystified by infinite sun. In summer most of them flew back to Seattle or New York or wherever. For some, the semesters seemed a vacation in a place they did not want to understand. And so most of my friends were not students at my college but kids who worked in warehouses, played in punk bands, and raced each other on the freeways. We sat on the cement patio outside King Taco and drank horchata and ate tacos de lengua and watched smoke from the deep fryer rise over the yellow roof. My friends rubbed A+D ointment into fresh tattoos and grimaced, and I told them just a little about my family and where I came from. Though they had never scratched their skin on rose hips, they seemed to understand, because their world was strange also. Los Angeles gave me a family for a while when my own felt beyond repair. It taught me about neighborhood softball fields and sunsets over train tracks and terra-cotta tiles warmed by the sun.

But if I went south to escape home, it didn't work. One moment I was at ease in the haze from my friends' cigarettes, beneath streetlights in the dew of an East LA midnight, searching a gutter for someone's dropped keys—the next, transported in my head to the splintery porch on Mountain View Drive, the wood grain illuminated by a bright moon.

A COUPLE OF years after I left for college, Kaela loaded up her car and rented an apartment in a neighborhood called Little Armenia, just east of Hollywood, less than two miles from the place where a young Mulholland planted a seedling oak beside a water ditch. The neighborhood ranked high on charts for violent crime, but Kaela left the plastic slats of her blinds swiveled open. In the mornings kids hung out on her doorstep. Above her building, just off L. Ron Hubbard Way, a giant sign flashed SCIENTOLOGY and cast blue light on her pillow. Ants covered the sink. Cockroaches laid eggs in the walls of her microwave.

Here, Kaela tried to become a model while her boyfriend burned holes in the carpet with his bong and hung a reeking marijuana plant to dry on the wall. Kaela pinned up tapestries. On her bed sat a stuffed leopard from Mom, and on the nightstand she tossed change and guitar picks and dental floss and coconut body butter and bowls of peanut shells. Beneath the bed lurked a kitten called Bill, rescued by the boyfriend from a gutter and brought to their apartment, where pets were forbidden. In a photograph taken in this room, the two of us stand with arms around each other's shoulders, heads together, a withering potted palm and two fast-food milkshakes on the table at our backs, and beyond that the open window, the sky purple, clutching a scrap of moon.

For weeks—before her boyfriend moved in—we slept in her bed together while I searched for a summer sublet. My college had somehow agreed to pay for my food and rent while I helped start a music venue. I showed up at Kaela's apartment in the middle of May with everything I owned shoved in my car. I had followed her directions scrawled on a sticky note tacked to the dash: take the 10 west to the 101; exit on Vermont Avenue; turn left on Lexington and right on a street that, despite its name, bore little resemblance to New Hampshire. Kaela's block hosted zero shade trees and a half-dozen varieties of palm. She lived in a studio on the first floor of a brown square. Everybody had a tiny patch of grass.

In the few feet of dirt outside her door, Kaela planted bachelor buttons and a jalapeño bush. She wouldn't get home from work until 1 a.m., and among the mint and morning glory, she had buried her keys for me.

I crouched to jostle the top layer of soil, which rose and drifted over my jeans. Two pimply boys who sat on the stoop next door turned to watch. They were André and Raúl, I quickly learned. André and Raúl were eating paletas, strawberries and cream. Hi! Was I Kaela's sister?

They were unfazed to see a stranger grubbing in the dirt. They knew Kaela. When Pop came to visit months before, he went to the grocery store and brought them a box of chocolate almonds. Did I need help? They rose and sauntered over, slurping their paletas, the juice dripping at my knees.

ALL AROUND ME was noise as pervasive as dust. In Los Angeles sirens were constant. Choppers broadcasted descriptions of fleeing criminals or lost elders from loudspeakers, voices talking from the sky. The traffic never faded, even in the middle of the night. Sounds of tires and motors and horns were omnipresent and diffuse, coming from fifty unseen freeways and boulevards at once, coming from everywhere and nowhere, in this way like the wind in my old desert, and also nothing like it at all.

The first time I went home after moving away, I followed 395 over land that became jagged beyond the last desert subdivision. Joshua trees prickled, and brown hills rose in a wall. It was January, before drought, before fire, and in Swall Meadows the willows and poplars stood leafless. Snow fell heavily over Wheeler Crest. I went on a walk with Pop down Mountain View Drive, up Swall Meadows Road. We walked like this nightly when I was a kid and then a teenager, even when I refused to pull the headphones from beneath my hood. The snow silenced our footsteps, and the air hung wet with clouds. Mount Tom vanished in gossamer. The neighbors' Christmas lights beamed halos, the valley stretched, ghost country beneath frost, and I wondered: Could I ever know silence like this, peace like this, anyplace but my home?

A couple of friends came by my dorm on the night I turned twenty, the summer before junior year. We wandered around campus and watched moths careen into streetlights. When the friends drove back to their suburbs, I walked under olive trees to my car, to sit behind the wheel without sparking the engine, while the tape player clicked and my mother's flute sang.

THERE WERE THINGS we both missed, Kaela and I, and things we remembered, which we could not yet discuss. There was a sense of trudging forward, as Kaela's friend had that night years ago, lost in the dunes, toward what we didn't know. Beyond Kaela's apartment loomed the Griffith Observatory, a giant white building, golden domed on the slope of Mount Hollywood. The Observatory looked over downtown and, when the smog blew clear, the ocean. Inside, projectors cast constellations on the walls, and you might catch a view of the stars—or so we were told. We could have climbed Mount Hollywood together and searched the night sky, looking for stars wheeling to their stations. We might have found an ocean with no monster. The fear of what we might not see kept us away.

I have not forgotten the evenings we passed, peeling foil from burritos on her stoop, wringing the juice from limes, cruising the flea market for matching pairs of red sandals. I remember waiting in line to buy groceries at midnight and staring at oceans of bumpers on the 101. For a little while we were alone together, outside the world of family or childhood, and we saw each other differently.

Perhaps the city was a better counselor for us than our mother's friend had been long ago. And maybe this new almost closeness was simply the product of time, of waking one morning and no longer being sixteen. If I spent years clawing toward sunlight from the bottom of a dry well, that summer I looked over the edge for the first time and saw my sister.

I saw my sister and I saw her pain. She rolled off her pillow, lit her bong, and filled the studio with smoke. Afterward, it seemed, time and distance telescoped. The green bolls her boyfriend gave her smelled almost like sap or sage. When she burned them to ash, the miles between that apartment and the house on Mountain View Drive could no longer be measured. The years between her and the story of wildflowers dissolved. Time turned to water, through which she could almost wade.

We stood on the curb in our matching sandals and blinked in the sunlight, and then she went to work at a restaurant in Beverly Hills, and I signed for a sublet in unit 525 of a hulking building on South Berendo.

My temporary home was four miles west of the concrete bed of the Los Angeles River, three miles west of downtown, and fifteen miles east of the ocean. Below my fifth-story window stood a dying tree and a greenish streetlight. A classmate had heard of a rough middle school on Berendo, but I never saw any threatening middle schoolers. My building had a security guard named Phil—the poor man condemned to that florescent lobby with its cruddy fountain and bowl of fake lilies—who talked to you for a half hour unless you had

your arms full of groceries. In the evenings the hallways filled
with the smells of bulgogi and frying tortillas.

The other bedrooms in unit 525 contained a raver couple, who went out Saturdays half-naked in flower crowns,
and a mother-daughter pair from Florida, who ate my ice
cream and quite possibly ran a fluff-and-fold business out of
our laundry room. A Japanese dancer lived on the sofa. She
tended bar nearby and slept most days. Her breathing and the
rasp of her grinding teeth filled the afternoons.

My building had three treadmills and a couple of weight
machines in the basement, and I got a parking space in a
high-rise garage a half block over—pure LA gold. The quiet
woman with whom I signed a sublease collected the rent
and disappeared. Eviction notices appeared under our door
from time to time, and once, a less friendly security guard
stopped beside my treadmill and informed me that the residents of unit 525 were banned from the facilities and must
vacate the building immediately. But that security guard was
almost never around, and Phil didn't seem to mind squatters.
When Kaela came over, we always had the gym to ourselves.
Sometimes her boyfriend, who worked at a medical marijuana shop, came along and wheezed away at the chest press.
Kaela ran at a frantic pace on the treadmill because her agent
told her jostling would bounce the fat off her face and accen-
tuate her cheekbones.

With or without jostling, Kaela had the figure of a beanpole, as Pop describes our family, and blondish hair, and the
smile of someone used to working the counter of a chocolate
shop in a tourist town, all of which got her a hostess job at

a restaurant owned by a housewife from a reality TV show. The restaurant's decor was white on white: ornate pillars, eruptions of lilies wider than Kaela's open arms. Chiffon curtains blew from the windows, and giant chandeliers hung over every table, aglitter with candles, fire and earthquake hazard at once. White pillows choked the booths, overstuffed and inscribed in silver. Kaela earned twelve dollars an hour guiding guests to their tables.

When I stopped by, Kaela fed me mints and bread. En route to the restaurant, I counted eleven private swimming pools in one block. Patrons requested that the staff serve their dogs using the restaurant's plates and bowls. Half the time the dogs ate more expensive meals than the kids. On the restaurant's social media page, among shots of chewing celebrities, a customer posted a picture of a plush white chair with a scuff on the armrest, captioned "Actually gross." A shot of an unacceptable cushion: "I would *die* if they tried to give me this gross seat."

"Did someone chew on the menu before sending it over?"

"Silverware from IKEA!"

"Am I at the county fair or Beverly Hills!?"

Often, the customers came in bruised and mottled. The restaurant sat beneath a plastic surgery clinic.

ONCE KAELA'S MODELING agent realized she couldn't stay upright in heels, he took her to the grocery store, and she walked the aisles, wobbling at the handle of a shopping cart. She appeared on various retail websites, each time with a differently shaped nose, her skin alternately pale or tanned, once with diamonds in her eyes and a pelt of CGI glitter. She was paid sometimes with money, most often with clothes. The more sober dresses were passed along to me.

I went with her, wearing one of these, to the premiere of a promotional video featuring a pop-rock band and commissioned by an electronics manufacturer whose mission it was to remind the world that "at the end of the day, driving around with your car stereo on is just fun." The video featured bikini-clad women in convertibles who navigated Los Angeles on a sunny afternoon suspiciously devoid of traffic, blowing trash, sick pigeons, and cardboard GOD BLESS signs. A woman who, beneath the eye shadow, might be Kaela, head-banged in the backseat of a sports car. Every fifteen seconds the camera made a sly pan around cleavage and naval rings for a flash of the dashboard entertainment system.

The other women from the sports car clip joined us on the way to the premiere. As we waited for our subway car, one of them asked, suddenly astonished, "Are we taking the subway?"

A photo exists of our group on an escalator, dropping into the city's guts, headed for Hollywood. My dress is gray and knee length and I grip the handrail. The video stars stand with heads thrown back and hands in hair. Their dresses are jewel-toned polyester, at once tight and slinky. They arch backs, pop spiked heels. I look as though I might cry.

A FEW TIMES that summer I chased the 101 to Woodman Avenue, crossed the concrete bed of the Los Angeles River, turned right on Moorpark, left on Tyrone, merged onto

Beverly Glen Boulevard, and then began winding, suddenly surrounded by trees, to Mulholland Drive, which climbed to a jungle of irrigated palms, until finally I arrived at an iron gate through which I was buzzed.

Here stretched a driveway that felt—though surely it wasn't really—as long as a city block, stuck on both sides with roses, and at the top a mansion so large and strange it has been rejected by my memory. I do remember sports cars black and slick as Rottweilers, a tennis court, a trampoline, a swimming pool with a waterslide, a security guard who leaned against the door and regarded me without expression.

This was the childhood home of a college classmate, the son of a minor celebrity, a lanky kid who described his taste in music as "anything that sounds good to my ears." He came to class late if he came at all and drowsed with his feet on the table.

I went over to the mansion a few times that summer when Kaela was busy. A life-sized statue of a butler stood in the foyer. The television hung immense and chattering. Certainly the ceiling wasn't really made of glass? Sometime during the previous semester this classmate cornered me and commended my work in "activism/charity," by which he must have meant my hanging out with people from greater Los Angeles. Among my friends were kids who cross-stitched pillows with EAT THE RICH and made a piñata of a fat cat in a business suit, which we clubbed to pieces on the sunbathers' lawn. College had taught me how to hold forth on the crimes of consumer culture and mass media. I fell asleep with my face in books about feminist backlash and the history

of punk rock and woke with highlighter on my cheek. I had
bad blood with the campus conservatives. I had bad blood
with the campus liberals. I worshipped Emma Goldman and
Howard Zinn. By junior year flossing my teeth felt like a fun
break from all this important thinking, all this debating with
other twenty-year-olds, all this holding forth.

The son of the celebrity explained that although his family
had "financially adopted a few dozen children from various
developing nations," he could hardly find time to finish his
homework, let alone fling himself into the urban scrum. I
guess he was nice enough. He liked to loll around the campus
radio station where I had a job and display the features of his
smartphone before anyone had smartphones.

When he invited me to Mother's Day brunch in Beverly
Hills, I thought briefly of Pop alone in Swall, and Anthony, by
then in a desert lock-in school for delinquents. Pop suggested
I collect jokes to send my brother. "They cheer him up," he
told me on the phone. Counselors at Horizon Academy used
terms like *run risk*. The school sat swathed in the Nevada
desert so that escape meant dying of thirst. Six weeks after
Anthony got to the school, Pop called to tell me my brother
ran anyway. "He ran without shoes and there were spines and
Russian thistles and everything."

Pop sent Anthony to Horizon Academy when Bishop became
unsafe for him in too many ways. The day he ran, Anthony
stepped stocking footed from a van on the outskirts of Beatty,
Nevada, the nearest town to Horizon Academy. Boys were
taken beyond the academy's walls for visits to the dentist in
flip-flops and socks, so they wouldn't do what my brother did.

I started the work of pretending not to care what happened to my brother, who'd sat in front of me on Pop's motorcycle, my arms around his shoulders, the top of his helmet bumping my chin. My teammate in backyard broomstick hockey, the softly snoring kid beside me in the tent. In my dorm halls, the fact of my brother disappeared when I talked to classmates I didn't want to know very deeply. No lost boy. A mother in present tense.

I decided Mother's Day was a good day for distraction. My classmate gave me directions to Mulholland Drive.

The kid's father was on tour in Europe. His sister was pleasant—a volleyball player, like mine. She passed along a tip on where I could get my hair cut for half the price of my rent. At no point did his mother look me in the eye. She handed me her phone and smiled into the camera with her arms around her children.

Anthony would have run all the way back to the rez, if he could. The desert floor bristled with tumbleweed, broken glass, rusted beer cans, gopher holes that swallowed his heels. He was once a running back for Bishop Union High, and he ran fast enough that the counselors let him go. Maybe they stood with open mouths, staring through sunglasses at the boy disappearing—though *boy* was not the right word. There was no longer anything childish about him.

"They were amazed at how far he got," Pop told me. "The counselors couldn't keep up with him so they called the sheriffs, and the sheriffs tracked him down and they caught him." They wrestled him into a van and took him back to that distant desert.

I snapped the photo of the mother and her children. And then I ate French toast at the counter of a Beverly Hills hotel, the walls the color of coral, the chandeliers leafed in gold.

ON THE OTHER side of the universe sat the future music venue I was supposed to help run, the empty storefront we named The Half. I got there via Western Avenue, potholes as large as the lids of garbage cans gulping at my tires. I passed La Mexicana Meat Market and Prado's Party Supplies. Signs on bus benches advertised relief from dolor de diente: forty-five-dollar emergency tooth extractions and an X-ray exam gratis. Men stood in front of storefronts with hands in pockets. Moms held the hands of kids with backpacks. I parked next to QuiQue's discount, which featured a giant sign announcing el servicio of sending money, with the best exchange rate, a todo México, Centro y Sudamérica.

Tidy houses sat behind fences, windows barred. The streets crunched with waxy leaves fallen from short, pale-trunked trees. When shops closed in the evenings, owners rolled down steel doors. One punk had the keys to a long, narrow room, a slot in a strip mall with "½" in the address and no restroom. That winter we'd put up flyers around the neighborhood asking locals to suggest events. Some of the punks were from the area, and they gathered old friends. We held meetings every Sunday, and often twenty or thirty people came. A rectangle of available space in Los Angeles is something of a unicorn.

Mostly high school students came, with bangs in their eyes, in purple hoodies and pleather jackets and black jeans.

They painted the walls with butterflies and a UFO and a rose garden and a peace symbol and smiley faces and music notes and a black cat with a picket sign. They painted words.

Go placidly amid the noise and the haste, and
remember what peace there may be in silence.

No drinking. No fighting.

Only positive vibes belong here.

I love you, my friend.

The kids wanted to know how old I was, where I came from, and I told them: I can't get into bars. I'm from a town that devotes a holiday to mules. We couldn't fathom each other's geography as I traversed the personalities of Los Angeles, followed freeways that sliced a million versions of home.

THERE ARE MANY kinds of locals in the home I'd left behind: cowboys and old hippies, tattooed fishermen and teenagers with skateboards and the stern middle-aged lady who worked at the DMV and flunked me on my first driving test. Los Angeles, too, had a million versions of locals, and I began to know the city through the ways they collided.

I was driving a couple of high schoolers around one afternoon when we passed a skatepark. Cardboard signs lined the fence on which someone had written in black marker: LOCALS ONLY.

"White people started coming here," one boy in my car explained, "and the locals didn't like that."

After a man found gold in the American River in 1848, miners and merchants swept in to California from twenty-five countries, ninety thousand in a single winter, one hundred thousand the next. They came from Mexico and Peru and Chile and England and Germany and France and Ireland and Australia and China and the rest of the world. When the gold rush began, there was a record of six Chinese people in the state, and at its close there were twelve thousand. Some of those who came from far away stayed and they made California into a million different places and also into the singular place that it is.

In churches I saw a portrait of the blue-cloaked Virgin of Guadalupe hanging on a wall. She is the Lady, the Mother, the savior who appeared to an Indigenous man, Juan Diego, in Mexico City in 1531, while his people died from European disease. Richard Rodriguez tells the story: "A clap before curtains, like waking from sleep; / Then a human face, / A mother's smile; / Her complexion as red as cinnamon bark; / Cheeks as brown as pérsimmon." The Lady spoke in Nahuatl, "like rain, like water flowing, like drips in a cavern," and the Catholic Church was never the same. The First People looked around at what the Spanish had done to their home and made something new.

"I defy anyone who tries to unblend me," writes Rodriguez on being mestizo, of Indigenous America and Spain, of Mexico and California. I drop the high schoolers at their houses and I drive to meet Kaela in Beverly Hills, in that white room where breeze throws the curtains. Californians began with the raw materials for mixing both ideas and flesh, but we have often since defined home not in terms of blending but of boundaries.

Why shouldn't we fight to claim what we believe to be ours? The Nuumu in Payahuunadu didn't own land, but they asked for blessings before going after pinyon nuts in trees usually harvested by neighbors. The place I loved was at least three times swallowed, and Owens Valley was a fleck in the mural of our state. Spain took from Indigenous America, and Mexico took from Spain, and the United States took from Mexico—or did we forget? Our lives rest on the sediment of construction, predation, and decay. The Spanish missions, once symbols of ordained authority and home to an empire's dreams, exist now as museums, as a unit in the California fourth grade curriculum.

To understand the home I fled, I had to learn about the place that had swallowed it. Between the San Gabriel Mountains and the San Rafael Hills stood a mission older than the city of Los Angeles. Padre Junípero Serra named it the Mission of the Archangel Gabriel of the Earthquakes, and diaries tell us the ground did shake in the first days the Spaniards saw this part of California. The suburbs of Los Angeles were built on ranchos originally granted to Spanish-blooded Californios by the Mexican government, back when the San Gabriel River was sometimes a dry bed and other times ran over its banks, the mountains pale with chaparral, the floodplains virulent with California brome, purple needlegrass, chamise, manzanita, silk tassel. Then came the railroads, and then the aqueduct, and in July 1953 *Life* magazine published a photo essay about the filling of an LA subdivision. "Four Hundred New Angels Every Day," read the headline beside a photo of moving vans and identical houses stretching out of sight.

Fast-forward sixty years. In Los Angeles I learned that a community gets the name "park poor" if it has fewer than three acres of park per one thousand residents, and that the LA city center has 1.6 park acres per thousand people—eight times less than the national average. My celebrity classmate lived on at least 1.6 acres of teased-up jungle. In the city, I didn't find omnipotence, a homogenous power, as I thought I would. Instead I watched a back-and-forth between predator and prey within Los Angeles itself. I watched the unfolding of decisions, made decades ago, about which locals would possess this place and define its future.

FOR ALL THE shows I'd gone to, for all the suburban punks who were my friends, Kaela knew more than I did about this world Mulholland made. She spent more time on the sidewalks, in the libraries, on the campus of the city college. She had a friend who lived in a high-rise apartment downtown, who looked from his window every evening to see the sidewalks fill with tents.

In learning to live in Los Angeles, Kaela invented what she called Street Face. Many nights she finished her job in Beverly Hills, changed out of her little black dress, and put on baggy sweats and a baseball cap for the hour bus ride home. When she stepped off after midnight, she put on Street Face. She did not smile. She made her eyes lightless, disinterested, a barrier to communication. She did her special walk, head forward, a sort of mannish prowl, and in this way she conveyed to the city the opposite of an invitation.

A producer of major action films came to Kaela's restaurant often. Bald on top, yellow teeth, stubbly white beard. He told her: "I love your look. I want to use you for my next film. Let's have dinner and talk."

She was nineteen. She ordered orange juice. Afterward he said he'd take her home, but he didn't drive in the right direction.

The director said: "We need to stop by my house first, because I want to show you these splash reels." As soon as they got in the door, he leaned her onto the couch and climbed on top of her.

She said, "What are you doing? I'm nineteen years old!"

The director told her: "Bitch, I've been sleeping with nineteen-year-old girls for the past fifty years."

In the city, learning to guard one's self, to put up borders, became crucial. There was the night when an improv comedy show ran late, and Kaela and I found the subway tunnel blocked by a metal gate. We walked four miles while groups of men idled by the sidewalk and tried to get us into their cars.

And yet as we grew cautious, we became porous. We watched parts of ourselves and the city combine. I sat in a folding chair in a backyard while a band played in the garage. Someone had picked a mound of limes to go with the Tecate and chicharrón; everyone tried to play king's cup, but no one could remember the rules. I drove with my friends for hours through traffic to get to the beach, passing twenty thousand houses, one hundred freeway exits, a dozen In-N-Out fast-food franchises before parking at the shore, the sky dim with fog. The boys dug holes to hide their beer cans. We watched the ocean leap toward our feet with the tide.

In what sense do we make our homes, and in what sense do our homes make us? Mulholland sunk his shovel in the banks of the Los Angeles River with what might have been love, or perhaps greed. Or, like lots of us, he approached his home with both. With soil and water and steel he made a world that the teenaged punks of Los Angeles must navigate today. Back at The Half, the kids in my car took the signs in their skatepark—LOCALS ONLY—to mean that the future of their neighborhood was still up for definition and that its residents intended to have a say.

WALLACE STEGNER SAID, "I may not know who I am, but I know where I am from."

The kids I met that summer loved a complicated home the way I once had, and they knew more than I did: they knew what they wanted home to be. They spent afternoons hanging their art on the walls of The Half. They chased flickers of a certain kind of future.

From Los Angeles, Kaela began to learn about choosing the future, and maybe I did, too. In that living room she shoved the film producer off her. She told him, "We're going outside, and I'm not paying for a cab—you're taking me home *now*." When she got out of the car, she slammed the Bugatti door so hard, the paint chipped.

For Kaela, Los Angeles was not only Street Face. Street Face she left in a drawer when she walked mornings past the metro station and the vape shop, past teenagers holding hands. André and Raúl kept her company in the garden, daring one another to eat jalapeños. They found Bill the cat whenever he ran away. In the months before a dream sent her out of Los Angeles, Kaela became less interested in bouncing the fat off her face and more interested in climbing to the Griffith Observatory. She broke up with the boyfriend who restocked her weed supply. She drove to a church on a cliff over the ocean, where a portrait of the Virgin of Guadalupe hung on one wall, and sat alone in the sanctuary. Time and distance stretched again and cleaved her from everything she missed, but looking back from sea level to an old home, she began to remember where she came from and where she might yet go.

When I moved to the city, friends gave me pepper spray and taught me how to bristle keys between my fingers. I did this when I remembered, when I parked at midnight and traveled five stories through the dim garage, even though I wasn't really afraid. Sometimes I violated all warnings, drove to the garage roof, and stood for a moment. I didn't look down at the alley or the dumpster filled with hunks of concrete. I looked to the skyline, where the moon hung over skyscrapers, holding some sort of vigil.

We came to what might have been a tenuous peace with the city, my sister and I. But the desert waited for us, beyond the palm-lined streets. Beyond the white curtains of Beverly Hills, beyond sea breeze and citrus, a boy ran in the sand. In stocking feet, through thistles, a boy ran not toward some bright tomorrow but away from the past.

10. A Child's History of California

TWO YEARS OUT OF college, I load everything I own into my car and drive nearly two thousand miles. I drive through carved red desert, a million acres of last year's corn, frosted plains of black soil where cows drift and a flat wind blows. The world is wrapped in blizzard when I pass a sign in the shape of my next home. MINNESOTA WELCOMES YOU blurs by through April sleet. In the driveway of my new apartment, my wheels spin in drifts until a neighbor lopes outside in a parka and pajama bottoms, carrying a shovel.

After college I tacked a US map on my wall and pressed blue pins into cities I'd never seen. Two in Iowa. One in West Virginia, Montana, Ohio, Pennsylvania, Minnesota. None in California. I left because it was hard to live sandwiched between freeways and pinched by high rent; because home was empty; because I had a romantic notion that my life was short on chlorophyll and it was time to get over desert, get to know the color green. Grad school would teach me all about the nuance of the comma. I would steep in the significance of the first person singular, though I wore the pocks of Mammoth High all over—I still can't tell you what a gerund is.

"Maybe I'll stay forever," I said to everyone before I left California, then extolled the low cost of living in Minneapolis, the prevalence of parks, the absence of venomous snakes, spiders, scorpions, wildfire, earthquake, avalanche.

By spring the weeping willows bud around the lake not far from my apartment, and then the Lazarus lawns spring up without sprinklers, and then flowers, and then leaves, as if the trees wave silk handkerchiefs. I'm riding to the grocery store when the sky cracks and a curtain drops and water courses off my bike helmet, into my eyes. Lilacs spill like curls over fences, and humidity cloys the wave back into my hair, red again, dye grown out, the skin on my knuckles no longer so dry it's broken.

I don't miss cities cupped in brown hills, I remind myself, nor my own harsher desert. Give me new culture, new habits, new colors and smells. Give me lumberjacks and blue oxen and gray wolves, if there are any wolves left in Minnesota. I live in a beater rental, the carpet an ashy pelt, the heater a hulking brown box in the middle of the living room, the floors so slanted my dumbbells roll away of their own accord. The place is punched full of windows, and a wet breeze buffets through the rooms.

The streets are tunnels of underwater green—an odd feeling, to look up and see branches after the sprawled cities of California, where not much gets between you and the sun. I buy a bicycle the color of the noon sky and name it Wheeler after a mountain I once knew. I learn to pump tires and fix popped tubes. I bike to the lake after dark and lie on beach pebbles, searching for stars, still coming up short. I ride thirty miles, I ride forty; the ground flattens and the country rushes by like a river. All the while the Mississippi flexes, a long brown muscle easing through downtown, rumbling over the St. Anthony lock and dam in low, yellow falls. This water is frightening and huge and not a place to swim, so unlike Owens River that I often forget and call it a lake.

I walk the circling streets of a Minneapolis neighborhood until I find a rare hill, capped with a water tower, eagles molded in the concrete at its crown and knights spaced around the sides, hands resting on the hilts of swords. The knights are stern, guarding the view. I am drawn to the hill daily, maniacally, starved for elevation. I climb dusk and noon and sunrise. Airplanes rumble over my head like homing dragons, their noses pointed groundward toward runways hidden in the trees. Here is an ocean of branches, buoys of water towers, the city shielded or suffocated, I am not sure.

In my Minneapolis apartment I hang a picture of my parents on their wedding day, Pop in green linen pants and a loose shirt, the two of them sitting on a granite boulder in front of an alpine lake, choppy after a storm. Rain fell during the ceremony and thunder rumbled behind Mammoth Mountain, shaking the church. The power went out, and Mom's brother played the piano in the dark. There was some difference in opinion over whether to get married in a church or outdoors. Mom wanted to please her parents. Potted pines were brought to the altar to appease Pop: a borrowed Sierra forest. The desert would have been harder to simulate.

The wind that ruffled the lake in that photograph must have pushed the clouds away. Her dress: simple satin. No makeup, no veil. Her hair is long and straight and dirty blonde. Toes peek from beneath her hem, one bare foot pressing Pop's boot.

Beside the hippie parents on my apartment wall, Pop's hot air balloon lofts above a meadow. I hang watercolors of mountain chickadees and coyotes by a Bishop painter and a series of snapshots: the redwood house, a close-up of an orange and speckled lily, the fine line of the Sierra, sky and mountains blue, the valley brown. Years later, I can see it: that apartment in Minnesota was a shrine to something I thought was gone.

One of the books I brought from home, *A Child's History of California*, is covered in rose-colored fabric, frayed after bouncing around attics since 1941. Chapter 1, "The Pleasant Land," begins: "This is the story of California. It is more thrilling than any make-believe story you have ever heard. It is more exciting than any moving picture you have ever seen." Inside the cover, a line drawing shows little upturned Vs for mountains and two blank expanses labeled "Desert."

My Minnesota classmates come from Georgia, Pittsburgh, New York. They are not bowled over by water and green. I try to explain. Rain in the desert calls for special activity: in childhood, this meant running madly in our underwear, whooping and leaping. Rain where it is badly needed smells like rain nowhere else and turns everyone into maniacs. In Los Angeles drivers become even more crazed, which is no small accomplishment. In Bishop, when monsoons swoop in during summer, people step outside and scream.

In my old world, I tell my new friends, green marks human intervention, sometimes tender and often brutal. For a while, I had found this normal. Then suddenly lack and absence became something I could not abide, and in this way California chased me away.

If I ever knew Minnesota beyond its clichés, we met in sudden downpour en route to the grocery store, or as I stood dumbstruck on the shores of Lake Superior, the water bluer than the Pacific, at least from that beach of tumbled red stones, the woods at my back, where, in the middle of the night in a tent, my friend asleep, I alone heard the wolves.

Yet I missed the midnight sound of sprinklers, which all over California ring the bell of summer. In school I wrote about drip lines, those black spidery tubes that spurted at the stalks of our carrots and tomatoes. When my classmates asked, "What's that?" I couldn't believe the question. Not much food grows in the West as we know it without drip lines or some similar mechanism transporting water, and I couldn't grasp a worldview that didn't hinge on an intimate knowledge of how not to trip over these black threads, how to splice them together and add an adjustable valve. Pop drags around a giant yellow toolbox devoted exclusively to drip irrigation, this smallest technological link in western infrastructure, which stands on a devotion to the movement and control of what is scarce. Our gardens model the aqueducts that feed Los Angeles and Phoenix and Las Vegas. They are metaphor for the flood of men and money and ideas that was the gold rush, that flowed into and out of California and left nothing the same. The drip line, perhaps, is a metaphor for my own departure from a dry place, my delivery, via a network of highways, from desert to a land where water still flowed.

Back home, technologies simulate what we lack in abundance. California is strange country, country of dearth—go there now, to almost any town or city, and find not enough water, of course, but also not enough jobs, not enough housing, not enough room in the jails and schools—yet California is known the world over as a place of excess in lifestyles, ideas, and dreams. See Disneyland. Silicon Valley. You know the story. In Prague once, after sharing his tenth tragic Czech legend, a tour guide looked at me, the only American in the group, and said: "We don't put too much stock in happy endings. For those, we have Hollywood." All I could do was nod.

But the story of California was not shaping up to be entirely happy, and I had fled for a place where people lived outside the reach of the drip line, outside that deep sense of lack. The need for water was filled before it was perceived; if dynamite were used here, it would be over something else. I could relax and breathe in the humidity; I had found a place where emptiness could not follow.

And so I tried to make Minnesota a home. I had brought with me an LA man, product of the inland, urban California desert, a lover of the Dodgers baseball team and carne asada and the strain of punk rock that evolved in some suburban garage. We settled in among the green, but as I shed my California skin, I left him for a Midwesterner. This new man was unfamiliar with black widow spiders, unfond of sleeping in a tent. He was immune, I believed, to the myths of the West, skeptical of the strange brown place that had sent me ricocheting, and I went with him into Lutheran basements, carrying banana bread for potlucks. He wore a tie almost always, and his dress shoes got muddy when he followed me off the trail. He didn't like it when I said "Jesus Christ" or "God damn." He loved landscapes with water, loved gazing at lakes, knew little of roaming around in the sagebrush. His family was kind and appeared complete, rooted in Minnesota, and with them I walked beneath branches and made small talk.

But I was an impostor, a misfit in this land and culture. I was greedy and irreverent, impulsive. In my Minnesota gym I got in trouble for breaking an unspoken dress code, wearing what I believed to be a modest sports bra and high-waisted tights. "You'll upset the older patrons," said the blushing trainer, a scrubbed boy from Wisconsin. I took to pacing my lone hill.

BACK HOME, ANTHONY has clawed through his locked-in high school in a different desert and lives again in a friend's trailer on the rez. The Bishop sheriff watches him slouch the streets. All his life, we have known only that my brother is brown. Years in the future, a DNA test will reveal that his genes are indigenous to the Southwest. This will not be a surprise—we all know which people have become his family.

Here, he sees his sense of loss mirrored. He is understood. There is trouble to be found on any street in Bishop if you look a little, and Anthony finds it on the rez. Reservation rumors bounce around. Even in Minnesota I hear stories from home of beatings and drugs, and I hear ripples of violence done in the past, of kids placed in boarding schools and denied models of parenting, of families without generational teaching, of lands and water removed that were means of moral and spiritual wealth. "When I got back, I couldn't even talk to any Indians," an Owens Valley Paiute recalled anonymously in an interview. Like many of the Nuumu, this person was taken, at age four, to a Presbyterian school in Fresno, returning nine years later to the Eastern Sierra. "My grandfather, I used to go visit him. I had to take an interpreter with me, so I could understand what he was saying. I lost my language altogether." People survive such a history, but they survive alongside violence—violence that is sometimes the only conceivable reaction to an inheritance of loss.

In Minnesota I dream that my brother is dead. He is dead and I am relieved, because there is nothing left to fear any longer. The worst has happened, has proven itself capable of settling onto our lives again. Dead, my brother is video-chatting with Kaela and me on my laptop at our kitchen table. The valley unspools out the window. He sits across from us with his shaved head and hard jaw. He wears a baggy white T-shirt and stares past us. Behind him is blackness. We are about to ask him where he's gone, what he knows, who he's found, when I open my eyes.

I wear through the soles of my tennis shoes, circling lakes while talking on the phone to my father.

He tells me about my brother, who is very much alive and smoldering. And he tells me about another kind of destruction—the drought. The snowpack on the Sierra Nevada is creeping toward a five-hundred-year low, the worst news for a state that anticipates well over half its water supply from snow fallen on these mountains. The snow is supposed to melt gradually during California's typical, dry summers, continually replenishing the reservoirs. Pop describes fields in the Central Valley lifting and blowing away, the stink of fish rotting on the bottoms of Bishop's empty ponds.

"It's bad," he says. "Bad. Maybe turning seawater drinkable. Desalination. We're going to have to start thinking along different systems." And I counter with the amount of energy required, the damage to the ocean as hot, brackish water is returned. What else? On the phone, Pop and I are quiet for a moment, and then we move on. We're used to our relationship with near crisis, just another part of home. To continue living, we have learned to think around disaster, for better or worse. Next autumn, as the drought ripens, Pop's well will run dry.

Seasons pass, and I do not go home. I do not want to see California dry up. I don't want to go back to an empty house or a town where my brother combusts. The dishes in my Minnesota kitchen find familiar spots on the shelves. My bike is stowed, and ice skates sit in a bag by the door. Minnesota delivers the coldest winter in thirty-five years. When the wind chill hits forty-eight below zero, the city launches warnings about frostbite. At the same time, Bishop's winter highs climb into the seventies—twenty, thirty degrees above average. In California these months are the warmest since we started keeping track in 1895, the drought—if you can call these years drought and not a new West, or perhaps an old West awoken—the worst in twelve hundred years.

IN THE FIRST months without Mom I was selected, out of pity, such a half presence I was in school, to go with a few classmates on a trip to Whitewater, Wisconsin, to attend some sort of conference. A thousand teenagers from all over the country sat corralled in a university auditorium large enough to hold three times the student body of Mammoth High, where we listened to lectures on I have no idea what. I wore a black T-shirt that read LOST IN WONDERLAND and made inappropriate confessions to the kids stuck in groups with me. I breathed damp air and thought I would choke.

In the middle of a lecture a man stepped onto the stage and interrupted the speaker. He asked that we follow him, in an orderly fashion, to the basement. We'd grown up crouching under desks with hands over the backs of our necks for earthquake drills so familiar they turned comforting. Our soft little hands would protect our spines from falling rubble, we were told, and of course this must have been true. But I had never seen a tornado. Was I supposed to guard my neck? Get under a bench? In the migration to the basement, I lost the other students from Mammoth High. Midwestern kids loped around me, kicking each other, laughing as we traveled underground. The tornado skipped our city, but before I knew this, I sat in a corner and waited to be lifted into the sky.

We get used to our home disasters. Or, if our homes are mostly disaster, we get used to home. At 2:30 a.m. in March 1872, in the Owens Valley town of Lone Pine, an earthquake—the third largest ever recorded in the contiguous United States—brought roofs down on beds and killed twenty-seven people, whose mass grave you may visit beneath a stone monument. The California state flag features a grizzly pacing beneath a red star. Online I saw a cartoonist's reimagining: a brown bear sits beneath the same star, atop a smoldering tree trunk, face buried in his paws.

In Philadelphia a friend who grew up roaming sagebrush beside me handed her driver's license to the cashier at a liquor store.

"California," he said. "California! You ever been in an earthquake?"

"Sure," she said, "lots of times."

"You Californians," he said. "You just *say* it, like it's no big deal. The ground moving! The ground moving under your feet!"

In San Diego I knew a woman who refused to walk on an overpass, because she lived in Oakland in 1989 when the Loma Prieta quake collapsed a double-decker section of the Nimitz Freeway and killed forty-two people. She remembered bodies crushed between layers of concrete. Like all Californians, she had been raised to anticipate the "Big One," the quake we're told will turn Southern California into a postapocalyptic horror film. We ask each other: What will it be this year? Wildfire, then mudslide? The promise of destruction becomes the wallpaper of our culture. It occupies our politicians, our artists, our bad dreams. In Spellbinder bookstore in Bishop, I have skimmed the shelf of books about my home state and found a common theme: *The Destruction of California, Ecology of Fear, Losing Paradise, A Crack in the Edge of the World*. The earth shakes, desiccates, burns.

Two thousand miles away in Minnesota, I remember the way my first wildfire glowed. I was twelve, out of school for the summer, and Pop had a turkey in the oven. We expected friends for dinner. They got word of flames rising forty feet beside the highway and asked to reschedule, and so we carried turkey sandwiches up the mountain and gave them to the firefighters, who were not yet fighting fire but waiting for fire to arrive, standing in the dust and brush and looking north toward the flames.

All day we cleared brush from around the blue spruce, raked pine needles, and dragged buckets of water all around the house. I remember the sun, round and red through smoke, my skin and clothes smeared by a rain of white ash. After dark, when the sheriff came around to tell everyone to evacuate, Kaela and Anthony cried in their bedrooms as they shoved clothes into garbage bags while Mom took the photos off the walls. We loaded the van with cats, a hamster, a cockatiel, my fire-bellied toad. We fled fire on the mountain. That time, Swall Meadows survived.

In Minnesota, the world is blanketed in snow silence. It's safe to say: I miss familiar disaster. I miss water's absence. I miss lack. In my Minneapolis kitchen I open a package of sage for cooking. I smell rain in the desert and I see the bristled valley rise.

All the while, California withers. The West is accustomed to drought. About eight hundred years ago, civilizations in what is now the Four Corners region of Utah, Colorado, Arizona, and New Mexico abandoned crops and dwellings and moved far away. They likely fled famines caused by droughts that did not abate, megadroughts lasting centuries. A more stable climate in the West beginning in the late 1800s encouraged cities to spring up in dry places, but this country is fickle. In the

West floods often follow droughts. Throw in windstorms and earthquakes, volcanoes and fire. Combine this baseline with a warming global climate, and you get greater extremes. It's easy to talk about all of this theoretically. In California people are bathing in buckets. Everyone is talking water, thinking water—because it's gone. From far away I remember a desert turned empty, and I watch loss spread over the land.

WHEN ANTHONY WAS little, long before he disengaged, went off somewhere, learned the trick of the dead eyes, I led him on hikes across Wheeler, and we came home with cheatgrass in our socks. We sat on a couch printed with maps, and I read him *What Was I Scared Of?* by Dr. Seuss. (*I was walking in the night and I saw nothing scary. For I have never been afraid of anything. Not very.*)

Anthony could recognize about half the letters on each page. He bobbed beside me on the couch and looked at the pictures while Pop clattered in the kitchen, tossing maps into bins for the next day's delivery. (*I ran and found a Brickle bush. I hid myself away. I got Brickles in my britches but I stayed there anyway.*)

I didn't know then what disasters still awaited my brother in his young life, and I didn't understand those of his past. I couldn't foresee the ways he would try to keep his world whole or how he would fail. We lingered on a page washed in green, where a fuzzy creature huddled in a bush by the edge of a cliff.

"I threw my old dad in the Brickle bush," Anthony said. "He got Brickles in his britches."

I asked him why he threw his birth dad in the Brickle bush.

"I had to," he said, "to save my family."

I SIT ON a wooden chair in a cafe in the quiet hours before close, as the lights of a dive bar glow past a wall of windows and the stars hang pale, the Minnesota night too cold for snow. I watch people come and go, the tattooed musicians, bearded beer dudes, quiet sketch-pad guys, yoga girls. I sit and I remember: the first time I set out to circumnavigate the lake near my apartment, I gave up and turned around. For all I knew, the blue ran for twenty miles. I could have rounded the lake in an hour, but in those first weeks I didn't know how to read water. The lake held islands cloaked in trees. I saw a muskrat swimming and not a single lizard. This was no moonscape, no saline bowl cupped by tufa towers. No dark spill, like the vast reservoir near Mammoth, storing water for Los Angeles. Nothing like the snowmelt that pools between peaks, a bathtub beneath lifted knees.

I think about this new world in negatives: the lakes of Minnesota exist in the ways they are not the lakes of the Eastern Sierra. The lakes of home, meanwhile, are like this—and then I remember fiddles and mandolins, a square-dance band in a warm hall, a hammer dulcimer thrumming. I'm on a shore where my parents pitch tents. I smell mud and chilly snow water and little frogs leap. I breathe thin air and I can see the pinked peak of Mount Morgan through the mesh tent door.

A student crinkles the pages of a textbook. The barista, whom I love, slightly, because she looks like Mom—something in the teeth and the smile—walks between tables, pausing to light candles. The flames swirl as the door opens, and the cold lunges for the gap. But I do not shiver. I am a child strapped to Pop's back as he swoops on a mountain bike. I am picking bouquets of rabbitbrush for the cat. Prancing on the top of the snow while Pop sinks through to his knees. Eating fruit salad in meadows after hot air balloon flights. Running the mountainside with Anthony, hauling him up the steeper rocks. Playing porcupines and foxes and digging dens in the brush, chasing stinkbugs, rolling in mud on the riverbank and tending injured moths, wandering pretend-lost in a real desert.

The ground shifts beneath me. And I know that eighth grade graduation, when I clutched a single stolen flower and walked that aisle in the gym, will never really end. You don't move out of Lupine Land. The things you left behind are no longer beautiful in the way they used to be, but you need them.

I ANSWER THE phone when my father calls, but I never call Anthony. I have no jokes to tell him.

What's come between us? Culture. College. Distance. Time. We are both, at the moment, pretending to be disinterested in our family. We are both, in our own ways, gone. And we can handle only so much loss.

I don't think about him until, unbidden, the child he was interrupts, and I remember: him persuading me to teach him all the bad words I learned in middle school. And I did, as we ran together up Wheeler Crest, against my better judgment. I did it, I told him, because he was a good brother. Remember riding up Sand Canyon, through brush that later burned, both of us crammed in front of Pop on his dirt bike, his arms wrapped around us to reach the handlebars. Remember how we lifted our feet as we flew through the stream.

11. Dust

"CAN YOU PLEASE COME through and try to speak to us?" a young man says. "Can you feel things, can you feel pain? Do you remember moments of your life?"

Lights flash.

The men stand in the dining room of a Greek Revival-style mansion on San Diego Avenue. They carry flashlights, and the beams strike the banisters of the staircase and the tripods of night-vision cameras, whose lenses paint the wooden floor and the chair against the wall a shifting green. On the chair sits a REM Pod, a black cylinder that measures changes in temperature and electromagnetic fields. The lights at the top of the cylinder flash frantically, and the men stand still.

"Talk louder," the young man says. He approaches the cylinder. Beneath his boots, floorboards creak. "At that red light. Talk louder. Just tell us hello. Can you just say hello?"

I am not in the Whaley House Museum with the ghost hunters but watching the clip from my little duplex four miles east. Five days a week, I walk to my job at the museum shop, down Sunset Boulevard and Juan Street, past turreted mansions painted seashell pink. I descend a steep hill and the

Whaley House looms, its whitewashed pillars and balcony and a palm beside the western wall. To the east, pepper trees Mrs. Whaley planted 150 years ago stand just taller than the roof.

San Diego's Old Town perches at the westernmost rim of the continent, close to the line between countries, the sea just out of view. The museum shop sits next door to the Whaley House and has yellow walls, candy-cane shingles, and a pale gray porch that I am required to sweep every hour whether or not dust has gathered, because a shopgirl sweeping a porch is supposed to look picturesque to the tourists who walk up and down San Diego Avenue in the evenings, stopping in one or another of the fragrant Mexican restaurants. Fresh out of college, I am supposed to sweep the porch and sell tickets to the museum, to answer questions for the tourists, and to dust the old-fashioned board games, the sugar skulls and Mayan chocolate bars and rhinestone rings in the shapes of spiders. I push the wastebasket beside the cash register forward with one foot if I notice visitors chewing gum, forbidden inside the Whaley House. I print their tickets and send them across the weedy lawn, past the pepper trees, onto the white porch. At the end of my shift I hide the contents of the till in the back room and slide a heavy window shut. The pink blossoms of a hibiscus tap the glass, and I cannot see the moon.

Four miles east of the Whaley House museum, men chase each other across the park next door to my duplex, drawing knives. On the weekend families picnic and toss footballs. Trash gathers around the sprays of agave that border my door, misted monthly with a white powder by masked gardeners.

Elizabeth worked at the Whaley House before I did and told me when a coworker quit. I moved to San Diego after college without a plan, and she'd been there already for a few years, because there was nothing for any of us to do but leave home after high school. A flea-chewed Mary Austin wrote of her visit to San Diego in 1888: "If you took a handful of the top soil, half of it hopped out and the rest of it ran through your fingers." She liked the city anyway, "the slow sea, the low foreshore, and the endless inner green sea of the chamise." By the time I arrived, the flea problem was superseded by a bedbug epidemic, and the chamise was replaced with burrito stands and bungalows packed among succulent gardens and resorts for Midwesterners fleeing snow. But the slow sea still heaved somewhere in the distance, and in a white-walled adobe office, Elizabeth introduced me to her boss, Edward.

His black hair stood slightly on end, forever startled. He asked if I believed in ghosts. In October heat a fan swirled the curtains, here in San Diego where climate control means opening a window—and I must have looked at him strangely. "I have to ask," Edward said. "I ask everybody. It's just that we have to weed out the people who get a little too . . . into it."

I was mainly into paying my rent. I imagined working with Elizabeth as a revival of our days at the old cafe, where we tossed bleachy rags back and forth across the dining room over the heads of tourists. But in the museum shop one person worked alone.

The shop, with its wooden floors, bright jewelry case, dark stairs leading to a bedroom full of boxes, sits empty for hours. Instead of sweeping the porch and straightening bottles of

Spanish perfumes and fanned displays of painted leather bookmarks, I huddle in the back room and read the history books we have for sale and listen to a disc of songs from the gold mines. (*But I'm a used-up man, a perfect used-up man, and if ever I get home again, I'll stay there if I can.*)

The shop nestles in the living room of a two-story redwood Mansard. Fifty years ago it belonged to a widow, unrelated to the Whaleys, a gatherer of debris from the streets and mistress of so many cats, who died in the kitchen of pneumonia and sometimes, I have been told, haunts the place. Out the shop windows across San Diego Avenue, a breeze flutters California bear flags, Mexican flags, palms. Street vendors hawk wooden turtles with bobbing heads and leather vests and cowboy boots and red-and-green serape ponchos, everything available for half the price twenty miles south across the border. Visitors wander into my shop after eating chiles rellenos and flan and buy ceramic skeletons and copies of *Whaley House: The History and Mystery.* A freshly sunburned woman from Missouri in flip-flops complains of blisters. A somber teen, crucifix around her neck, gazes at rings in the jewelry cabinet. A friendly middle-aged couple from Connecticut want to know my favorite beach—I tell them it's called Garbage, accessible by climbing a rope down a cliff.

Whaley House docents dress for the mid-nineteenth century: vests over cotton shirts for men, hoop skirts and sleeves to the wrists for women. They lean against the pillars on the porch or knit in rocking chairs by the open front door and take turns leading tours. There, right where you're standing, sir, the gallows loomed before this house was built. And there a six-foot-three French Canadian called Yankee Jim was hanged for stealing a boat. He came to San Diego from the mines. He kept his feet lodged in the wagon as long as possible, and when the rope around his neck finally pulled him off, he swung back and forth like a pendulum, the local paper reported, until he strangled to death. You can visit his grave in El Campo Santo after the tour, one of the state's oldest cemeteries, just a block away—low light, rustling olive trees, cactus clusters. Not a bad place to take a date! If you'll follow me through these doors—notice the doorknobs down below hip level, because people were smaller back then—this is the dining room. That green wallpaper, see the crosses gleam in the oil lamps—expensive stuff in 1857. Pay close attention in this room, folks, especially the ladies, because here the Whaleys' great-granddaughter Marion found a crescent of ant poison on the floor and ate it. Thought it was a cookie. She likes women, so you, ma'am, in the long skirt, you might feel a tug, little hands—that's Marion hoping to be lifted up. Now if you'll file through here, we'll head upstairs. You may feel a chill on this staircase; this is where the spirit of Yankee Jim lingers. That's not a draft, not in San Diego! In these bedrooms, the porcelain dolls, the furniture and mirrors, those bedspreads, are all original to the period. Things were made differently back then; imagine your box-store duvet lasting 150 years! Here's the parlor, sheet music waiting on the pump organ. And there's the love seat where Violet Whaley bled to death, in the corner—her husband ran off two weeks after the wedding and left her, damaged goods at twenty-two. Of course it's been reupholstered.

The tour ends. The visitors trot across the lawn to the shop, eager for a souvenir. Joan Didion suggests that we Californians are inclined to "traffic our own history . . . a new kind of cash that did not depend on crops." We stumble into a "fable of confusion," as she calls the myths Californians fashion for themselves. Some come to the Whaley House because they have an interest in the past—in the way land changed hands, was mined for new meaning, stripped, discarded—but mostly they come for the ghosts. In life, Mrs. Whaley was tan skinned and frowning, hair parted and pulled tight over her ears in a low bun. Mr. Whaley wore a mustache and a goatee. In a family portrait, a baby girl lolls in a tent of polka-dot fabric. A flat-eyed boy stares past the frame.

The visitors report back to me on the ghosts they have seen. In death, they tell me, Mrs. Whaley stands somnolent in the backyard where her garden once grew, and Mr. Whaley peers forever over the bannister, down the dark stairs. Their son, a ladies' man, sidles up with a vanilla cigar. Dolly, the fox terrier, skitters across hardwood floors. The Whaleys' daughter, Violet, shot herself in the chest with her father's revolver in the outhouse out back, and sometimes young women report an aura, a trailing sadness, outside Violet's room.

Sun glazes the shop floor. Elizabeth tries on the spider-shaped rings between tours, her waist pinched and a hoop swinging around her ankles. I count dimes while canción ranchera—trill of trumpets, the crescendo of a grita—drifts across the street from Café Coyote, where the hostess greets customers in a giant green sombrero. Children inspect replica hoop-and-stick games in blank confusion. Their parents buy

T-shirts that read GOT GHOSTS? and hand me their phone cameras, pointing at the screens. A fingerprint on glass, they tell me, is a woman running; a bolt of light through a window is the face of a man. As for those of us who sell tickets—we believe or we don't. Or maybe we're not sure. One coworker describes falling backward down the stairs leading to the porch. Something, she says, or someone, caught her before her head hit the ground and left finger-shaped bruises on her forearms. Elizabeth has never seen a ghost, isn't sure if she believes, but once in the parlor someone played with her hair when she was alone.

At night, it is my job to shutter the shop. That means latching the jewelry cabinet, counting the till, and climbing steps to close windows in the lightless bedroom, now used for storage. The windows are far from the door, and I stumble past grinning calavera tote bags and jars of mango salsa and candles painted with saints. Sometimes I make it across; other times I have to wait for Edward to come to lock the door for me and walk me to my car. I need to hear the sound of somebody's boots on the floor when I'm up there alone.

In the ghost hunters' video, in the green haze of night vision, a young man calls for Mr. Whaley. He offers whiskey and records a whispered "yes."

"Do you miss your family?" the man asks the dark dining room, the glittering REM Pod. "Are you with your family?"

The answer is static.

In white noise, the men find voices. Sometimes the voices speak names. Sometimes they beg. "Please leave," a woman seems to cry. The men come close to tears. They lean into the cameras and report pressure on their arms, on the backs of their necks. They writhe with chills. The cylinder crackles and falls quiet.

Years before I worked at the Whaley House, a week or two after Pop dropped me at my college dorm, Kaela called my cell phone. She was crying because she and her friends had been playing with a Ouija board. She was seventeen; this was her year of parties, of stealing lingerie from the tourist boutiques in Mammoth. When I heard her crying on the phone, I left my dorm room and went to sit on the floor in the hall, which was dark except for a glowing green exit sign.

"I said, 'Mom, what is it you used to call me?' and the board spelled out *s-h-o-o-t-i-n-g s-t-a-r*," Kaela said. "That's what Mom used to whisper in my ear before I went onstage to perform in a play. That was our private nickname."

She asked the board if there was a heaven.

Yes.

If there was a hell.

No.

If there was anything she should tell Kendra.

T-e a-m-o.

Te amo, the last thing she said to me the night before she died. As my sister spoke, I thought of her voice above the congregation at Mom's memorial that day in March, scrawny, just a child and singing, while I sat silently in the first pew and could not even cry.

Listen, listen, listen to my heart's song. I will not forget you. I will not forsake you. I went back to my homework and I tried to believe in the powers of a Ouija board. Because what we wanted then, what we want still, is just to talk to her, to feel some trace of her in the world.

We set her ashes to flow in a creek lined in aspen and pine. Pop shook the glass jar while I stood some distance downstream and studied the bark of a Jeffrey pine. Whatever lingers I will not find through the ghost hunter's lens. It rustles and runs and hangs, half-remote. My mother does not have a headstone, no plot beneath the Sierra. She is diffuse, hiding somewhere I have yet to find. Her voice does not wait for me in the quiet museum after close. I do not find her cold hands; I find no trace of her bright mornings and storms. In sickness, she bought bunches of silk flowers—forget-me-nots, delicate, her favorites—and gave the bouquets to her children, coworkers, friends. These people wept when they received the little vases and they held her hands. We keep the bouquets on our desks and shake the blossoms free of dust.

PART 4

MOONRISE

12. Rim of the World

I SIT IN A PLASTIC chair beneath a white canvas shade that does not cut the heat. I sit beside my father in a little town in the western foothills of the Sierra Nevada, on the green grounds of the Mountain Sage cafe and nursery, amid groves of horsetails and yellow coneflowers, and we sweat through our sunscreen. At the front of the tent beneath the half-filtered sun, a woman from Oakland with long salt-and-pepper hair says, "We have a problem!" She yells, "Water!" She yells, "Extreme drought! Extreme drought! Extreme drought!"

In the heat of this June, the Swall Meadows blaze is still years in the future, but the drought that desiccates the valley and prepares it to burn is well under way. I've driven up and down the state, visiting drought-smacked towns—places where folks take their showers in a bucket, where working in the yard provokes a cloud of dust that drifts a half mile, and neighbors admonish each other with signs: LAWN MOWERS ARE FOR LAWNS, NOT DRY GRASS!—but nobody's got a lawn anymore.

I drove across the Central Valley, heat glittering outside the windshield, past dust devils and black specks of distant cattle. I passed signs every hundred yards: NO WATER = NO JOBS.

I passed ranch houses, tumbleweeds caught against fences and heaped higher than my head, a lone tractor in a fallow field.

In the old mining towns of the Sierra Nevada foothills, the dry air smelled of lilacs. The windows of the old general stores were broken. I drove over buckling ground, beneath oaks so tall they seemed prehistoric. Time after time I rounded a curve and the highway swooped around another reservoir— Don Pedro, New Melones, McClure—each a crater in red earth, drained to a mud puddle.

In a grocery store on the central coast, a cashier said hopefully, "Looks like rain. That's exactly what we need. Fill up the lake. Give the ducks a place to live." But the rain never came. I walked onto the concrete wall of a reservoir to read the graffiti spray painted there: RED ROB. DAN THE MAN. ONLY HELL MY MAMA EVER RAISED. STAY ALIVE, DON'T DIVE. I saw dried, muddy footprints spaced far apart like a person running. Someone had painted in white R.I.P. TYLER. FLY HIGH. I LOVE YOU WITH ALL MY HEART, BROTHER! MY LIFE WILL NEVER . . . And here the words became illegible. I stood and looked at the place where somebody maybe fell to his death and I thought about how an empty reservoir is a relic, a memory of a time with water.

On a farm I met a shepherd who sold half his flock that drought winter when hay became too expensive to keep them alive. The sheep he sold were born on his farm and irreplaceable because of the grazing patterns each had inherited: ninety ewes tied by blood to the foothills. They had their own systems of knowledge, the shepherd said. In their sheep brains they carry a catalog passed down through generations. They know which plants are edible and which will make them sick. He could have kept the sheep, let them overgraze and push the drought-stripped land toward erosion. Instead he hoped for rain next season.

I left the shepherd and his shrinking flock, and I visited my mother's first California town, before she crossed the mountain and came to the East Side.

There in the bristled middle of the Sierra Nevada, the shelves of the general store were dusty and bereft of all but a few dry goods and souvenir T-shirts. The cashier—stout with white hair and a baseball cap, skin cancer removed along with half a nostril—bemoaned the struggles of the ski resort, the basis of the town's existence, after years of scarce snow. The school where Mom taught was long gone. A one-room museum stood in testament to the town's past as a nexus for folks fearless on skis. In a deserted campground a few miles out of town, in the last campsite before the woods began, I imagined bears rummaging in the darkness beyond my tent walls. I looked into the woods and followed a trail toward the Siskiyou Reservoir, wondering whether I retraced her steps.

In Groveland, sitting with Pop beneath the futile canvas shade, I'm beginning to understand what compelled me to make this drought tour. It isn't easy to stay bound by the private pieces of your own story when everyone around you is losing something. Rebecca Solnit writes that disaster forces us back into the fold. It reminds us that we never experience loss alone, that we share our lives and we share our homes. I come west to fallowed fields and cardboard signs in windows reading PRAY FOR RAIN. I come in time to watch systems unravel, to catch a hint of some wrong future in the water tanks casting shadows on dead lawns, in towns where the aquifer has dropped below the reach of all but the deepest industrial wells.

The Mountain Sage cafe and nursery sits on Highway 120 in Groveland, a town of six hundred in the western foothills, across the Sierra from Bishop. Groveland got its start during the gold rush and used to be called Garrote, which means to strangle a person with wire or cord. Now Groveland is a couple of cafes, a plant nursery, an ice cream shop, hotel, and thrift store along a highway that leads into Yosemite. A year before my visit, the Rim Fire, largest in the history of the Sierra Nevada, devoured more than four hundred square miles, including 10 percent of Yosemite. The Rim Fire started near Groveland, allegedly after embers from a bow-hunter's camp blew onto a drought-dry hill.

Fire isn't new to California. In the western Sierra Nevada foothills sits a dusty little town that burned down seven times between 1854 and 1866 until the local women got tired of waiting around for their husbands and raised funds to buy a firefighting hand pump. Accidental fires were started by candles and cigars, and then they were started by trains and, now, by downed power lines. Droughts aren't new in California, either, but the kind of drought that fueled the Rim Fire hasn't been seen here in over a thousand years. Scientists believe droughts and storms in the West will get more extreme as the climate shifts. In other words, it's hard to say how many times we'll have to rebuild.

Pop planned to meet me here for the weekend, for this conference about drought and fire. He rode his motorcycle through a pass, camping gear stuffed in his saddlebags, while I waited for him to arrive. Mountain Sage is half coffee shop, half gallery, flowers and seedlings sprawling outside, and here I sat beneath a fan while my iced tea sweated onto the table. Kids' drawings of the Rim Fire covered the walls. In one, animals ran from flames. In another, scribbled smoke swallowed the mountains.

Pop walked through the door in black leather pants, his head a white orb, then pulled off the helmet and began to change out of his riding pants in the middle of the cafe. The forest rangers and dreadlocked tourists from the Bay who lounged on couches, comatose in the heat, didn't care; who could be bothered to ask for the restroom key? This is what remains of the Wild West: a tall man pulling up his Wranglers inside a shrine to fire.

We camped close to town, and in the morning before the conference, we hiked a dirt road through the foothills. Here and there the soil resembled grayish cornstarch. "Dust pits," Pop said, called "death pits" by mountain bikers—a place of false stability, loose powder that can sink twelve inches below ground. From a high point we looked over hazy foothills, mostly brown. "Pure fuel," Pop said, looking at the brush that covered everything. Walking back to our campsite, past small houses shaded by oaks, Pop pointed out the ones that would just go in a wildfire, if—when, he said—fire comes to Groveland again. "That one. And that one." Anything, it seemed, with a tree nearby, offering relief from the heat.

And of course we talked about Swall, not yet burned. "Just one spark," Pop said, even though he'd installed a fire pump. "I'd sneak in the back way on the motorcycle to save it, if I could." But maybe we should still remove some of the family photos, just in case.

The speaker at the front of the tent wipes sweat from her forehead.

She yells that snowmelt from the western Sierra Nevada mainly feeds San Francisco and the Central Valley, while snowmelt from the east feeds Los Angeles. Without imported water, Los Angeles proper might be home to five hundred thousand instead of almost four million. When not enough snow falls on the mountains, we pump groundwater, depleting twenty-thousand-year-old stores.

As we remove water from rivers and streams, she says, those systems die like dehydrated bodies. Eighty percent of California's native fish species face extinction in the coming decades.

"Humans are sixty percent water," she bellows. "What river are you made of?"

The Central Valley was once a freshet flooded by three ancient lakes—four million acres rustling with willows, cottonwoods, sycamores, oaks, and crawling with grizzlies, tule elk, wild horses, ocelots, mountain lions, beavers, foxes, brown bears, wolves, coyotes, swans, wrens, salmon, antelope, pelicans, ducks, geese, and cranes. We diverted the rivers that had fed the lakes for a million years, plowed up the beds, and planted cotton.

California's farms now feed a quarter of the nation. This state is home to 12 percent of the US population. If you add up water to grow our food and make energy for our travel and shopping, each of us in California requires about two thousand gallons for one day of life. We built dams to accommodate growth, and in turn that growth never stopped. Ninety thousand people lived in California in 1850, 1.5 million at the turn of the nineteenth century, and over 33 million at the next.

"So who gets the shaft," asks a lawyer who takes the podium next, "when there isn't enough water to go around? That's what we have to figure out in California," he says, where water is "about as emotional and religious as can be."

Westerners have hauled glacial ice from Alaska, plotted to tow icebergs from the Antarctic, and eyed the Great Lakes. The Colorado River Aqueduct, completed in 1941, runs 242 miles from the Arizona border to the inland reaches of Los Angeles. The California Aqueduct of 1997 runs 444 miles, from the Sacramento Bay Delta to the farms of the Central Valley and on to Southern California.

"Not the law, but the land sets the limit," Mary Austin wrote in 1903 at home in Owens Valley, ten years before the water was taken away. Now, it seems, this is no longer true. Twenty million people in Southern California get over half their water from hundreds of miles away. Since 1850, Californians built more than twelve hundred dams—one or more for every river. Sometimes we make the rivers flow backward.

"SWEETWATER IS A lovely campground," Mary told me across the counter of the Groveland Yosemite Gateway Museum, the day before the conference, before Pop arrived.

"Just lovely. A little stream and meadows." She handed over a photocopied map, the ink blotted. Mary was tanned and gray haired, a volunteer at the museum. Groveland had been her home for decades. In the past tense she mentioned a husband who once followed her along trails, with whom she must have visited Sweetwater, and maybe that's why she remembered the place as especially beautiful.

Most weekends Mary stood behind the museum counter pointing visitors toward ivory hairpins and tiny christening gowns. In a small theater she screened films about the nearby Hetch Hetchy Reservoir, a part of Yosemite yielded to municipal interests in 1913, which runs for eight miles and stores water for San Francisco and its sprawl. Mary lived alone in a house she refused to abandon during the Rim Fire, when the order came to evacuate. Now she pulled out a tablet and showed me photos she took herself: smoke hanging over her little peaked roof, the museum's parking lot filled with fire trucks.

The Rim Fire earned its name because it approached a lookout called Rim of the World. Driving to Sweetwater, I stopped at the lookout to peer over miles of pines. Ranges rose like waves to the horizon, everything burned bald. This was the rim of something, if not the world I expected to find.

IN THE TIME since Mary last visited, Sweetwater Campground had gone to charcoal. Drought snuffed the stream. Pine trunks stood blackened. Near the entrance, a sign warned: TREES CAN FALL AT ANY TIME.

I pitched my tent on yellow grass and tossed my string cheese and tortillas into a metal bear box. The sun went down and the mosquitoes came out, and by flashlight I read a book by two scientists at UC Berkeley. The scientists study extremes, years of flood and then drought. They study wildfire and the way drought causes longer, harsher burns. Wildflowers erupt every spring in the Sierra Nevada—paintbrush, poppies, tiger lily— and with extra effervescence after fire. When I was a child, months after a wildfire burned a meadow near Mammoth, the five of us walked through lupine that rose over my head.

The Berkeley scientists also study butterfly migration, determined by the lengthening and shortening of days. Butterflies pollinate wildflowers, which bloom according to temperature. When temperatures rise before days lengthen, as in drought years, the butterflies and wildflowers appear at different times. They do not overlap; the flowers do not multiply, as in my memory; they do not hang as thickly from the walls of Lower Rock Creek Canyon. And then it seems the fires are just fires, and the earth blows like powdered bone.

Lying on my back, I could see the silhouette of a ponderosa pine through the tent's mesh roof. The pine seemed to lean. It appeared firmly rooted in daylight, though when I thumped its trunk with the heel of my hand a flake of burned bark drifted down. With stars between its branches, it overhung my patch of ground. But I did not move the tent, because all around me stood tall trees, partly burned.

I woke to the buzz of weed whackers in the grass around the vault toilets. Rangers ambled like ghosts, creating defensible space. In the hazy morning I ate a granola bar at a picnic table mottled with guano, not lingering to light the camp stove. It did not hurt me to leave Sweetwater behind.

I drove a narrow road that burst through burned woods and skirted cliffs without guardrail. Yosemite reeled past the windshield, and far below, a pocket of water appeared. Hetch Hetchy was once a valley, but now it is a reservoir kept in place by a concrete wall nearly thirty stories high. In this valley, long before work on the reservoir began in 1914, the Central Sierra Miwok gathered black acorns and buried their dead.

San Francisco officials proposed to dam Hetch Hetchy after an estimated three thousand people died in an earthquake and subsequent fire in 1906.

"Dam Hetch Hetchy!" John Muir wrote. "As well dam for water-tanks the people's cathedrals and churches, for no holier temple has ever been consecrated by the heart of man." The cliffs that rose around the valley, Muir wrote, seemed to "glow with life." The water running over the mountain was "the most graceful fall" he had ever seen. Muir and his newly formed Sierra Club promised to defend Hetch Hetchy Valley "if it shall take until doomsday."

Now the reservoir supplies water for 2.6 million people.

Ellen Meloy once tried to tour Hoover Dam. She waited an hour for a shuttle bus, and when it arrived, she didn't get on. She drove away.

At the Groveland museum, Mary assured me that Hetch Hetchy was still beautiful. But I did not believe her. I traveled, after all, to see what California could become. Hetch Hetchy was lovely in photographs, maybe, or to tourists, but not to those who knew what the water concealed.

In a small roadside lot I covered my cooler with towels to hide it from bears and I walked at the side of Hetch Hetchy.

Western whiptail lizards ran from my shoes, and Harlequin lupine, purple and blue, blotted the shade beside the path. Mary had warned of rattlesnakes in the shadows: Don't sit on a boulder and dangle your feet. Don't reach over your head to climb for a better view.

I entered a tunnel and moved toward a bright orb. Water dripped from the roof and pooled. Some deep-dwelling bird called shrilly in the dark. Then, sun in my eyes, the falls flowing like a pitcher poured from clouds as I stood blinking.

LATER, BACK IN the museum and reading about dams that have made places into something else, I found pages of photographs taken of Hetch Hetchy before 1926 when the reservoir filled. "Remember Hetch Hetchy," the heading read.

When Joan Didion wrote her book about California, she tried to find the "point" of the place, to "locate some message in its history." But I did not want to see the pictures of Hetch Hetchy Valley before. A part of me did not want to receive this message made from loss. I did not want to remember or to know. Remember wildflowers and sleep full of dreams and her voice, somewhat harder to call back now. I had made my temporary return to California, but in many moments I wanted to leave. I was afraid that the meadows, the cottonwoods, the abrupt granite rise of Hetch Hetchy might look too much like home, might force me to see again a world that could be so swiftly changed or destroyed.

CALIFORNIA MIGHT HAVE gotten its name from a sixteenth-century Spanish novel about a mythic island, a paradise ruled by Queen Calafia, a sort of Lupine Land. The name comes from the Arabic word *khalifa*, as in "steward," as in "Behold thy Lord said to the angels: 'I will create a khalifa on Earth.'" And so he created people. The prophet Muhammad said, "The world is beautiful and verdant, and verily God, be He exalted, has made you His stewards in it, and He sees how you acquit yourselves."

In San Francisquito Canyon, fifty miles northwest of downtown Los Angeles, William Mulholland engineered a dam—one of many to hold the city's water, including water from Owens Valley. The St. Francis Dam, Mulholland believed, would protect the city from shortages during drought. On the windy morning of March 12, 1928, Mulholland responded to a call from a troubled dam keeper, took a look at the brown water seeping from a crack toward the bottom of the western abutment, and dismissed the leak as benign.

The St. Francis Dam broke three minutes before midnight. Twelve billion gallons moved down the canyon at eighteen miles per hour, a black mass 120 feet high, chewing boulders and trees. An estimated six hundred died, most of them farmers, dam workers, and their families. A survivor said the breaking dam sounded "like a cyclone." His house "disintegrated," taking with it his wife and three daughters. Stripped naked, riding the roof of a floating building, he jumped to a hill that rose higher than the flood.

Does the law or the land set the limit? After the St. Francis Dam broke, people living nearby put up signs that read KILL MULHOLLAND. But I don't know whether Mulholland the individual is entirely at fault, or whether it was the ambitions of his culture that led to the construction of such a dam, a project once applauded—remember, the greatest good for the greatest number—its risks and weaknesses not yet understood.

We've lost count of the bodies buried in mud when our reservoirs don't hold. If the 710-foot concrete wall that is Glen Canyon Dam breaks, as it almost did in the summer of 1983 after storms overfilled Lake Powell, a 580-foot wall of water will lumber through the Grand Canyon at twenty-five miles per hour. Three hundred miles downstream, the flood will destroy Hoover Dam and eight other reservoirs, sources of water and power for thirty million people in Las Vegas, Phoenix, Tucson, and Los Angeles.

Who will be the scapegoat then? When the floods and fires begin to overpower infrastructure and disaster-response resources, when the world turns strange, when we look around for a figure to lambast on yard signs, who, besides ourselves, will we find?

In the West, water's absence is our problem now. It won't be our problem forever. Some of the worst floods in history came nipping after the worst droughts. In the winter of 1861–62, rain fell in California for forty-three days, putting Sacramento, the state capital, under ten to twenty feet of water. Such floods are typical every one or two centuries. And yet today, Sacramento has the worst flood protection of any city in the country.

California's Central Valley consists of the once vast floodplains of the Sacramento and San Joaquin Rivers. Scientists call the region a giant bathtub. The land is rich for farming because for millennia that bathtub drained and then filled when storms made the rivers overrun their banks.

As the global climate warms, the scientists predict, the storms that occasionally tumble off the Pacific and slam California are likely to amplify. As warmer winters bring more rain and less snow to the Sierra, the percolation of water into reservoirs becomes abrupt—no longer the gradual, summer-long melt on which we depend, which our reservoirs are built to withstand. Thousands of miles of levees protect farms and cities in the Bay-Delta and Central Valley from floodwater. Some of these levees were built during the gold rush by miners and Chinese laborers using shovels, picks, and wheelbarrows and haven't been much improved since. This is part of the reason the US Geological Survey considers a major flood a "disaster waiting to happen."

If the storms that once drowned Sacramento return tomorrow, they will bury the Central Valley under ten to thirty feet of water—never mind the accompanying mudslides and hurricane-force winds. The cost, the USGS estimates, will be three times what the state expects to spend recovering from the Big One, the massive Southern California earthquake that's been promised all my life. Such a flood will destroy a quarter of the homes in California. From the national hub of food production and technology, 1.5 million people will try to evacuate.

"God, don't let people be killed," Mulholland said the night the St. Francis Dam broke, woken from sleep, a widower then, his own wife dead from cancer for thirteen years. "Please, God, don't let people be killed." Bodies washed up on the beaches of Mexico.

• • •

THE LAST SPEAKER at the conference is a man my father knows. He used to be the caller for the square-dance band in which Pop plucked Irish folk songs on a stand-up bass and Mom played her flute. As the caller stands at the podium, I remember his voice in the lakeside dance hall, its windows glowing. My friend Daniel roamed with me outside, and we saw the shadowy movement of a bear. We spun between the adults as they followed the direction of the caller—shake right hands, right-hand star, the other way back, left-hand star. Gents drop out and ladies go, swing a little bit on the heel and toe. I remember Mom holding me up to the microphone, my terror at the task of announcing the name of the next song, and then the caller coming in just under the fiddle. Heel-toe, heel-toe, slide, slide, slide.

The caller has been a ranger in California state parks for twenty-seven years. He is a historian, and he is here to tell about the survivors, the plants and animals that make it through. He describes orange-and-yellow fire poppies, endemic to California, found in the first wet season after fire, and sequoias, whose cones need the heat of flame to release seeds. Jeffrey pines, which grow in a row above the redwood house, cultivate protective bark and shed lower branches as they age to prevent fire from climbing to their crowns.

Pop leans over to whisper: he suspects the row of sentry pines above our house in Swall are 250 years old. Beyond surviving fire, they tell us we are halfway safe from avalanche. The fact that the mountain has not slid with enough force to destroy them in more than two centuries is a comfort if not a guarantee. In those plastic chairs, in that heat, we listen to stories of destruction, but we cannot imagine the river of flame that will flow over Swall Meadows Road.

Then it's time for discussion. A man in a baseball cap and checkered shirt stands. He won't give his name. He lives in another foothill town not far from Groveland and wants to know, "What's it gonna take to eminent-domain Hetch Hetchy and keep that water in Tuolumne County"—in other words, away from San Francisco. A lawyer tells him the proximity of a community to a source does not guarantee rights to water, which is something the people of the Eastern Sierra already know.

People are concerned about megafarms in the Central Valley paying low prices for water. Someone points out that the cost of water for agriculture is subsidized by California taxpayers even though the food that's grown here feeds the nation. Nods and grumbles all around. A man describes a trip to Los Angeles for a doctor's appointment, telling us how stressed the traffic made him, how he couldn't see the sky for the air. He frets over efforts to make seawater drinkable and what it could mean for California's sprawl. "Imagine this state with unlimited water," he says. "Just because you can do something doesn't mean you should."

A landowner from nearby Mariposa—a town where butterflies once crawled inside the ears of Spanish explorers—fears meters on groundwater. "Property rights," he says. "People are very concerned." And a rep from the local water company tells him the state will eventually enact some kind of metering.

"Well," says the man from Mariposa, "private landowners will come out in droves and shut down that kind of legislation. It's my water comes through my pipes."

The forum ends with a line at the podium four people deep. At times everyone talks at once. Someone behind me cries, "Whiskey's for drinking, water's for fighting over!" and others pick up the chant. A woman leaps to her feet. "Water doesn't function in a growth-driven capitalist system!" she shouts. "It's a limited resource! It's, like, what are we thinking!"

WE RETREAT TO a park, where Pop kicks off his shoes, sprawls on patchy grass, and puts his hat over his face to block the sun. I look toward the playground—a jungle gym, a slide, a turret with a blue-and-yellow dome, paint peeling— and realize I've been here before.

"Sure," Pop says. "You used to play in this park. We stopped with Mom anytime we drove to San Francisco."

The park in my memory is different from the park now, in drought. I remember thick grass, the woods a dense home for fairies, and, though perhaps this is conjured by almost twenty years of distance, I remember a tree shading the blanket that Mom spread on the ground, its branches spilling white flowers.

Back at the nursery we wait for a local bluegrass band to take the stage, and in true California fashion, our forum of apocalypse becomes a festival. Kids with balloons scramble. Men and women who stood red faced at the podium recline on beach towels or hop up to dance. Everyone buys tacos and pineapple juice from a vendor and no one shouts about whiskey. I see Mary, who smiles under the brim of her floppy hat and asks if I have time in the morning for one last hike. She describes a favorite trail she used to walk with her husband, shaded by pines, and I wonder whether this, too, has burned.

Then she asks how I liked Hetch Hetchy. It was beautiful, I tell her, just as she promised.

Hetch Hetchy Reservoir was not dry. Hetch Hetchy lay full as a bath, full as its creators intended one hundred years in the past—this after driving through a parched state and seeing everywhere lack. Mulholland's reservoir in San Francisquito Canyon, before its walls broke, must have stood this still, this fathomless, this eternal. As the car curved and dropped toward the water, I noticed tears in my eyes, and for a moment I did not understand what was happening to me.

What happened was the arrival of a beauty deep and corroded, a thrust of granite, the stooped head of a god, and then water, a dark bowl full from melting snow. I could almost see the country as it once was—how much taller the kneeling granite and longer the shadows. Yet I could also see with the eyes of the engineers who created a pool of roughened glass, a gift for the future, fashioned from concrete for the love of their city.

Looking over the gathered water, I knew what had gone beneath. I could not help but imagine the drowned valley, the lost. What alit without warning as the surface rushed toward me was the beauty of the thing that took another's place.

Hetch Hetchy Valley was full in a way I had not expected. I saw destruction in the transformation. I wanted the dam gone, wanted the old country, wanted snow meandering to the sea. Some things I will always long for. The car conveyed me toward the water mostly by gravity, and I had to brake hard at every curve. The road pitched and turned, and I felt the blood in my veins sling side to side—suddenly I was very aware of this blood and its movement, the dark blood filling the reservoir, shining in its trap, and I remembered the dreams I used to have as a child when I flew from my bedroom window through parted curtains as the mountain swooped in moonlight. The valley shone beneath me, and I felt I could drift over that land forever.

I could not drift over the valley forever. But what if I flew back, looked for her and found traces, found the place changed but still beautiful?

This is what happened to me, for a moment. But the moment passed, and I could only move toward water. I imagined I could break the laws of physics as in those dreams and pass beneath the surface, between skeleton trees, over moss-covered boulders, among trout. Would I find only darkness? Does sun filter across things discarded, broken fishing poles, rusted hubcaps? Would I find promise, dropped treasure, light glancing from fish scales? If the water were not so dark, I might have peered over the edge to see pines reaching for the surface. Or perhaps those trees are buried too deeply to be visible any longer.

13. Walk Home

WHILE I'M WORKING AT the Whaley House, Anthony turns eighteen and gets sent to jail. The jail is forty minutes south of Bishop in the little town of Independence, named for the army camp established in 1862 when the soldiers came to eliminate the Paiutes from Payahuunadu. Anthony goes to jail because of some shenanigans with somebody else's car. I imagine a room, bright and windowless. Outside, beyond fences pricked with barbed wire, the mountains gleam. He can see them when a guard lets him into the yard. Maybe he sketches their outlines on the ground.

ONCE WHEN HOAVADUNUKI was sick, he gathered navitanidu roots, he remembered, "which I boiled and put on my sores. Soon I recovered." Again he cured himself "by drinking a tea made of a plant—kohigamavarugutu—which I got near Owens River." And once he was visited by a stick doctor, who twirled a fire drill "until the end was hot and he put it to my stomach until it burned me. . . . This man, this doctor, probably helped me some but it was my own power, Birch Mountain, which saved me."

Then the settlers came and the bodies of water and the mountains and the ground where the Nuumu harvested navi-tanidu took another meaning, and what had once been medicine became someone's property. To the ranchers, who saw the place for the first time, the land meant agriculture and mining. No doubt the ranchers followed a set of instructions taught to them long ago and never examined in this desert light. The ranchers saw beauty in Payahuunadu, but they were of a culture that often forgot what to do with beauty. They believed themselves ordained to make the land yield all they needed and more, the greatest good for the greatest number.

In March 1863, eight months after the army made camp in Independence, a post rider on the west side of the Sierra Nevada loaded saddlebags with mail and rode east. Days later a rancher saw a light in the dark valley, a fire beside George Creek, an oxen roasting, figures moving before the flames. The next morning the rancher watched as the Paiutes traveled south. Back at the army camp he told a captain what he saw: thirty-seven men walking single file, dressed for war.

The post rider was headed for Aurora, Nevada. Presumably his route passed through Owens Valley. The captain assumed that the war party intended to head off the rider and ransack the mail. He assembled twenty soldiers and a handful of ranchers to act as guides. Hours before the rider was expected to arrive, the posse tracked the Paiutes south to a ravine west of the heaped rock of the Alabama Hills, where a gunshot echoed and a bullet pierced a rancher's hat just above his skull.

One Paiute fled into the mountains, and sixteen fell. Their white assailants lost a horse and injured one of their own men.

"We chased them toward the lake," a soldier wrote. "Some of the Indians got within forty yards of it, a place of safety, so they thought."

The Paiutes stood against the western lakeshore. Dirt clogged their rifles, and they pounded the ramrods with stones as they tried to reload. As the posse drew closer, the Paiutes dove. They swam. Night fell, and a hard east wind blew, pushing the swimmers back toward shore.

Perhaps the men believed, as they ducked beneath the brine, that darkness could save them. For a moment the gunfire may have stilled as the valley shifted from purple to black. But then bright silver over the Inyo range—the moon.

Every historian I've encountered describes it rising full over the mountains. But when I look at the lunar calendar for that day in 1863, I see that the moon was new, the sky black and full of stars.

But let's remember as the historians do. Maybe the first to invent this detail responded to some impulse to illuminate a piece of the past that might otherwise remain shadowed. Not just a story but a motivation. The reason history shunted one way and not the other. A direction hinged on collective choice.

I imagine this place in full moon has looked the same for millennia, the crest of the Sierra and the pale tuff of the valley made to glow. If the Paiute men in the water looked back, they might have seen silhouettes along the lakeshore. Did the whites on the banks imagine the post rider alone and ambushed in the desert? Or did they forget him and follow rules taught to them as boys, rules meant to dictate how land should be lived on and water used, and who should reap the rewards? Did they say to themselves, To shoot these fleeing men in their backs is to secure the greatest good for the greatest number? Did they follow a code passed to them in boyhood and carried in a charred part of the heart until that moment?

The bullets flew, methodically, toward splashes of silver where the swimmers raised their faces to inhale. Sometimes those on the shore heard a cry. A shadow may have risen from the water. A rancher is said to have shouted, "Die, damn you," as he shook his fist and aimed for the man who would not—"Die, damn you, in the lake!"—and fired again. The east wind pushed the bodies to shore.

BY APRIL REINFORCEMENTS filled the land of flowing water. They carried a mountain howitzer—a slender, portable cannon that fired explosive shells almost a half mile—and fifty Minié ball muskets, which they gave to men in Aurora in case they should be called to the valley to fight. The *Visalia Delta* declared: "When the infantry and howitzers, now on the way from Los Angeles, arrive on the grounds, short work will be made of Mr. Indian."

At the same time a party moved north, led by Captain Moses A. McLaughlin.

McLaughlin is said to have ordered soldiers to shoot two horses that were making too much noise in a corral. On his way to Owens Valley, his party spent a night in a mining town on the Kern River. Here, the captain received word that a group representing several tribes camped nearby, including Paiutes rumored to have harassed white ranchers and rustled cattle. McLaughlin and his soldiers visited the camp before sunrise, accompanied by a local chief.

"I had the bucks collected together," McLaughlin wrote. "The boys and old men I sent back to their camps." He marched the remaining thirty-five—we understand, from his later writings, that these included boys of thirteen—a short distance away. The men and boys fought the soldiers with hidden knives and rocks and sticks. The soldiers ran them through with sabers.

In Owens Valley, under McLaughlin's command, soldiers guarded streams and sought out food stores, destroying three hundred bushels of nuts and seeds cached around Bishop Creek. The Paiutes abandoned "range after range, spring after spring, so closely followed by the troops that they were obliged to throw away even their water jars," McLaughlin reported. Some fled into the neighboring desert of Death Valley, "where they were forced to subsist upon cactus and carry water at least a day's march."

THE PAIUTES BURIED grandparents and children. Chief George, signer of the original peace treaty, came into Camp Independence, and now the soldiers found him thin, his face drawn. In days he returned with three hundred half-starved people. Others followed. A prospector shot and scalped two men and a little girl fifteen miles from the camp, though the party traveled with white flags.

By July 10, 1863, more than a thousand people had gathered. McLaughlin recommended "that they be removed to Nome Lackie, or some other Government reserve where they would be prevented from further outbreaks, or that a military commission be appointed to try and punish those found guilty, which would, I think, result in putting to death every male Indian over twelve years of age." He assembled the people on the parade grounds, gathered a ring of soldiers around them, and commanded the Paiutes to sit. He announced that their people would be taken out of the valley; that if they tried to run, they would be killed.

Maybe the chiefs understood they were headed to an alleged reservation 225 miles southwest, where the government promised to deliver food and farm equipment. They could not have known that this land was owned by Edward F. Beale, a prior superintendent of Indian Affairs and the father of California's reservation system, who bungled the state's earliest reservations while acquiring plenty of private land. Beale had already told the government he would "on no account rent to the hostile and vicious Indians whom you have lately removed" from Owens Valley.

"We took a bath in the morning and in the afternoon went to the soldiers," Sam Newland recalled. "In the morning they put our women and children in wagons and had us walk behind surrounded by soldiers. . . . We thought surely that they would kill our women and then us, for we had no weapons. That night we were very much afraid and some of our people escaped."

Wagons held as many pregnant women, elders, and children as could fit, along with what would soon prove to be insufficient food and water. About seventy soldiers kept a brisk pace. July is the hottest month in this valley, when temperatures surpass one hundred degrees. The group approached the southern tail of the Sierra Nevada between the prickly, reaching arms of Joshua trees, named by Mormon settlers for the prophet who led them west. They crossed the mountains at Walker Pass, ascending two thousand feet.

According to Captain McLaughlin, "The sufferings upon the route were intense."

"I have the great and good news to tell you," a correspondent wrote to a San Francisco newspaper on July 31, 1863, "that yesterday morning the Indians . . . were removed from our beautiful valley."

"Many of the young girls were assaulted and afterwards murdered," a Paiute woman recalled.

"Some went on bravely," another woman said. "Some were too feeble and weak and fell. I saw them lay down to rest or sit down to rest for want of water or food. I saw the white men with long knives stick the knife into their sides." That woman escaped with her mother. "We crawled close together in the brush, taking care that the two soldiers who were looking for us would not find us. I saw them coming near, just fifty feet away. I felt chills run through me, death was to claim us. . . . The soldiers turned away, took another route, and we knew we were safe."

After a march that lasted eleven days, the soldiers left the Nuumu in the desert, where they remained for two months. "They gave us a big pile of flour, rice, and ham and then wheat from a large granary," Sam Newland said. "But all this was soon used up." For a while, the people gathered pine nuts to survive. Then they turned around and walked home.

FIFTY YEARS AFTER the Paiutes made that march through the desert, the water left. As he imagined his farm's final season, a white rancher wrote to the Owens Valley paper: "Today the trees that bore that crop are again white with blossoms, but the petals of these blossoms will fall on parched ground." The ranchers who lost their homes to Los Angeles might have been the grandchildren of those who beckoned the US Army to ensure that a certain valley would be known not as Payahuunadu but as Owens, the name of a man from Ohio. "The boughs will never more bend under their load of fruit," wrote the departing rancher. "The water is gone. It flows southward to the Great City. Be it so. The sin is not ours."

Forget the past, Rebecca Solnit writes, and you will not understand the present. But how does a person walk forward with history humped on the back? "The art is not one of forgetting but letting go," Solnit writes. "And when everything else is gone, you can be rich in loss."

Wovoka, a Nevada Paiute, had a vision. Amid a solar eclipse on the first day of 1889, Wovoka saw his home returned to what it once was. He said, "When the earth shakes do not be afraid," and he made the Ghost Dance: movement in a circle, a rite to restore the land and bring the dead back to life. After five days and four nights, the dancers bathed in a river. The ritual spread across the plains. In some accounts, Wovoka rose into the air above the chiefs who visited him and hovered, his face peaceful.

If you can point to trouble, you can also walk backward until you find its source. I don't know whether people in Payahuunadu practiced the Ghost Dance. I believe some lives spin this circle without relief.

Before he went to jail, when he could not bear to come home, Anthony lived on the banks of the river where we floated in inner tubes as children. Pop met him with a brown nylon tent and a few twenty-dollar bills. "The bugs are bad, but the nights are warm," Pop told him. "You can sleep here, under the willows."

Anthony built his tent on dirt and reeds. He slept in the tent with his pit bull, Bear. Other people lived beside the river, too, and his belongings disappeared. Often he had no food. Sometimes he asked Pop for help and sometimes he didn't.

So many people have found so many meanings for this place, have leached it and gotten sustenance as well as poison. The settlers tore the grasses. The city guzzled the lake. There is arsenic in this dust. And now we, angry children of the present, find ways to lash at it, too. Perhaps my brother tried to devour a place that became impossible to tolerate for all it did and didn't contain. Just as I might have drunk down the waters of Hetch Hetchy or years before run out of my bedroom and ground my teeth on granite, perhaps he tried to consume a place that remained beautiful as it became terrible. He tried to swallow the past.

"He has nothing. He's homeless," Pop told me, and he laughed the way he used to laugh when we caught him crying behind his glasses during cheesy family movies. "He's chosen to be homeless in the valley."

14. Dawn of Tomorrow

WHILE I SELL TICKETS to a version of the past, I begin reading books of history. Not *Whaley House: The History and Mystery* but the collected letters of soldiers and diaries of settlers and ethnographers and interpreters for the Indigenous and encroaching populations of the West. I begin reading books about people and water and features of the land that changed and disappeared. This is the beginning of wanting to understand the senseless, and who belongs, and what it means to live in the eddy of history.

I want to see the grave of the man who made the future. I want a word with Mulholland. And so I leave San Diego to surf the Ventura Freeway and exit beside railroad tracks and Golden Road Brewing, passing Dinah's Chicken, El Sauz Mexican Cafe, and a billboard asking DOES GOD EXIST?

I drive through the world's largest wrought-iron gates and park at the side of Cathedral Drive on softening asphalt in late July, in Glendale, four miles north of Kaela's old LA apartment and six miles north of mine. Forest Lawn Memorial Park lies before me, three hundred acres perfectly mowed. I stand at the steps of the mortuary, Tudor style with a swooping brown-shingled roof. A quarter-million people have been buried at Forest Lawn in the century past, many of them Hollywood stars, famous artists, musicians. Beyond the mortuary I see no grave markers on the rising swaths of turf, no dark monuments to endings, because the man who designed Forest Lawn found rows of headstones too grim for the LA climate. This place is an experiment in the virility of grass, a green blanket tossed over the earth, a picnic spot for giants.

Around me Los Angeles swarms. To look from the parking lot of Forest Lawn to smog-dulled hills in the distance is to look at the body of a caterpillar quivering with ants. The very air vibrates with machine life. Cathedral Drive hums in the heat, and with uneasy gratitude I enter the mortuary lobby, where the air-conditioning gusts flower scented and the walls lull in pale stone. A few silent men sit on benches. Beyond the lobby through open doors, I find the flower shop and wonder whether I should purchase a lily. I don't know how to approach this grave, but humility and devotion don't seem like quite the right gestures. Perhaps an azalea, flower of abundance, or a pink carnation to acknowledge a debt. Lavender, stubborn weed of drought-stricken yards—lavender, for distrust. Or a daisy, for innocence?

A woman with lined lips and bangs curled and shellacked above her forehead works the counter. Her name tag reads ILIANA. She is maybe my age, maybe a daughter of Los Angeles, a young woman at work for the common dead, for the wealthy and the famous and the very long in the ground. I ask her how I might learn the location of a grave. When I spell Mulholland's name, her face registers no recognition.

I wait among the chilled mummies of orchids, dangling rosaries, kits for polishing bronze, while Iliana looks up the grave in a back room. A grandmotherly lady stands behind me holding a bouquet of white roses, and I wonder if I ought to be ashamed, if I have no righteous purpose here. When I think about what we leave and what we carry forward, I think of Mulholland, and some nights I wake as a sleepwalking child, dragging the past behind me like a blanket. *There it is. Take it.* Mulholland's message for the future. But the offerings he's left are not simple to accept.

"Repeat the spelling of the name?"

Iliana can't find a record of the grave. I fumble—so many *l*'s—and glance to the grandmother. Sorry.

"He's a historical figure," I tell Iliana. "No relation of mine."

"If he's famous, his location might be private," she says by rote. "We might not be able to tell you where he is."

Strange to think of Mulholland being anywhere, so still for so long—strange to think of a life landing like a stone tossed into the Pacific, a splash, a system of waves turned ripples, large and then small and then gone.

But not entirely. Iliana returns with a photocopied map. Her fingernails, as red as roses, click. She's highlighted a square on the paper in the center of Forest Lawn. Mulholland's grave is public, is not remembered by his city in a way that attracts either ruin or worship.

Back into heat, over grass roasting in a dry July. For all the cemetery's posing as a park, no sidewalks line Cathedral Drive. You can walk over graves, markers flush with the lawn and running right up to the curb, or you can walk in the road with cars. These hills once lay "sere and brown," an early Forest Lawn brochure informs us, until a San Francisco businessman took over the land. "The cemeteries of today are wrong because they depict an end, not a beginning," he wrote in his Builder's Creed. The dead of Forest Lawn embrace their beginning out of sight. Here we herald death a dawn, then hide it, and extol instead a lawn on life support, sprinklers perhaps more numerous than the deceased.

Here lies a section of the cemetery dubbed Triumph and Faith, abreast of Ascension, Humanity, Harmony, and, beyond that, Immortality, Righteousness, Inspiration Slope, Dawn of Tomorrow. Turn west to Victory, south to Summerland. The Mystery of Life garden is all green grass and white marble. Carved figures wrapped in robes embrace and lament. They grasp and scold and raise arms to the sky, crammed together on an island of stone.

Tourists file into the garden. They chatter and laugh; I briefly despise them and then I remember that I, too, am a tourist here. "This place is full of scenery!" a teenager says to his friend as he photographs the statues.

Forest Lawn is a chain establishment, this green sweep one of eleven in Southern California. "I believe in a happy eternal life," wrote the builder. And what did he build but what he called a cemetery "as unlike other cemeteries as sunshine is unlike darkness, as eternal life is unlike death." So often I don't know whether Los Angeles is hideous or beautiful. A family passes by speaking Spanish. The world is rolling *rrr*'s and birdsong, and for a moment I am unsure, as I am often unsure in California, whether I am in chaos or at peace.

"Those men of long ago were brave and daring to try to cross the dreary deserts. The men of today were just as brave and daring to try the great task of changing a desert into a garden," *A Child's History of California* informed its audience in 1941. "You, in turn, will do your share to make and keep California, the golden happy land." The book is not clear about how, exactly, the children of 1941 might do this. It seems no one has quite answered the question, even today. Perhaps some other kind of daring altogether is called for.

Mulholland, you claimed many times to seek only the greatest good for the greatest number, and for a mind capable of such feats of memory and mathematics, this equation seems sadly simple. "The inevitable is the inevitable," Mulholland said after the aqueduct's completion. But did he believe he could rewrite every ancient law? He built the aqueduct thirty years after John Wesley Powell returned from the parched West, to report "broad districts of country which can never be settled" in the way easterners knew. In the end, Mulholland, you were bedfellow to the boosters who forced that country to resemble the world of elsewhere, boosters who in 1881 promised farmers they held "the power in their hands to make wilderness and waste places glad, and to make even a desert blossom as a garden with roses." You did not believe that the land sets the limits and undoes them, and so the unborn will learn your lessons for you. You did not see mystery, you did not learn from the people for whom the brown land was home, from the men who built a sweathouse out of waidava, the old telling stories to the young, the boys sleeping in a corner; did not learn from the women who gathered love grass and rye and fed their families through the winter.

When asked about his politics, Mulholland replied, "Conscience, progress, a chance for every man."

The seizure of water he engineered rode piggyback on the prophecy of the first California governor in 1851: "That a war of extermination will continue to be waged between the races until the Indian race becomes extinct must be expected. While we cannot anticipate this result but with painful regret, the inevitable destiny of the race is beyond the power or wisdom of man to avert." This is another way to say the greatest good for the greatest number. But the inevitable is the inevitable only when you fail to see the world differently. Mulholland, you continued the governor's war, further eroding people busy with the task of surviving history. This was never about us, Mulholland and me, my old grudge turning obsidian or softening like asphalt in the sun. Our cagey dance across a century enfolds much more than my own sorrow.

Not many visitors on the slope of Ascension today. The grass lives its green life only for me. A placard marks one native oak, somehow allowed to remain. From the bottom of a hill, I see white walls, a fortress, and now all that's left is to climb.

I ONCE IMAGINED Mulholland buried in a field so large it absorbed the sounds of the city, so that as I sat beside a weathered headstone in the heat of July, eighty Julys after his death, the world fell silent, a vacuum of time and consequence. In daydreams I walked across the field under a huge blue sky with a view of the ocean. I don't know where the vision came from. You can't see the Pacific from Glendale.

Mulholland might have dreamed a person like me, born into a future he seeded, but it seems he didn't think into the distance very far. You die, Mulholland, and all that you brought into being shudders around you. Here, he resides among the blossoms of the beds he fed. The dead of San Francisquito Canyon washed to sea. Our beaches buffer ripples still.

It isn't easy to see your way out of the culture that swaddles you. It is easy to put a KILL MULHOLLAND sign up in the yard and move on. But those of us living in the fire or flood path, which is to say all of us, do not have the liberty to do the easy thing. Whatever the hard and good thing may be, I am not exactly here to say but to show how I and others have failed and tried. Mulholland, I excoriate your decisions once and for all, but I do not exonerate myself, and I do not know the next thing to do.

At the top of the hill, at the end of Cathedral Drive, I stand in the grass and behold a fortress. Mulholland rests in the Great Mausoleum, in a wing called the Sanctuary of Meditation, slot 6395. He isn't far from Sunrise Slope, where tomorrow turns over and over.

Perhaps his slot is lavish and adorned, but I don't have the chance to find out. The Great Mausoleum is closed. "Come back tomorrow starting at nine," says a woman, just locking heavy doors. But I do not want to find Mulholland down dim halls. I turn and walk back the way I came. And I am sorry that I will not sit in the grass and look up at the sky as the city heaves around us.

15. Sunset

ONE VISIT HOME I opened a gray metal box in the attic of the house on Mountain View Drive. I was looking for a document to bring downstairs to Pop, working at the kitchen table. Here among the family birth certificates and immunization records, I found a book, bound in cloth, filled with pictures and Mom's handwriting, smooth cursive becoming sloppy as her pain grew. *For Robert Atlee, my husband*, she wrote inside the cover and drew a little heart.

I carried the book down the rickety attic steps and into the garage that still smelled of kittens.

She gave him the album on their last Valentine's Day together, in her last month of life. In the first photograph, two mountain bikes rest on wet soil, one supporting the other as it leans. Clouds build in the sky. Sometimes, even in the driest places, rain falls.

In the foreground rocks and sand scatter, the kind of soil I find difficult to navigate because of the way sand wrestles a back tire out of my control and sends my bike wobbling. Not long ago I tried to ride a mountain bike for the first time in ten years. It's Pop's favorite, after all—you get a view of the country but also speed, that flight feeling. These days I've finally gotten over the childhood memory of crashing into chilly Lower Rock Creek, down in the gorge, trying to keep up with Pop on an afternoon ride in the fall. Mom was with us, worried but hiding it, aware that his lessons—how to predict a thunderstorm, how to climb out of a pit in a meadow, how to ride through loose sand—were just as important as her own.

The album she made for my father moves forward in time. The two of them lose the suppleness of their thirties and, together, begin to gray. Still, she smiles in the pictures—here we are with parrots perched on our shoulders, their feathers, the lights that illuminate our faces, incredibly bright.

There were tips to help Pop raise three kids alone. *Kaela needs to learn to keyboard before the first semester of tenth grade.* A will for the trivial. *Keep my pots of marbles for a grandkid, okay?* Permission to continue living. *Remember, if there's a woman you like/love—you know what to do.*

She knew, for ten years, that the autoimmune disease at work on her liver could abruptly turn to cancer. What was it like to live with that knowledge, to raise us with cheerfulness in the face of her own fear?

"Mom's energy has dispersed," Kaela once told me. "She's a different kind of being now. She's gone on to do other work."

Mom, I don't know what work your energy is up to in the big, broad universe. But I do remember the work you did in our little cobbling of mountain towns. The early morning you learned you'd gotten a big grant funded for an after-school program—how you jumped up and down in your underwear and threw your arms around Pop. I know if you were to come back to us, as you sometimes do in my dreams, you would run to me like the mother and daughter I saw racing toward each other across my college lawn. I watched the two of them fly beneath elms with open arms until I had to look down at the grass.

When her coworkers came to our house to say goodbye, she walked them to the door, despite what those steps cost. She made me display my finished homework where she lay beneath blankets, a struggle then to stand, before I went to Bishop with Elizabeth to wander in the park. From the couch she watched Kaela's freshman theater troupe perform the musical they put on in the high school auditorium the day after she was gone. She listened to her daughter sing, *I'm alone in the universe*—and what else could she do? She maintained the ritual of family dinners even when the tumor in her abdomen crushed her stomach so she could eat only one or two peas. Sitting up straight, she asked us about school while the oxygen tubes trailed over the wood back of her chair. Almost cruel, those dinners, when all I wanted was to lurk alone in my room. But you, Mom, were not done with us.

She wrote, *I had ideas, funny poems, newsletters, and grant applications to write. I wanted to grow old with Robert. I wanted to see my children graduate and become happy, loving adults.*

At her memorial in the Methodist church in Bishop that March morning, Pastor Caddy began, "This is Jan's service. Now some of you, if you use your imagination, you're gonna see Jan running around, making sure everything goes the way she has planned because she has planned the music, she has planned the readings, and she has put this service together."

"These messages will come through my voice," Caddy said. "But these are Jan's words." And then singing, as he lifted a hand to the choir, to the congregation spilling into aisles full of folding chairs.

In her album she predicted more than she could have known. *Someday maybe Anthony can have a big dog. His sweetness with pets is worth cultivating.*

How could she have envisioned Bear, the brindle pit bull who has been with Anthony through nights under stars, beside the slow winter river? Anthony saved up so Bear could get surgery to correct a congenital eyelid problem and never travels because he worries so much about leaving the dog. These days Bear runs around the Bishop park on Monday nights when we gather to watch the community band play in the gazebo. The horns and woodwinds waft, the conductor stands sincere before a retired clarinetist, a teenaged drummer. Pop's white head glows above the others as he lifts his trombone. Bear drops dead when Anthony points a finger and says "Bang!" and rain falls lightly through the cottonwoods and we smell the desert and listen to drops in the trees and watch the sky blacken beyond the lights of Main.

Please hold on to what is good and be okay.

Perhaps her notes in that album were less requests than plans, manifestations of a future she set in motion, even when she knew it would unfold without her.

PART 5

SUMMIT

16. Three Points of Contact

THE EARLIEST LESSON I remember receiving from my mother and father is this: anytime you find yourself higher than you'd like to fall, maintain three points of contact with whatever is keeping you aloft.

Do this while shimmying up a shoot in Little Egypt or scaling the boulders that ring Mack Lake. While scampering, almost flying down the shattered granite of Half Moon Pass. While climbing onto the flat expanse of the Volcanic Tablelands or careening off the top of Tungsten Peak, racing the shadow of Tom stretched by sunset, the valley going gold to purple, then silver with the moon.

Don't get carried away. Remember that you can't really fly.

This is the idea: If a foot slips from a rock lip, your hands will save you. If a knob that seemed sturdy snaps under your fingers, you've got your feet planted, or you've got one foot planted and one hand with which to hang on. If you don't maintain three points of contact and one of your holds fails, as your holds are bound to fail from time to time, that is when you fall.

Maybe you fall a little distance, but you fall wrong and hit your head. Or maybe your ankle twists and it's the start of the season and still getting frigid at night and the sun goes down.

Maybe you fall a long way.

So don't fall. If the place that shaped us braced us for instability, we had guidance in navigating unsteadiness. You could say we learned how to fly in the Sierra Wave. The inevitable is not always the inevitable—the future is a thing we make, and you can try to show up prepared. You can take care.

My parents understood. You can't climb without the risk of falling. Beyond three points of contact, they did not try to guide us, though Pop repeated that lesson anytime we came to a point in a climb he called "hairy," presenting the possibility of the long kind of fall. We were not a family of technical climbers—we had faith in our limbs. Mom ascended the granite jut of Half Dome in Yosemite before I was born, levitating with ropes over glacial polish, but she taught us to scramble, using the friction of soles and fingers wedged in an ice-widened crevice until we rose by the strength of our hands, as if we were the very cirrus clouds that hovered over our heads.

Kaela and I have not forgotten the lesson, though we put it to use in different ways. And though we met the concept together, contact, to us, has not always meant the same thing.

On hikes Kaela pauses to commune with wildflowers and sense the energies of stones. These days she meditates and cooks for groups of women at silent retreats. She gives too-long hugs. "Quick hug," Anthony says when he greets her, patting her back gingerly. "Quick hug." She still does some modeling, but she spends most of her time in glasses and loose clothes. The kind of contact she looks for is intangible, auras invisible to me.

I have ricocheted home for a summer visit from Minnesota. These days I go into the mountains to press my insignificance against a mammoth weight. I watch the mountain loom in inanimate slumber and I let it sleep. There is nothing I am searching for, just aching muscle at the top of a rock pile. On most trails I race ahead until Kaela is a dot. I chant in my head to keep my legs moving, pukeorpassout, pukeorpassout, and I don't rest until I risk losing sight of her altogether. A thruhiker on the Pacific Crest Trail taught me this mantra when our paths overlapped for a few hours on a day hike Kaela and I were taking out of Independence. His trail moniker was Tasty; he lived off dehydrated food packets of the same name. Tasty's beard grew long and scraggly, and the sun roughed his skin to pine bark. He found himself, ecstatically, in the middle of a five-month 2,650-mile journey from the Mexican desert to the Canadian border. Four-fifths of the people who begin the Pacific Crest Trail quit before they finish. "Don't quit," Tasty said, "till you feel like you're gonna puke or pass out. You won't. Your system can handle more than you think. There's nothing wrong with being uncomfortable."

I am, on Pop's suggestion, conditioning my hips to a new pack in preparation for our upcoming ascent of Mount Tom and have filled the pack with towels. At the top of the last dusty switchback I look west over the interior of the Sierra, the peak-canyon-peak rhythm of pines and snow and stone that stretches to the Central Valley. I stop and wait for my sister.

MOM HAD SAID, *Be sure you get the kids up Mount Tom.*

They had talked about doing the climb as a family, Pop said. "You know, when you guys got big enough, and then there was always something going on. She always thought that would be cool, and we never . . . we never made it up."

On a Sunday we decide to climb.

Prickly poppies and lupine flare orange and purple, bits of silk among stone. Approaching Tom that August evening, Kaela and I dodge tiny petals of granite prickly phlox unfurling at our feet, while Pop crushes blossoms and does not notice. The light drops. In August tourists swarm the Eastern Sierra and buy maps with fervor, sending Pop north and south from Bridgeport to Pearsonville, restocking visitor centers and gas stations. All that day he drove, folding long legs behind the steering wheel, a name tag pinned to the blue button-up shirt he keeps bunched in a bin in the back of the van. Pop does not have time to climb Mount Tom, but this is my last weekend home from Minnesota—and so we approach in the dark and search for a place to camp beside Horton Lake. Our head-lamps illuminate the crumpled beams of mining structures and wooden cabins wrecked by avalanche. Tomorrow we climb.

Kaela and I have climbed other mountains with Pop, most of them less daunting than Tom, and we know he will always underestimate the scariness of a peak. He says he need never travel, that he could spend a lifetime and see only a fraction of the folds within these mountains. The spell of the summit overwrites the difficulty of the ascent. He misremembers a climb as easy in the hopes that he can persuade someone to join him, to share the view. This works out better for Kaela and me—wary when he is cavalier—than it does for out-of-town relatives. A four-hour hike turns out to be eleven. What Pop describes as barely steep becomes, to them, a promenade with death. "This is where your cousin"—or his brother-in-law or a friend from the city—"refused to go any farther," he observes on some sliding face of rock.

AFTER THE WATER left for Los Angeles, a rancher's wife wrote in to the *Inyo Independent*. They had decided to sell, decided they could find some other place that felt like home. "And then one morning I awoke early. The sun was coming up over Black Canyon and its first long beams had just touched the white cap of Mount Tom and dyed it that exquisite rose which we all know so well," the woman wrote. "I don't want you for a keepsake. I want you as you are, to care for and cherish. I don't want to let you go, I don't want to go away."

In history books about Bishop, Mount Tom—Winuba, as the Nuumu named it—fills almost every picture. "As I return to Bishop I find little that remains of the pleasant town I knew as a boy," wrote a California historian, Richard Coke Wood, who came of age during the water wars, who remembers his car searched in the hunt for the pipeline's dynamiters. "Only beautiful old Mount Tom to the west of Bishop remains as I remember it—never changing but still changing its appearance each season of the year and even each hour of the day."

The crucial choice Bishop businesses face regarding interior decor is the season and light in which to feature Tom. Enormous, in full color, it adorns the sides of garbage trucks. In the portrait in Astorga's Mexican restaurant, sunset strikes the peak magenta. Framed, the mountain oversees the chamber of commerce, the Mule Days office, Spellbinder bookstore, the optometrist, and Pop's dentist. Great Basin Bakery offers a Mount Tom turkey sandwich. The Mount Tom pizza at Upper Crust heaps with jalapeños. On a poster in the DMV, the peak makes a public service announcement about the dangers of teen drinking. My father hangs a Tom poster in the office scattered with his maps. The windows overlook a parking lot, a few poplars, and, beyond that, the mountain itself, ever-changing beside its likeness. The streets are named according to the perspective they provide: Longview, Grandview. "Most of my friends have gone," wrote the historian, but Mount Tom "is always there to greet me and to welcome me back as an old friend when I return home."

In darkness we make camp beside a lake we cannot see. I have looked out my window at this mountain all my life, but I have never slept at its base. Sun wakes us in our tents, and I unzip the nylon door and peer outside at the neighboring peaks of Basin and Four Gables. Pop cooks oatmeal on his little stove, while Kaela assumes sukhasana, legs crossed and eyes closed beside the water, and I cannot help but disrupt her calm to swat mosquitoes from her shoulders.

We fill water bottles from the lake. Sixteen switchbacks lead us through dust without a lone pine for shade. We abandon the trail at a dry basin and survey the south ridge, our route of ascent, and here we meet a gray-haired woman as she returns from the summit.

"I met one group on my way down," she tells us. "They gave up and turned around. Didn't trust the rock."

KAELA TELLS US how, hitchhiking across Paraguay, she filed her flight plans, then asked the universe for the clarity to know which cars to climb into and which to wave on. Pop and I couldn't speak to this beyond observing that she made it back alive.

Ask Kaela how to pray, Mom wrote to Pop in the album she left behind. *She can pray with you.*

Something softer has replaced Street Face. "Focus," Kaela says. "Intention. Never use the word *hate*. The universe will produce what you manifest."

Once, we'd caught our old house empty between renters, and we stayed for a few nights. Kaela was just back from South America, I had just finished college. Our bedrooms, upstairs and across from each other, were carpeted in the same pale blue. We unpacked suitcases into dressers that once held overalls and dinosaur T-shirts. Most of our things had been discarded or boxed in the attic, but traces remained. A picture of Mom, smiling in the yard, her arm around the shoulders of a snowman, hung on the refrigerator. Family photos along the stairs: Pop's balloon hovering in a blue sky; our family in front of yellow aspens; Mom in the eighties, tan and smiling and looking slightly silly with a perm.

In my bedroom a sheet of song lyrics was still tacked to the wall. The faces of Kaela's high school friends hovered over her closet. Above my desk, a ten-year-old rose drooped its dusty head. Strange for a vacation rental, but gutting the place was hard enough that it had to be done gradually, and meanwhile the house waited, as if we all might return.

Sometimes in those days I saw my brother on my visits home; sometimes I didn't. On the rez, he collected tattoos. "I've got thirteen," he said on a rare meeting at Keough's, standing waist deep in steaming water. "I always use clean needles." He'd marked his body with burn scars from the heads of cigarettes and coins heated with a lighter, spotting his hands and arms with wrinkled, shiny patches, his skin a map of his past. A chief in a feathered headdress covered his calf. The outline of California stretched from collar to jaw. Inked on his left shoulder were bear paws, matching the tattoos of his friends. On a forearm the word *family*. C-A-L-I ran across his right wrist, L-O-V-E across his left, and one shoulder said *Atleework*, in cursive. On his back, our mother's dates, her fifty-two years—*RIP, Jan.*

Perhaps because of the way loss collects in shadows, he stayed clear of Swall as of some plague.

This was life now, life as we could never have imagined, familiar and utterly changed. Dinnertime, our first night home, and a friend Kaela brought back from a New Year's camping trip in Death Valley stoked the fire too high and lay spread-eagle on the living room floor, where our family once convened weekly to negotiate chores. Kaela's friend was a Londoner so tepid it seemed the desert might swallow him up. I suspected Kaela had to carry his pack over the dunes.

He did not eat with us because he did not eat anything cooked. Kaela would not eat food from the microwave or from cans. At the dining room table, in front of windows overlooking the valley, she closed her eyes, cupped hands over her plate—rice, steamed vegetables, the things we were taught to eat by parents no longer there to eat with us—and silently blessed the food. We claimed our old seats at the wooden table, across from each other. Nine years earlier, Anthony squirmed at my left while, to my right, Mom undermined his campaign against tomatoes: no video games until you've eaten at least one. Pop planted elbows on the table and encouraged us to do the same. "Keeps your back straight!"

My sister and I missed the same things. We shared memory, thrumming like an organ.

"Why do you hold your hands over your food like that?" I asked her. And she said, "What's wrong with blessing my food?"

Why did I care how she ate her food? Why couldn't I keep the quills out of my questions?

In this house, once, mornings made the windows over our parents' old futon blaze as if full of fire, and I thought day came everywhere with so much color and light. But that night, the early dark of winter snuffed the sun behind Wheeler, and dusk assembled between the rafters, and I wanted to retreat to the silence of my room. This new version of Kaela touched too much. She took the hands of old women sitting alone in the Bishop park. If I am ever an old woman sitting in the

Bishop park, I wanted to tell her, I will not be waiting for a stranger to hold my hands. I will be thinking of mountains I have climbed and books I have read.

"She never felt lost—simply out of touch," Austin wrote of her own childhood. "For her 'belief' was always so thin a shell to the spiritual urge that it was shed with comparative ease." On that night I understood belief as shell, as the sand dollars we picked up on the shores of the Pacific on visits to Nana and Fafa, pale wafers easily crushed beneath a sandal. Belief was shell, belief was a sandcastle that must be constantly resurrected because it stood on nothing.

Sprawled on our living room floor, my sister's friend talked of cleansing his colon with juices. Having lost his glasses in the dunes, he squinted constantly. In Britain, his family amassed wealth. After a meltdown at the Fukushima nuclear power plant, he bought Kaela a plane ticket from Los Angeles to London, to escape for a few weeks the radiation shimmering west from Japan. I pointed out that the jet stream diffuses radioactive particles globally, but that night there was not room in Kaela's world for my kind of knowledge, or room in mine for hers.

What was broken, we set about fixing in different ways. Older sister of existential rage over late capitalism, of anarchist meetings in student unions; younger sister of organic coconut oil and stones collected from a globe's worth of trails. Gone was the party girl—here instead was a hard-core nouveau hippie. Which was harder for me to understand? The nature of a piece of obsidian, in my universe, was deduced by the study of its radioactive decay, not by talking to stone.

I took up the weapon of language against the world, while Kaela tucked quartz, amethyst, aragonite, beneath her pillow.

At the table with my sister, I knew only a steely satisfaction with the cerebral, a world devoid of mystery, the terms of life a sad certainty. Mystery of any kind, I was certain, was clutter, tertiary to the truth. Kaela hovered hands over her food with a peace that made me want to chase her around the house with a microwave and send the bits of broken shell that made up her castle—a figment she seemed to think a bulwark against any tide—sprawling. Because no bulwark held the tide of change and loss, and once again we sisters witnessed a violent amalgamation of our ways of being in the world. I tried to convey to Kaela the significance of hours spent wrangling words into an undergraduate thesis baggy with theory. She talked about what I imagined to be half-nude enclaves of wayward white Americans in South America, which she called conscious communities—prayer flags, lots of deep eye gazing—and I said acidly, But what does that *mean*? If I don't understand the word *conscious* in this context, does that mean I am *un*conscious? Is the goal of your subculture to alienate those outside its jargon? Is my level of consciousness yours to judge? Must we all be conscious of the same things?

When we were little, Kaela had thrown tantrums, grated on me with her noisiness, and I offered cruel comments. "Good morning, *boy*," I greeted her. This was the foulest insult either of us could imagine, and she'd collapsed into tears. *Yesterday Kendra offered to babysit Kaela for pay*, Mom wrote in a letter to Nana when Kaela was one, and I was nearly three. *So, for three cents Kendra took over the baby and I went about my chores with my fingers crossed and ready to pounce. But she did fine! She imitated what she has seen Robert and me do with Kaela—handing her toys, asking what the doggie says, and hugging her. When the job was done, she felt compelled to remark, "Well, Kaela, one day I will sell you."*

That night at the table our voices rose. A few hours together, and things fell apart.

The house was dark after dinner, Kaela and her friend talking by the fire. Dark, and quiet, so that putting plates away I could hear everything.

My sister talked of fifth-dimensional beings, of auras, of chakras and the power of crystals. "I met one in South America," she told her friend of the otherworldly souls. "He looked so normal. I'm grateful he allowed himself to be seen." At times, she said, these beings vibrate at a frequency so high we cannot see them; they pass as a gust of wind. They come to Earth to do good. Their genes reside in our bones.

"Extraterrestrial genetic material," she said, and I was quick to climb the stairs until I could no longer hear her voice, passing baby pictures—my eyes a blue-gray you might call cold, hers green-brown, open wide and beseeching.

FOLLOW ME. PUT your hand here, your foot there. Keep your belly to the rock. Maintain three points of contact.

Our parents' desire: *You must learn to climb.*

Place a foot wrong and your head hits a rock and cracks like a melon. On some family outing Anthony somersaulted over a bluff and reared up from the dust, red streaming down his skull as if from a showerhead. Scalp wounds bleed out of proportion to their severity. Mom wiped his face with a T-shirt, and he forgot by the time the cut scabbed over.

"All that long stretch between Salt Lake and Sacramento Pass, the realization of presence which the desert was ever after to have for her, grew upon her mind," Austin wrote in her autobiography. "Not the warm tingling presence of wooded hills and winding creeks, but something brooding and aloof, charged with a dire indifference, of which she was never for an instant afraid."

You must learn to climb carefully.

We might have broken bones, might have died, but there are worse ways, worse fears for adults to pass on to children than all that tuff and granite can do to a body. Fear, for so long, we glimpsed only in corners, like the shadows between rafters on the ceiling, a rustle in the brush at dusk—hunting time for mountain lions, when you knew you ought to be inside, and yet the five of us lay on our backs on Mountain View Drive to watch the moon rise.

MOM WANTED TO climb Mount Tom. She loved the way old stone cradled the towns into which she poured her life. She had wanted to climb the mountain since she and Pop moved into the redwood house and saw the ridgeline through the window above their bed, or perhaps even before, on her first drive through the valley, safe in her young years.

As tall as Bigfoot, his hat, loose shirt, and pants all the color of dust, my father swings hiking poles. Crickets chirp dully in the heat. My sister stoops and closes her hand around a frosty chip of quartz while I keep pace with Pop's long strides.

How sturdy the mountain appears from a distance. On the side of Tom, hours blur. We trust the rock in the way you might trust a dog that once forgot himself and bared his teeth. Granite chunks slide from beneath my boot and careen into the blue, an instability that surprises me after a lifetime spent gazing at the summit from nine thousand feet below. "No need for ropes," Pop says later when a friend asks what to expect from Tom. "But you need experience with boulder fields or you could break an ankle."

I add, "Or die," and he nods thoughtfully. "Or die."

Because you can always die in the Sierra. Usually you can tell if a rock will shift before you trust it too much. Always you must be ready to jaunt your weight onto a different arm or leg should a part of the mountain give way. Maintain three points of contact. Kaela and I no longer need the reminder. We climb with enough space between us that a dislodged and tumbling boulder won't squish the person behind.

Pukeorpassout. Pukeorpassout. The mountain sheers to cliff, and our path dwindles to a three-inch ledge. "That's enough for your foot to be fairly comfortable," Pop says. "Just hug the face of the mountain." We traverse spider-like. A nook for a break, no shade but a view of the taupe backside of Tom. We eat string cheese, drink from dented metal water bottles. "That chute looks promising," Pop says, and points to the endless rise.

MOVEMENT OVER PRECARIOUS ground clears space for something quiet to occur, for contact with the mind's undertow, even if in this quiet you are only running calculations that direct hands and feet, somewhere beneath the current of thought you can observe and corral.

Mary Austin read her first geology book in a crook of her favorite cherry tree. "I remember how, as I read, the familiar landscape of Rinaker's Hill, the Branch, the old rock quarry, unfolded to the dimensions of a geological map—the earth itself became transparent, molten, glowing."

That molten earth is solid, for now, but heaped unsteadily on this mountain. Aristotle suspected that some sort of Earth-like creation had existed forever. The Roman poet Lucretius, in 57 BC, also wasn't sure Earth had a birthday and likewise wondered whether it would someday disappear. Martin Luther, in the sixteenth century, taught that Earth was younger than six thousand years. In 1650 the archbishop of Ireland decided that this planet came to be on the evening of October 22, 4004 BC. In 1715 the astronomer Edmond Halley explained that Earth's age could be determined through the saltiness of its lakes. By the late nineteenth century geologists generally agreed that Earth was one hundred million years old. In 1926 we settled on 4.55 billion. Much remains unclear, including what happened between one hundred million and one billion years ago, a period missing from many regions' geologic record. We don't know for certain which is older: our planet or the moon.

What ambles through my mind as I climb: how little we understand, how little we can count on, how we fumble for some logic by which to conduct our lives. Pop might be called an Epicurean, described by the philosopher William James as "snatching what it can while the day lasts," happiest with the chance to chase the sublime. My mother might have been a transcendentalist, an Emersonian, believing that God is love, believing that human beings possess something we might call a soul, that whatever the soul is, it is moral, that it resonates with the greater universe. "For all things proceed out of the same spirit," said Emerson, "which is differently named love, justice, temperance." Neither of my parents knew these terms. Leave all this fretting over definitions to me. And what am I, in flight between?

What does any of it matter, if not to tell us how to climb, why we climb, what we climb away from, and what we hope will be waiting when we come back down?

In San Diego I sold tickets to the past, but I didn't believe in anything that lingered. Hand on stone, foot on stone. I can never ask my mother where she found comfort in the days after her students walked onto a frozen lake.

Mary Austin couldn't bring herself to pity the child who watched her father and sister buried in a hillside cemetery. She never had any disposition, she wrote, to feel sorry for Mary. "One doesn't, you know, for children to whom God arrives under walnut trees." She might as well be gripping the rock beside me, skirts ragged, chin sunburned. Look down from this mountain, she says. She has tethered me to something I can no longer escape or deny. Remember Austin as a child on the hill, beneath the walnut tree, all her world alive and conscious. "All these things come back with the shattered brilliance of light through stained glass. . . . How long this ineffable moment lasted I never knew. It broke like a bubble at the sudden singing of a bird, and the wind blew and the world was the same again—only never *quite* the same."

Remember the woman who stood naked on a boulder over water.

Was it an understanding of the self connected to a universe, a mountain, a town, a river, that Austin felt beneath that walnut tree? Pause to perch on a ledge, turn. Watch father and sister getting too far behind. How do I approach you, mountain that I love, that I speak to without expecting your reply? How do I stay beside you? How do I weather the turning of the world when the world turns, winces, destroys?

To cross the boulder field without breaking bones is to see a vista that pushes past perception. It is to reach for the future of the valley below, to see it as mystery, to see my life as a part of that mystery.

At last.

Father and sister catch up. Kaela hoists long legs over Tom's shattered staircase. And it hurts to think about everything this place might have been, without Mulholland, with a different idea of good, a different kind of meeting between newcomers and First People.

Sometimes it seems the past has poisoned the future. This is only partly true. It remains to be seen where we go from here. I'm afraid of fire, but I'll go back down, back into the thick of the dry brush and branches and everything ready to burn. I'll be there with water. Mulholland once said the inevitable is the inevitable. But Mulholland was wrong.

Perhaps to climb over shifting stones is to find some comfort in uncertainty, the absence of inevitability. We see the mark of water in the desert, its fossil carved in land. The unexpected forms the bones of this land. And in the void of that uncertainty the future and its meaning might be ours. Many have gone. But some have walked home and remain.

NO ONE KNOWS exactly how the Sierra Nevada came to be—when the range began to rise or the valley at its eastern base to fall, the mountains to crumble, to carve avalanche chutes above Swall and shed the boulder called House Rock. Each year the range grows taller. The soil on which we live deepens.

I will not forget you. I will not forsake you.

What did you know, Mom, of the infinite, of wild gods and change? She married my father in a thunderstorm, committing herself to as much of a future as she could snag from shifting continents, the fast-rolling Wave cloud, fast-spilling time. She disappeared before I could outgrow the childish wisdom that a parent can always answer, and sometimes it seems that she hides, withholding those answers, and I will spend my life searching. At other times her disappearance proves to me that no answers exist at all. If she took comfort from the mountain, was it the stony bulk, the intractable presence, silhouettes witnessed by sixty generations, or was it scree slipping down the face to become the valley, rocks falling and breaking, the eventual return of ocean to a desert or a swath of snow impenetrable, all that eternity impenetrable, that gave her peace?

THE SUMMIT OF Tom resembles the shattered surface of another planet, fragments of gray rock heaped and pointing to the sky. Snow huddles in shadows, lingering through summer. At our backs the Sierra unfolds. And before us Bishop lies impossibly small, as if I could lift it, its pastures and potholes, its mobile homes and creek-cut park, and hold it in my palm like a marble. Somewhere below roams my brother and his dog—he's out of jail, though not off probation, not ready for such a climb—and beyond lies the future, out of sight.

Pop and I reach the summit together. A moment later Kaela appears on the crest. Instantly she is crying. We sit together at the highest ring of rock. Red flecks the gray: ladybugs "from a big hatch in the Central Valley," Pops says, "blown up helplessly by the winds." Kaela folds her legs into her chest and hugs her knees.

In this broken gray-rock world, Kaela says, "How can you not feel this?"

And I know futures dissolve like continents, that flight plans aren't always enough, that Mom never had the chance to look down from this mountain. *In case I don't get to tell you. In case you don't get to ask . . .*

"We do," Pop says with a half smile, and he looks toward Swall, toward pines and specks of houses smattering Wheeler Crest below. He doesn't know what comes next. He has kept a promise.

So now, off I go to climb, she wrote to Pop all those years ago. Maintain contact, she might have said at that pinnacle: with rock, with something beyond rock, with each other.

17. Wings

DAYS AFTER CLIMBING TOM, Pop and I drove down-town, windows open, scooping up summer. He turned off Line Street into the residential blocks of West Bishop, passed the Methodist church and Bishop Union High, turned onto Keough Street, and slowed in front of a little single-story ranch house, white with blue trim, wrapped by trees, a FOR SALE sign sunk in the lawn.

"What do you think?" he asked me. "Hard to find some-thing downtown with enough room for an orchard and a garden. Walking distance to the bakery and the library and the park."

We closed on the house four months later, in January.

THE MORNING AFTER escrow closes I walk across the yard and into the rising sun, toward St. Timothy's Anglican Church with its red door, where a statue of a priest offers up his porcelain hands in the courtyard. Cows moo in the dis-tance. To the west the day pours into the mountains until they grow enormous, ballooning in color and water and light and so buoyant I fear they might rise and float away from me forever.

I sit by the fire at Pop's house that evening after he goes to bed. The house. My house. I imagine the yard, the orchard, chicken coop, vegetable garden, berry bushes, clothesline. Imagine writing on the porch with a view of the liquidambar.

The yards on my street are filled with folding chairs and chopped wood, bike frames, birdhouses hanging from the trees. At least one mailbox is cow shaped. A giant wicker penguin guards a front door. Sidewalks end in patches of yellow grass. You have to walk in the street, but that's okay, because time passes between each passing car.

We measure the yard. I hold a yellow legal pad while Pop paces the winter lawn. He's almost as useful as a yardstick— one of his strides is about three feet. I jot numbers, draw boxes. X's mark the orchard's future: peach, plum, pear.

The place sits four blocks from the First United Methodist and a half mile from the hospital where I was born, two miles from Pop's house on the outskirts of Bishop and two miles from Anthony's mobile home. Pop will collect the rent and answer the tenants' calls when wasps build nests in the eaves until I finish school and move in.

"It's a good little house," he says. "It just needs some TLC." We fix a clogged kitchen drain for the tenants. I think of my father before I was born, stapling a tarp over the roof of the fire-ravaged restaurant where he slept in the freezer and peed in a hole in the ground, and I feel spoiled.

"You can be my roommate!" I tell Elizabeth. She still lives in San Diego and dreams of the mountains. Kaela threatens to drive over from Santa Cruz and host meditation classes in my yard. The house on Keough Street tumbles into my life, its fidgety water heater, its many windows, the center from which I will head into desert and mountains and along the tendril of the river, and for this, although it is old and small and not remarkably well maintained, the house is glorious.

Of course, I will buy my utilities, like most of us in Owens Valley, from the Los Angeles Department of Water and Power.

My neighbors are teachers and bakers and well drillers and firefighters. Across a field and over a canal sits the Paiute reservation. Early in the 1930s, as the valley's economy tanked, Los Angeles and the federal government tried to move the Paiutes to another part of California. "I explained how hopeless the future seemed for their valley," wrote a field representative for Indian Affairs in 1933. "These Indians are bound to Owens Valley by every tie of sentiment which may bind a man to the soil; they are used to the dry atmosphere; they know every foot of the mountains on which their eyes open in the morning." The government offered better jobs, better farms, better schools, and a better climate in the lush, irrigated, booming Central Valley.

"They made it perfectly clear to me," wrote the representative, "that they would rather die in Owens Valley than live prosperously elsewhere."

"This valley is my family's homeland," said Harry Williams, the historian who showed me trenches dug by his ancestors to water the desert. "I will be buried here and blessed here."

Once, Hoavadunuki left Payahuunadu and went to Sacramento. There, he said, "I saw my mountain in a dream. It rose up in the east and looked for me." The mountain said:

"You must come back soon to your own country and your own people. Nothing will happen to us. We will always be just where we are." And so he came home.

He said, "Few Indians leave their own country who do not return."

And here live his descendants, a people who walked home, who carried their families back to the valley, where mornings overflow.

In the beginning, there was water. This is the start to many tellings of the Nuumu creation story. In one version, Coyote placed the people next to Owens River, and thus they became themselves; thus consciousness revolves around place instead of chronology; thus stories move over the country, not over the years. Good spirits live in the high mountains, and from here life force flows as tributaries to the beings on the valley floor, just as the snowmelt creeks feed the river. Stories and names carry the locations of springs in the desert. Built into the language is the key to living in this particular place.

They remained, but the landscape changed around them. If land is both language and life, what becomes of a people when the nahavita that once sustained them no longer grows? What becomes of a people who became themselves when placed beside Owens River, when Owens River is carried away in a tube?

They become many things. Gardeners, historians, scientists, builders, lawyers. Many contend with the city for an ancient right. On shaky ground, they remain.

Strangers from all over the world have learned how to love this landscape, and they feel at home nowhere else. Still, they can't imagine that feeling multiplied by sixty generations, what it means to live on ancestral soil and play a part in determining the future of that land.

The settlers cheered when the Paiutes were marched out of the Independence army camp for the desert. The earliest California governor prophesied their obliteration. Of the First Peoples of the California deserts, a military scout wrote in 1859: "The time is coming when their places shall know them no more."

He was wrong.

Mulholland's vision was limited to the people he could imagine, without much effort, inhabiting his city—his civilized nineteenth-century city, as his granddaughter put it. A certain kind of people, a certain kind of life, a love of a certain kind of progress. I don't think the world as Mulholland dreamed it would have been much of a place for me—caught between ways of seeing, preoccupied with the concept of good as subjective— or a place for my father, who insists on going around with holes in his pants. Certainly it was no place for some of my neighbors, the ones written out of the books when the water went away. When Mulholland told a reporter that he wanted a chance for every man, he really wanted everything—the whole lake, the whole river—for men who saw the world as he did.

But if Mulholland taught us anything, he taught us to anticipate change. He taught us to imagine other versions of reality, to consider how, and why, something different might have been, or almost was, or could be. The future of a place will be determined by the people who, by birth or choice or accident, know that it is home.

• • •

ANTHONY HAS A special voice he uses to snap directions at Bear, the same voice he once used to talk to our little pug dog, Ricky, when Anthony lay on his back in the kitchen and called "Chicken!" and Ricky ran and slid over the redwood floor, toenails clicking, wagging his round, gray body in half and hopping onto Anthony's chest.

My brother is twenty now. He plays on a community softball team. He's paying off his mobile home. His girlfriend weaves beaded jewelry in the tradition of her family and does triathlons and works as a middle school health technician. Anthony has a good job repairing major appliances. He never misses work. Pop walks the creek and turns down Anthony's street to loan him this or that tool, and Anthony tinkers under the hood of his truck in the driveway while the dogs wrestle. Not long ago, he came over and fixed Pop's washer.

His resting expression might scare people who don't know better, and yes, he slams the door to his giant green Chevy and peels out of every parking lot, but he'll spend all day freezing, digging and tugging and hauling your stuck truck out of the Buttermilks.

"Oh, your brother!" folks in town say when they hear my last name—the bouncer at the bar, the old lady at the next table at Las Palmas—and I am instantly beckoned into the fold, the family he has gathered, our home.

His hair hangs braided down his back. He wears a plaid jacket, a Raiders baseball hat. Sometimes Pop takes us to the Chinese restaurant on Main, and Anthony orders orange chicken. He doesn't want anything else, despite Pop's enthusiasm for heaping his plate with a little of everyone's food and mixing it all together—"So I can try all the flavors at once!"

There are many ways to know this landscape, and with his friends my brother shoots clay pigeons, facing the ancient Whites, and rides dirt bikes up the foothills. He goes mudding when it rains, comes home with the big green Chevy spackled brown to the windshield. He has a life here and it's a good one. It appears he has grown into a man.

I ask my brother if he remembers the kid who found nobody waiting at the bus stop and started for home without fear.

"I wasn't scared," he tells me, "until the cop pulled up and said, 'Hey bud, you all right?' And then I started crying. But I knew the way to go. I knew it like the back of my hand."

Ellen Meloy described a maze in the Mojave Desert as "dark stones in rows, paths of pale bared ground between them." No one is completely sure what the maze is for. Perhaps it was meant to make bad spirits lose their way, to guide good spirits safely on. "What if, after death, your soul had to travel across the desert, much like the treks of your lifetime," Meloy wondered, "and you had to know the way or be lost and forever thirsty?"

What restored my brother's sense of direction? It might have been our father, the one who never left, who kept the woodstove warm through winter, who set his son calmly walking this old path. It might have been the mountains, unmoving, changing in ways we anticipate—white in winter, blue in summer, black with passing fire. I remember that long-ago evening when we read Dr. Seuss together, when he threatened to throw danger into the Bricklebush. "I had to," he said to me, looking up, little brown-eyed boy with his bowl cut. "I had to, to save my family." And now, what would he save? What family would he protect from fire? The one that birthed him, or the one that raised him, or the one he found on his own in the valley? Or all these?

He's here to stay. Doesn't like traveling out of town. Even when he slept by the canals, cold winter nights, fleeing or devouring something, he was home. Pop waited on the mountainside for his son to calm. And the found family, the men and women of Bishop, of the reservation—this family waited, too, took him wooding, shooting, dirt biking; offered trailers and loans; and refused to abandon the boy by the river, believing he would someday decide to come inside and be warm.

My brother has gotten good at fixing things. The indestructible kid has learned what this valley has to teach, lessons some of us have just begun to figure out. Someday he will tell me. He will coach me through breakups, through failures, through solitude, this younger brother who is so wise. "An old soul," folks around town say about my brother. He will have strong opinions about my hiking boots. "What are *those*!" he'll say when I try to wear them out on a Saturday. He'll teach me how to play pool, shoot a shotgun, safety on until the last moment. Someday he will drive us in circles, down Line and behind the park and through the rez in the Chevy, Bear panting in the back. We'll dance until the bars close, walk arm in arm down Main Street in the cold. We'll sit in hot springs at Keough's beneath a full moon. He will teach me how to live in our home.

But I don't want him to hurry as he walks again toward the child on the shoulder of 395. It's enough that he remembers lying on our backs on Mountain View Drive at moonrise, slapping ants from our shoulders, blotting heat from the pavement with our skin. Sneaking clothespins onto her shirt. Breaking the crust of the dirt beneath the apple trees with a shovel to dig Ricky's grave while on the mountainside Pop gathered stones.

A FEW DAYS after closing on the house, I walked down Keough Street with a friend who'd left her home in Los Angeles to live in Bishop for a few seasons. I showed her the house after sunset, its windows dark, the tenants out of town, and she put her hand to her mouth and stared, as if she could imagine years passing there.

You're lucky, my friend said, to know the direction home. Then we walked back to Main, past a flood of tourist headlights, past Dusty's Pets and Alex Printing and a couple of smokers outside Rusty's Saloon. Amigos Mexican Restaurant darkened its neon call for Corona. And I was shaken suddenly by the smallness of this town, the strange welcome and warning of the place, which sometimes shares itself like drifting pollen and other times seems to shrivel like a dead seed.

Pilots know that anabatic winds lift out of valleys in daytime as the air above the ground warms. Anabatic winds rise up a mountain slope and dash off into the atmosphere. Those air molecules drift and disappear. Then every evening cold, heavy drafts sink back into the valley. If we conceive of the wind as an entity, if we believe Mary Austin that weather is really spirit shifting in the void, we might say that at night a spirit returns to its place at the base of the mountains. The air is changed, but the same winds come home.

YEARS AGO, AN avalanche killed a man as he skied on the face of Mount Tom. His wife remained in her house on Swall Meadows Road, an A-frame with a view of the place where he ceased to be. She fired a pitcher and painted the clay with the mountain's likeness and gave it to my parents. I don't know whether the sight of that ridge offered up her husband's presence or reminded her that she was alone. Perhaps it did both.

Once, rocks fell on a friend of mine while she hiked in the Inyo Mountains, driving her tibia into her heel. When she could walk again, she took me out to look for horned lizards. This friend builds cinder-block basking platforms for lizards around her house and recognizes rattlesnakes by their scars. She has spent years sitting in meetings with Los Angeles, monitoring the city's ongoing presence in the valley, placing herself in the path of its endless thirst.

She doesn't even limp now, and soon she'll go into the mountains again. What does it mean to live here, I asked her, despite the scar tissue?

"Depending on the day, my relationship with this valley feels like a one-sided love affair, a bigger commitment than marriage, a responsibility I'll never live up to," she said. "It's the first place I turn to for solace. And that means home."

"The mountains are on both sides and the valley is in the center," a Nuumu woman explains. "It's like a cradle."

On still mornings, from Swall Meadows, the valley glows with diffused light, and when I ask Pop why, he says,

"Dust, woodsmoke." Bishop rests crowned in a dirty halo. To imagine this place as home again is to chase a golden future, to tie myself to a land that leaps away from the past yet remains tethered. To return is to live once again beneath the smashed body of a little Beechcraft on the mountain, to wade in a reservoir of loss, to recognize the great loss of the land, the chain of depletion that has played out here, our lives meeting a longer story. Those purple marbles glowed when trouble came to Lupine Land. They called the children home.

After escrow closed, I jumped in with the book club that meets at Spellbinder, the bookstore on Main. Five appropriately weathered people introduced themselves; we ate cookies from a box and talked about magical realism in Luis Alberto Urrea's *The Hummingbird's Daughter*. Later in the discussion one man realized who I was. Sadness entered his eyes—he said, "Your mom."

He was on the board of education. They were colleagues. He took my hand and held it in his big warm worn palm and looked at me as if he were reliving something.

That night in the bookstore I almost said, "But it was so long ago," as if only my family carried that loss. But home has brought these people together, and my story is tangled with theirs.

Beryl Markham wrote the first book I read about flight. She wrote that a handful of miles "can be no distance in a plane, or it can be from where you are to the end of the earth." This distance, she claimed, "depends on the depth of the darkness and the height of the clouds, the speed of the wind, the stars, the fullness of the moon." It depends, she wrote, on whether you fly alone.

"If it had to happen, I'm glad it happened here," said the fireman in Swall who turned the hose on our block while his own house roared to ash, and he meant among people willing to pull him out of his bed while the roof burns.

My friend and I walked, that cold night in Bishop, and I remembered a photograph propped on a bookshelf back in my apartment in Minnesota: Mom in the redwood house, me five years old, my hand on her shoulder, head tipped toward her, a black bow in my hair.

I will not forget you. It's a picture of something everybody loses in some way, or never has at all. The world caught in that picture remains—not the people in the photograph, the woman to be found nowhere and the girl gone with her—but the feeling.

And Mom's grin. I don't know what it is to imagine your students slipping under the ice, to imagine your children growing up without you. But I can gesture at what it meant to be her, how it felt to be what she was: a life stirred among others, contained by mountains. And there are many moments, these days, when joy is absolute.

The cold air pinched our cheeks, bright and clear as resin dripping from the butterscotch bark of the Jeffrey pines, perfuming the night. The town opened. I've fed a thousand ducks in this park. In the pet shop we begged for rats and lizards and sometimes got them. I have followed my father to the cliffs above Mack Lake, looked over dark water, and jumped.

A friend of Pop's is hiking the Pacific Crest Trail. She mails a postcard from Northern California, a dried flower taped to a map where she'd written a quote: "Once you've realized that you can be, do, or have anything, what will it be?"

I'll tell you what it will be: a life on Keough Street. A moon, stark and clear. Snow to cover the mountains, winters that freeze, summers that boil, autumn green along the sea. Rain that falls in November. Fish to swim the rivers.

Richard Rodriguez stands on a California shore with a friend days before her death. He says, "Odd the convergence of loss and rescue at one place."

NOT LONG AGO Pop reminded me that Mom's sixtieth birthday was not far away, that within the next five or so years she would have retired from her job with the schools in Mammoth and might want to live in Bishop instead of on the mountainside in Swall—which would make her my neighbor. Pop said, "How different our lives would be." Every once in a while, for just a moment, he imagines her into place.

Mom, you occupy absence, never gone from my thoughts for very long but also not aged past your fifty-two years, so that when Pop places you close to me I am jolted. Your loss becomes concrete; you are no longer made up of so many memories, so much distance, that you abstract. Again I graduate from high school, graduate from college, and there beside him is your empty chair.

Tonight you took me outside and showed me the moon with a big circle around it, she wrote to my father. *It may be one of our avenues to communicate, like you said!*

After the fire, when a friend of Pop's learned that our house survived, he looked at my father with a half smile and pointed with one finger to the sky. It's what they all say: someone's watching over you. The moon shone awfully bright in those days, but who can't look to the face of the moon and find a trace of what's missing?

And yet, in the first spring without her, I, sworn teenaged atheist, felt what I could only describe as her presence in the predawn sky over Wheeler and Tom, looking west from my window in the depths of night when I could not sleep for fear of the sleep she had entered. A paleness along the ridge and, above it, the stars. It was the same ridge that burned years later, but perhaps because I had seen it so still and softly glowing, so touched by peace, I was able to look at it blackened and not despair.

Some who love this valley remember its first name: the land of flowing waters. Now we see it washed in fire. We live in a landscape damaged beyond repair, and we see our loss magnified the world over. We are here regardless, learning how to keep an eye on mystery and miracle, where they flicker beside disaster.

Kaela reminds me, years later: the night Mom died we asked to know that we could go on. "The four of us walked to the top of the hill together," Kaela remembers—the place Pop once called sacred, safe from stalking mountain lions. "And we were sitting in that spot, you know that spot where we go at the top of the hill. And the clouds were thick and covering the moon, and suddenly they parted and there was a rainbow around the moon, the light reflecting off ice crystals."

Listen, listen, listen. Wind in the Jeffrey pines, and at that curve in the road, Wheeler Crest soaring at our backs, I held Anthony's small, soft hand and Pop's chafed one. It was hard to stay with them when I wanted to be the night wind and fly away, but the meadows beneath us and the windows of our neighbors glowed. And there was something good in not being alone.

The day we climbed Tom, before a FOR SALE sign made the future, the mountain stretched muscles we forgot we had. The ache was femur deep and we moved with stiffness, as if we were growing wings. On that day I wondered if I might be crushed by rock. In another way, the climb was easy. I could see the summit and then I could see the valley floor. There was always only one place to go.

18. The Hardest Part of Flying

FROM THE HIGHEST STEP on this ladder, I can see the rooftops of neighbors, leafless trees, Tom and Wheeler snow covered, soft for all their steepness, and the almost dark blot of Swall. The ladder rattles when I move; it has dents and chips in its gray paint and it leans against the trunk of the liquidambar outside the house on Keough Street. I stand at my perch in Mom's work jeans and jacket, a saw in my hand because I'm supposed to be pruning a branch. Sawdust catches in my hair, my old blue hat tied under my chin on the first day of a new year.

This morning Pop craned his neck at the liquidambar. "That long branch is over the fence. One good snow will take it down and the fence with it."

We've pruned most of the trees in the yard, Pop climbing up the ladder with the chain saw, then a hiccup and the branches float, plunge, cascade, shake with impact, budded tendrils scattering over the dry lawn. Where the saw slices, pale wood rings a red center: heartwood, pure of knots and rot. The redwood house, Pop reminded me, is built from heartwood once used for water tanks in Los Angeles. This house on Keough

Street was once a miner's cabin, trucked over from Tonopah, Nevada. How many ways we redefine a place.

When the chain saw runs out of gas, Pop unscrews a cap and tips the orange fuel can to the hole. He is twenty times faster than I am with blades and engines of any kind, expertise picked up decades before on the Bishop airport tarmac. He tries his best to explain to me how the motor engages.

"It's a pull-rope start," he says, "and you have to position your body correctly so your weight is centered. You have to use this smooth, full-body movement to turn the motor over fast enough to make it fire. The starting is tricky. It's a balancing act. Most people say, 'I'm not strong enough to do that.' They're strong enough, they just don't know the technique."

We've worked since morning as the winter sun rose, then slid along the Whites and hovered. Pop drags flayed branches to a pile, shedding flannel layers. Dexterity drains from my hands, but sun warms Mom's jacket when I stand with my back to the light. Here, the day never loses heat altogether as this bed of stone lifts us closer.

I am up the ladder to learn a lesson. "You're going to live here," Pop says. "You've got to learn to take care of it." And he's right, and I want to, but I'm afraid to start the chain saw in the air when on the ground I can only make the thing gurgle and stall.

There is lots to learn. Before we began, Pop called a man named Bill, the tree guy—one of the many guys in Bishop with handy designations: the chimney guy, the lawn guy, the cooler guy—all of whom know my father and, when they come over—talk with him in the shared language of useful guys. "This is my daughter, she has to learn to maintain this house. Watch, Kendra, how Rick checks this meter." The guys nod, then return to the fuse box or whatever is at hand while I draw frightful diagrams in a notebook.

This morning Bill the tree guy showed up and stood in the yard in tan pants and jacket, windburn over his face and hands. He circled the liquidambar, which by Pop's guess rises eighty feet. "What a tree," Pop said. "That tree's the most valuable thing about this property."

Prune gradually, Bill told us, otherwise the tree puts too much energy into recovering and shortens its life. Nip anything that looks dead and brittle, that's too low, pointed down, crossing other branches. Lose whatever is not firmly attached to the trunk.

It was from Bishop that Pop watched Swall Meadows go, imagined the redwood house burning, and it will be a while before any of us can think of Swall and think only of home and not also of fire. After the fire, hiking Wheeler Crest became easy. The ground lay bare but for black stars, the remnants of bitterbrush that used to snag our jeans when Pop and I made a quick dash to House Rock to look over the valley.

Later we walked the few streets of Swall past lots once choked in ruins, now open space. Pop told me who planned to rebuild, who planned to leave. The bones of Dan and Linda's new house rose, two by fours and plywood, and I stood with Pop in their driveway and looked at the mountains through the gaps in the frame just after sunset, Mount Tom gray and dusted with snow. How strange to walk between walls that are almost, but not quite, what you had before. How strange a task to fill a new house with the spirit of the old.

We climbed to our spot on the hill, that place maybe sacred from mountain lions, and sat in the dirt, cheatgrass lodging in our socks. I forget when I am away how familiar the valley looks from right here.

On that walk around Swall Meadows, I saw that the Fairy Glen was gone, the water birch cut away. If enough snow fell in the spring to quench the creek, Pop said, the glen could grow back, changed.

MY FATHER STANDS with his hands on the ladder's metal frame and holds steady. He looks up—he watches for any sign that this tower is not secure. I remember returning to the redwood house after the dinner shift in winter, the hearth still warm.

Pop waits for me to make the cut. Finish pruning today, he says, and we can hike Tungsten tomorrow, safe from rattlesnakes thanks to the cold.

I am almost out of story to tell. I have come, after all my circling, to the present. I want to carry my father and brother and sister and mother and everyone below these peaks to the next season, the thaw, then the months of fire, then the golden fall, and back into winter. For so long I have been allowed to live with them in this story of not quite history. I am afraid to leave them at a place of peace, for I have learned that peace is tenuous. But they resist, cling to the moment, plunge me toward the future on my own.

Over dry grass, light and dark mingle. For all its falling branches and my failure to start the chain saw, this day has run itself out in beauty. Now we roll over into dark, and the dark will come cold. Pop will stoke the woodstove to gleaming. So many boughs lie in a pile bound for Bill's wood chipper, and now this limb of the liquidambar must go. *Take good care*, Mom wrote in that album. But how do you slice a living branch from a tree your father has called priceless?

First you make a little notch below the place where the branch joins, so when it falls, it doesn't pull bark with it. Next, position your saw an inch or two from the trunk, leaving what Bill called the collar, so the tree can cleanly heal.

I press the blade. Sawdust sprinkles over Pop's canvas hat.

Maybe because I am high up on this ladder, I remember: When I was a kid, I understood that I could fly. Not in a way that compelled me to leap from heights, though the urge was strong enough. How fun it would be, Pop has often remarked, to soar like a hawk, to kick from a mountain into air and skip the treacherous down-climb. If you have climbed anything at all, you know it is easier to go up than to come down.

The distinction between flying and belief was not important. That is the way I knew I could fly, when the world had yet to sort into daylight and dreams, into what we make up and what we wake to, the feeling of flying on a bicycle down Mountain View Drive interchangeable with a bird's flight, and miracles rose every morning with the sun out my window. Mom sang her morning song—*Good morning to you-do-doodle-do!*—and pulled the curtains, whisked off our sheets so light flooded our beds, and caught us in wrinkled pajamas, shrieking but really all eagerness for the bike ride to Bishop where we sat at Caddy's knees with hair crushed by helmets and cheeks roughened by wind. And so I could fly. I carried the knowledge like a marble held up to a reeling world.

I think of that picture of my father as a young man flinging himself into the sky, his face tossed back to the sun, an unbelievable leap—what must the wind have felt like, thin in oxygen and clear of the years that followed?

Once, I asked Pop what it meant for my mother to consider the end of her life.

Life is a short gift, she told him. Once, she told me, she watched a bee alight on the leg of her friend, an entomologist. The bee perched, extended a long, pink tongue, and licked the man's knee.

Pop said she was glad to have been here, to watch the bees.

From Bishop we look north and up to Swall. From Swall we look south and down to Bishop. I have tried to keep an eye trained on the fortune that puts any of us here. In a year, amid the heaviest Sierra snowfall in recorded history, this drought will end, if drought in the West can be said to end. Jackrabbits will struggle through heavy snow. In spring Owens River will drown fishermen. The world turns over, and nothing stays the same.

I will not forsake you. The saw wobbles, its pale, varnished handle cold in my hand. Below, Pop braces the ladder as teeth bite wood. East, then west, then east, then west, the saw tracks the range and habits of the sun. The wood shudders, the long branch tips. Any moment now the sun will fall west, then east, then west, and how high on this ladder my perch, how much I can see in last light. One friend believed me when I told him: I can fly. I stood beside my bunk bed, built by Pop, cut from pine. When I slept in this bed, my feet pointed west, my head pointed east, and if I rolled to one side and faced the window, I looked full into Wheeler and farther to Tom. Oh mountains. My hand on the wood of the bunk, of the branch, and Daniel, oldest friend, stood before me, his back to the window, his red hair wild in the light. My father below, ladder firm in his palms. "I believe you," said Daniel, and this I will always know. Oh mountains. Oh valley below. I believe you; I can fall; I can break arm or leg, back or rib. I can burn. That I understand. But I am not sure I have forgotten what I knew when I was a child.

THREE DECADES AFTER my father filled his last fuel tank at the Bishop airport, a small restaurant called Thai Thai took a lease in half of the terminal building. Windows overlook the runway and the White Mountains beyond. Colorful fabric stretches over the fluorescent lights, and Pop's friend from the community jazz band riffs on a saxophone in the corner. A door at one end of the restaurant leads to the operative half of the terminal, where pictures of gliders hang on the walls.

We drive out to the airport and order curry every so often, and Pop dresses up in black jeans and his blue map delivery shirt. On a warm evening in autumn, we walk onto the tarmac while we wait for our food. The planes rest, and I know he misses Zippy, the silver RV-4, old stick-and-rudder, tail dragger, long ago sold.

"You want to know what's the fun of flying?" he tells me. "It's the banking of the turns. It's the swooping, like a bird, where you can bank left and bank right. You can dip. You can drop. It's all that motion, that range of motion. That sense of vertigo, you know. That weightlessness."

He describes landing at this airport, dropping wing flaps to slow the plane and making a broad U-turn—downwind, turn base, turn final—then descending on a glide as the peaks regain their places in the sky. We watch the mountains lit half-gold, half-purple by the sunset. We wonder aloud if we should go back to our table. And then my father spreads his long arms and runs between the planes. His shirt flutters; his sandals flap.

He calls back to me, over a shoulder.

"Landing," he says, "is the hardest part of flying."

RESEARCH AND INSPIRATION

DURING THE CREATION OF *Miracle Country*, I was influenced by countless works of literature, scholarship, storytelling, and other mediums. The following were especially essential.

The oeuvre of the musician Joanna Newsom gave me courage to begin exploring the emotional and aesthetic power my home holds over me.

Richard Rodriguez's *Days of Obligation: An Argument with My Mexican Father* and *Brown: The Last Discovery of America* helped me expand my interpretation of the West, as well as my relationship to family, culture, history, and landscape.

Ellen Meloy's *The Anthropology of Turquoise: Reflections on Desert, Sea, Stone, and Sky* and *Eating Stone: Imagination and the Loss of the Wild* comforted me when I was terribly homesick for the desert and helped me articulate the preciousness of landscapes at risk of being dismissed as worthless.

Rebecca Solnit's *River of Shadows: Eadweard Muybridge and the Technological Wild West* and *Savage Dreams: A Journey into the Hidden Wars of the American West* taught me to tell nuanced stories about the past that help me imagine different ways of inhabiting the present.

Robin Wall Kimmerer's *Braiding Sweetgrass: Indigenous Wisdom, Scientific Knowledge and the Teachings of Plants* expanded my understanding of reciprocity with homeplaces and living with respect for beings beyond my own species.

Wallace Stegner's *Wolf Willow: A History, a Story, and a Memory of the Last Plains Frontier* and *Where the Bluebird Sings to the Lemonade Springs: Living and Writing in the West* helped me understand my relationship to the rest of the world as a being shaped by where I come from. From Stegner and so many others I have learned the power of living deeply in a place.

Visit KendraAtleework.com for a complete bibliography and notes.

ACKNOWLEDGMENTS

I'M THANKFUL FOR the people of the Eastern Sierra, past and present. For the friends who propped me up for six years while I wrote this book: Suzanne Calkins, Lauren Oxford, Clio Beauvoir, and Zoe Almeida. For Victoria Blanco, who pined away with me for our respective deserts. For Emily Strasser. For Elizabeth Scott. And for Jeroentje.

I'm thankful for the Ellen Meloy Fund for Desert Writers, my favorite people to read to in all the world. For the Minnesota State Arts Board Artist Initiative grant, and the Bread Loaf Writers' Conference waiter scholarship, and the Anderson Center, and the MFA program at the University of Minnesota, and the Gesell family, and for Holly Vanderhaar. For Kimberly Drake, who started the job of teaching me how to write, and for Patricia Hampl, Dan Philippon, Julie Schumacher, and Charlie Baxter, who continued it. For all the good folks at Spellbinder Books in Bishop. For the Eastern California Museum. For the Donald M. Slager Sunset Foundation Scholarship and the Tina Jones Family Silver Lake Resort Scholarship. For the people who helped me understand my home better, who work daily on behalf of this place: Ceal Klingler, Sally Manning, Harry C. Williams, Phoebe Nicholls, David Carle, Kathy Jefferson Bancroft, Alan Bacock, Anna Hohag, and Sophia Borgias. For Glenn Nelson, who helped me with Nuumu language. For Sunstone Press for keeping Mary Austin in print and sharing her autobiography with me. For Paul Fremeau, who answered a million questions about weather, and Louise Kellogg, who helped out with geology. For the firefighters who battled the fire in Swall, and for Rosanne Higley and Bob Sachs who told me about it. For Linda, Dan, and Jessie O'Dell for sharing their experience of the fire and for caring about our home. For Nana and Fafa, who taught me a lot of ways to love California.

For Kathy Pories and the wonderful team at Algonquin and Workman, who made this book exist, and thus realized the first and largest dream of my life. And for Janet Silver, a friend and a champion, whose patience and vision and love allowed this book to become itself.

I'm thankful for Kaela and Anthony for coming home with me. For Pop, for all the landings.

And for Mom, who asked me to fold my first published piece of writing into a paper airplane and throw it into the night sky. *I'll get it*, she said—*somehow*.

QUESTIONS FOR DISCUSSION

1. Every family creates its own culture, its own version of normal. What aspects of the Atleeworks resonated with your own idea of family?

2. What did you notice about the parenting styles of Kendra's mom and dad? How did they differ? How did they align?

3. In *Miracle Country*, California is presented as a land of optimism and innovation, of hope and forgetfulness, of tragedy and disaster. How does the Atleework family represent, and also differ from, the qualities of their home state?

4. The Los Angeles Aqueduct was built, and the water was taken from Owens Valley/Payahuunadu, because the people with power at the time had agreed to pursue "the greatest good for the greatest number." The author considers what "good" means and who gets to define that. Can you think of instances when you've observed something being taken for granted as good that might not have been?

5. Why do you think the book is titled *Miracle Country*?

6. What do you picture when you think of California? How has the way you think about the desert changed after reading *Miracle Country*? How has this affected your ideas of California?

7. Kendra had to leave home and do her own research to learn the story of the Indigenous people of her valley, the Paiute/Nuumu. What do you know about the history and contemporary reality of Indigenous people where you live? Why do you think many people are not taught this about their own homes?

8. Kendra decides to move home to Bishop for many reasons. Which ones stood out to you the most?

9. *Miracle Country* is as much about the author's home as it is about her life and family. What effect did the pairing of a personal story with the story of a place have on you?

10. *Miracle Country* is in part about living deeply in a place: committing to making it better and not just depleting it of resources and moving on. In what ways is your own home a deeply lived-in place? In what ways is it not?

11. Which family member's relationship to home most resonated with you? Why?

12. Is William Mulholland, the engineer of the Los Angeles Aqueduct, a villain, or should he be forgiven for upholding the values of his time?

13. How would you describe Kendra's feelings about losing her mother by the time she moves home? What are the different roles loss plays in *Miracle Country*? How does the author's attitude toward the loss of her mother change by the end of the book?

14. What role does Mary Austin play in the book? How does she help us understand the place and especially the women, like Kendra and her mom, who love it?

15. What emotions and ideas about your own home did *Miracle Country* stir?

KENDRA ATLEEWORK is the recipient of the Ellen Meloy Desert Writers Award, and her work has appeared in *The Best American Essays*, the *Los Angeles Times*, the *Atlantic*, and elsewhere. She received her MFA in creative writing from the University of Minnesota and now lives in her hometown of Bishop, California, where she is still really good at catching lizards.